THE LIVERPOOL WAY

For Owen, Olivia and (Sir) Alex Thomas
Albert Williams and for Sarah Roberts, born to be Red.
For Paul Reynolds, who kindly watches over Liverpool
supporters everywhere.

THE **LIVERPOOL** WAY
Houllier, Anfield and the New Global Game

JOHN WILLIAMS

MAINSTREAM
PUBLISHING
EDINBURGH AND LONDON

First published in Great Britain in 2003 by
MAINSTREAM PUBLISHING COMPANY (EDINBURGH) LTD
7 Albany Street
Edinburgh EH1 3UG

ISBN 1 84018 709 3

A catalogue record for this book is available from the British Library

Typeset in Bembo and Frutiger
Printed and bound in Great Britain by
Creative Print and Design Wales

Contents

CHAPTER 1

From the Glory Game to Broken Dreams

IT WAS 30 YEARS AGO TODAY

The start of the 2002–03 football season in England was a period of hope and expectation for Liverpool football club and its global fan base. Under manager Gérard Houllier's short reign Liverpool's league position had continued to improve – from fourth to third to second in 2001–02 – and Houllier himself had recovered from serious illness in 2001 to lead the club to the quarter-finals of the Champions League, a run of only 2 defeats in 21 League games in the second half of the season, and a real tilt at the League title, scuppered by Double-winning Arsenal under Houllier's friend and rival Arsène Wenger. At the end of the 2001–02 season Houllier had looked gaunt and tired, his team fading with him as the winning post approached. With the manager now fit and back in command at Anfield, with another stab at Europe ensured, and with three major new signings on board, the Anfield club was surely primed for a realistic assault on the Premiership crown. The Treble-winning cup season of 2000–01 had been a marvellous journey for Liverpool fans, but the real trip for this club has always been winning the League title, not secured since 1990.

In fact, 2002–03 was to prove a difficult season for Liverpool, and for Houllier. This is the story of the Liverpool club and its players, that season, and the events and people behind it. But it is also the story of the changing game in England, because the 2002–03 season was a pivotal moment for English football. For one thing, it was 30 years since the publication of Hunter Davies' extraordinary inside story of a year in the life of another famous English football club, Tottenham Hotspur. Following the publication of *The Glory Game*, Davies, himself a Spurs fan, has remarked many times on how English football had since changed – in few ways for the good – and how incredibly easy it had been then for a writer to gain access inside a major English club. *The Glory Game* opened up the English game for an intelligent readership like no other work had done before, or has done since.

Incredibly, Davies managed to persuade the club to allow him to travel to matches with the Spurs first team, he sat in on team talks and post-match post-mortems, attended player parties and social events, interviewed the top stars and their wives, and also Spurs directors, coaches and fans. He even got reasonable returns from his questionnaires given to the club's players. His account is a unique insight into English football in an age before top players became inaccessibly and impossibly rich and before football clubs began to 'manage' the media in ways gleaned mainly from the advertising industry. No one would have quite the same kind of freedom again.

Tottenham, back in 1972, were not the fakers and no-hopers they have since become. They still had high hopes of winning the League Championship – they had won the Double, after all, in 1961 – and had just paid a British record transfer fee of £200,000 for West Ham's Martin Peters. They were a top club.

Spurs also won the UEFA Cup on Davies' own watch and, in contrast to today, playing in Europe in the 1970s was still about winning trophies and surviving together on inhospitable foreign fields. There is little talk in *The Glory Game* about the financial rewards of European competition, or of foreign coaches or managers – or much talk about team tactics at all. The new foreign technocrats, among them Gérard Houllier, would arrive in England much later. Back in 1972, Bill Nicholson and his Spurs staff were staunchly English – and largely untrained, with coach Eddie Bailey teasing his spoiled charges for their use of hairdryers in the changing rooms and calling for the spirit of the trenches to deliver whenever the chips were down. Over at Anfield around this time, Bob Paisley was similarly recalling tank battles in the war in an attempt to motivate the team at Liverpool's European games. It was reasoned that blood and guts could still see the English through in tight spots abroad when the call came, in war or in peace, to go 'over the top'.

Top football players' business interests in 1972 were arcane, if they existed at all. Some players owned timber firms and builder's merchants; there were fish and chip shop owners; and garage proprietors abounded.

This is the era, remember, of men like West Brom and England's Jeff Astle, a striker who broke Everton hearts in the 1968 FA Cup final and retired to run his window-cleaning business. Astle also met an early death as a result of brain damage he sustained after heading too many sodden footballs, and many players from this period – Liverpool's Tommy Smith for one – retired with ravaged and abused bodies. These were, indeed, dangerous days for football stars.

Of the 1972 Spurs roster, only England internationals Martin Chivers and Martin Peters really pointed to the different way ahead for football players. Peters had already confessed investments in something called Martin Peters Promotions, while Chivers complained bitterly at one point about the footballer's lot, especially that players were being exploited by the press: 'Newspapers use your name to sell copies. They should pay through the nose instead of getting it for free.' Chivers was seen by the Spurs coaches of the time as a talented but work-shy striker with ideas above his station. Beyond the still-disorganised George Best industry there was, however, still relatively little player promotional work in the English game in the early 1970s, and certainly not in a young Liverpool team that was in transition again under Bill Shankly. But a bubble-headed Kevin Keegan was only just around the corner, a man who would signal a very new age for industrious and entrepreneurial English footballers. Chivers was only just a little ahead of his time.

Another 1972–3 exchange, brilliantly reported by Davies in *The Glory Game*, is between an early grifter, Paul Trevillion, the Spurs goalkeeper Pat Jennings and young defender Steve Perryman. With the benefit of hindsight it now carries plenty of symbolic weight. The agent is trying hard to sign Perryman to a deal for a special new 'tackling boot' – the midfielder's playing strength is tackling – and also to convince the experienced Jennings that his best saves might be better explained by a new brand of goalkeeping gloves rather than by the Irishman's mammoth hands: 'From this minute I want you to deny you have big hands, OK?' This was an era, of course, in which even top goalkeepers were simply not pursued for endorsements: Ray Clemence at Liverpool, for example, seldom even wore gloves. The highly rated Jennings was utterly fazed by this kind of hard sell.

More importantly, both players were flummoxed by the obvious commercial deception involved. Perryman seemed honestly aghast that anyone might even suggest that a football boot – rather then technique and practice – could improve tackling, while Jennings is equally ill at ease at being pressed to hide or deny his slab-like hands. The deal stalls. It is hard to imagine today's playing crop showing quite the same sort of concern. But Trevillion also had other big plans: one involved placing a blue cross, front and back, on Leeds United shirts, and a new club nickname for Leeds – the Crusaders. In the pre-branding days of the 1970s this seemed like madness; it seems a little more plausible today.

TEN YEARS AFTER

Flash forward once again, and the 2002–03 football season in England also signals another important anniversary: the tenth anniversary, in fact, of what many people regard as Year Zero in English football. It is exactly a decade since BSkyB's colonisation of the English game, and the emergence of the newly marketed FA Premier League. During these celebrations a very strange view of history emerged. Throughout the 2002–03 season there were awards and recollections about the sport of a sort which came close to suggesting that nothing of any real value in English football – Blanchflower's Tottenham; Yeats's Liverpool; Law's United; even Ball's Everton – had existed at all before the early 1990s. Satellite TV was in charge here and, at least as far as Sky Sports was concerned, English football history was mapped out solely from the availability of copyright TV footage and by the ever-present voice of Sky's own voice of the Premiership, Andy Gray. Sky now *owned* the Premiership.

One of the results of this skewered version of history is that a club such as Liverpool, for example, is routinely depicted on Sky as a striving 'nearly' outfit, one that actually has never won the League at all. How could they have been League champions: Sky's archive footage begins with Liverpool's defeat by Nottingham Forest in August 1992, and neither Graeme Souness, nor Roy Evans, nor the current Liverpool managerial incumbent, *Le Boss*, Gérard Houllier, have managed to pilot Liverpool home since. In this new satellite-driven world of TV football, nothing before 1992 really matters – 18 Liverpool titles effectively written off. Perhaps, like the glory, glory Spurs Double of 1961, it just didn't happen?

Later in the 2002–03 season, Alan Shearer, a man with just one League-winner's medal to his name, was voted the most influential player in the history of the League. *History?* To some of us it seemed like we had been playing for about five minutes on Sky – not long enough, in fact, to have enjoyed even a single run through of Richard Key's hideous wardrobe of multi-coloured presenter's jackets. But about one thing there seemed little dispute. Forget Spurs and 1972: in just ten years since 1992, the professional game in England, at the very highest levels, had enjoyed the sort of economic and cultural boom which was of quite staggering and unprecedented proportions in the post-war period. The new Premiership had undoubtedly been the catalyst for an amazing growth in popular interest around top football in England, after a long period in the 1970s and 1980s when the game had been in crisis and decline and when public discussion about the sport often centred only on concern about hooliganism and crowd control. Even Hunter Davies, tellingly, was spending time reporting among the Spurs football skinheads back in the gritty football times of 1972. But had 'new' football been a complete success? That is quite another matter.

PREMIER PLUS?

The Premier League was set for record-breaking crowds in 2002–03, with attendances up 60 per cent since 1992 and close to a 50-year high, built around the massive new ground developments at Newcastle and Old Trafford, stadiums which were now playing to a staggering 99 per cent average capacity. More than 13 million entrants each season now troop through the turnstiles for top-level English football. With more new, larger stadiums planned for Arsenal, Liverpool, Manchester City, Tottenham and maybe even Everton (you think?) in the next few years, no one would now bet against the game busting the all-time English crowd figures for the top level, set way back in the post-war shilling glow of the era of Matthews, Finney and Liddell, in 1948–89 – if this period ever really existed, of course.

All this football boom mania still seems incredible. It feels like the return of sport and the mass society – but in an era of escalating ticket prices and increasingly privatised play and fragmenting leisure patterns. It is the sort of mysterious and lucrative trend that had administrators like Liverpool's Rick Parry positively itching to lay the first brick of the proposed new 60,000-plus-capacity Chez Anfield on nearby Stanley Park, because he knows that this contemporary football miracle has been no cloth-cap revolution. Instead, it is one involving more women fans, the booming national fan bases of the bigger clubs, and the rise of the new football-mad middle classes and affluent public-sector professionals. None of the mud flung around about the game in 2002–03 – about greed, corruption, poor playing technique, the playing up of the hooligan fringes – seemed to stick to the Premier League elite. The crowds just kept on coming, gorging themselves on the sport's apparent 24/7 media appeal.

Richard Scudamore, chief executive of the FA Premier League, offered the usual marketing blurb about 'the world's leading players' and the 'atmosphere and spectacle that is unrivalled in any other league' bringing in the new punters – and some of this was true. What's more, unlike the gormless Martin Chivers, David Beckham, and his style-conscious mates, are rarely out of the fashion pages or the Sunday colour supplements these days, feeding the incessant media babble about global football and its new millionaire icons. Beckham recently clocked in as the highest-earning European footballer – taking home just over £10 million a year. Liverpool's Michael Owen makes a cool £6 million, and often he's been playing nowhere near his best.

By the middle of 2003 Becks – England captain, new man, hairdresser's model and global brand – and his family had pretty much taken over the popular British press, front and back. Would he stay at United to mend his bridges with a reluctant Fergie or fly off to Spain to explore new markets? When he finally agreed to join the 'galactic' star roster at Real Madrid, there was barely a dry eye in the corridors of the British gossip mags, nor a white Real shirt that could now not be sold somewhere in the Far East. If Ronaldo could shift 500,000 Real shirts worldwide with his kind of dentistry, what might the matinee-idol jaw-line and the pop-star persona of Beckham manage to move now? We all stood agog.

The non-stop marketing and soap-opera lifestyles of some of the top players in England – we even had by now the trashy TV hit *Footballers' Wives* to spice the mix – matched by expanding stadium capacities in England, the glamorous foreign imports and a safer, more attractive, climate inside grounds kept the crowds moving up. No one was easily put off attending Premiership home games in 2002 because of fear of the digestive effects of the meat pies or even that some clown might turn around the next corner looking for satisfaction. It still happened, of course, the football fighting, but usually in the car park of a distant carpet warehouse somewhere, where only the combatants had gathered. So, as a sad troop of sizeable English football clubs went belly-up to the administrators in 2002–03, the fans higher up the food chain continued to fight for stadium space. What does it all mean? And where – and when – would it all end?

SIGNS OF THE TIMES

For the game's many critics today, if Hunter Davies' elegiac depiction of the relative innocence inside White Hart Lane is 1972's literary football masterwork and a symbol for the sporting times 30 years ago, then the football books which best signify the new era have taken on quite a different, much harsher, tack. John Sugden and Alan Tomlinson's recent *Badfellas*, for example, exposes and explains the financial irregularities, mismanagement, double dealing and political chicanery inside the world governing body FIFA. These 'English professors', as the FIFA hierarchy disparagingly refer to the authors, remind us all that even 30 years ago there were still plenty of corporate crooks around in sport and in the very highest places.

But if FIFA is allegedly riddled with inappropriate sponsorship power, posture politics and brown-envelope electoral malfeasance, at home it was Tom Bower's book *Broken Dreams* that really stuck the knife into new football in 2003, with its trenchant critique of the corruption of the sport's new money men, its depiction of the incompetence and cowardice of the FA in allowing the big clubs to shape football policy, and its exposure of the complicity of Blair's government in helping to promote a winner-takes-all culture inside the game, to the detriment of the smaller clubs. Bower's text trawls over plenty of old ground and is overblown and full of pompous moral indignation, but it is still a devastating attack on the modern game and its supposed guardians. Bower had plenty of material to work with. In 2002–03 the FA was in disarray, with the Premier League running roughshod over the regulator's desperate attempts to rein in the power and greed of the top professional clubs. When, in the autumn of 2002, FA chief executive Adam Crozier overstretched the FA's own commercial ambitions and also tried to resist the influence of the Premier League inside Soho Square, then he had to go. It looked like a classic – and damaging – case of the parental regulator being forced out by his own spoilt children, the disorderly (un)regulated.

There are no easy meeting points here, no comfortable spots on the fence in the debate about how the English game had developed since 1972 and then had taken on quite a different trajectory since 1992. Passions run far too high for that. But let me argue this: over the past decade, in the Sky TV era of rocketing players' salaries and social transformations, top English football has changed, but not quite as completely as its supporters might want to suggest or, indeed, as damagingly as its opponents would have it. The people running the sport have certainly become more greedy and duplicitous, less open. This much is true, beyond question. Too much money is at stake now and too little has been done to ensure transparency and honesty in an era in which regulation has generally become a dirty word, a barrier to the 'effective' workings of business, rather than a necessary brake on avarice and corruption. Allow the market to run its course unhindered in sport or anywhere else, and business will cut corners and smaller outlets will struggle. Which makes you wonder why, when some of its professional member clubs were clawing at the pauper's gates in 2002–03, the FA directed its attentions instead to raising a mammoth £750 million for the building of a new national stadium in Brent.

TV is at the heart of some of the biggest changes, and some of the strongest conflicts, in the modern game, of course. TV has globalised the game, blown the Champions League into the sort of cash cow that has destabilised the balance of reward between foreign and domestic football, and added to the structural tensions that have empowered the largest English clubs and stretched their ambitions way beyond the normal national boundaries and constraints. Sure, satellite television has pumped big cash into the Premier League and trawled some of the world's top talent to England – which is a big plus – but it has also moved the kick-offs around until any notion of a rational fixture list is now impossible to sustain – a major price. Despite a commitment to show all the Premier League clubs and to share the TV money around, the biggest clubs, like Liverpool and Man. United, can wait weeks – sometimes months – for a 3 p.m. Saturday start these days, the familiar weekend rhythms of live attendance seemingly shattered for good.

Man. United fans protested this last point in 2003 and were even supported by their club, who now wanted to televise their own home 3 p.m. Saturday starts, giving warning that its time will come, irrespective of the interests of all the smaller clubs seeking a live audience at the same time. But while Sky and the BBC have messed around with the scheduling of the game – probably too much – a brand new set of rhythms has also opened up for the weekend TV football watcher. And don't think for a second that these are two distinct markets, the 'live' fan and the 'armchair' fan, because it is the fans who regularly *attend* games who also regularly buy into Sky's extraordinary football coverage. Again, swings and roundabouts: I want my Sunday football supplement – and give me the top clubs on the box. But, please, why do *we* have to keep changing our kick-off times?

But, essentially, despite the buckets of cash, the corruption, the greed and the artifice, the fundamentals of the game itself remain pretty much the same. OK, on the field there is more feigning and cheating these days; but there is also less violence, and more variety and new, complex relations drawn out now between the local and the global. In season 2002–03, for example, that old traditional English stronghold, Bolton Wanderers, fielded, for the first time in the club's long history, not a single British player. Stand back and think about that for a second. Local hero Nat Lofthouse might have mourned the absence of local talent at the Reebok Stadium, but what is remarkable is how this old, parochial – and sometimes racist – Lancashire town has taken to its new global heroes, the irrepressible Jay-Jay Okocha and the skilful Frenchman Djorkaeff. And Bolton stayed up in 2003, largely on the back of the togetherness of the players and fans – and the ability of its foreign legion. Amazing.

And there is much still in common today with 1992, or even with 1972. Football's supporters are still drawn by the drama and heroics of its stars, no matter where they are from; its followers are still moved (yes, sometimes to violence) by the passion of their commitment and by the indignity and pain of defeat or the indescribable high of victory. Not much has changed here either. The corporate market has grown, for sure, and more female fans get a chance these days and black people are less at risk of being abused at the match – both good things. But those who think the stands have simply been taken over by the corporate elites or by the moneyed middle classes don't watch from the same places I do, or hear and see the same things I still see and hear these days at football. In fact, the words of another great football writer, Arthur Hopcraft in his book of 1968 *The Football Man*, often still apply as much today as they did 35 years ago. Hopcraft interviewed fans from the Liverpool Kop and argued that, for them, football is not a sideshow, a mere entertainment. What happens on the football field matters. He went on, describing the English game in the late 1960s thus:

> It has conflict and beauty and, when these two qualities are present together in something offered for public appraisal they represent much of what I understand to be art. The people own this art in a way they can never own any form of music, theatre, literature or religion because they cannot be fooled as they can in those other things. Crowds can be vindictive and brutal, but they can seldom be deceived. They know about their football intuitively, as they know about their families.

The English football ground in 2003 is still no place for faint hearts or for those too easily offended, or even for those who don't really care. Because, even in the twenty-first century, football still provokes and tears at the sensibilities and emotions of its fans. It still hurts and transcends. It is still, after all, the people's art.

GREETINGS, FROM JAPAN AND SENEGAL

2002 was World Cup year, of course, the finals held for the first time in Japan and Korea. The big stories in the UK were that England fans might actually behave themselves and that a persistent offender, Roy Keane, might not. A pre-event bust up with Ireland manager Mick McCarthy sent the United nark home to walk his dogs, possibly the most televised piece of pet husbandry ever recorded.

Like Keane, Gérard Houllier was also uninvolved in the tournament for the first time for many years. It hurt him to stay at home. Steven Gerrard was also out injured, but a palpably unfit Michael Owen and also Liverpool's Emile Heskey were both there for Eriksson's England, as was a nervy and mistake-ridden Jerzy Dudek for Poland and Didi Hamann for the surprisingly successful Germans. Also in the Far East, as it later turned out, were a couple of Liverpool players we did not yet know about.

This might conceivably have meant Ireland's Damien Duff, a long-time Reds target. Instead, discouraged by Blackburn Rover's escalating asking price for Duff, and deciding to resist the option of re-signing the reformed Nicolas Anelka from Paris St Germain, Houllier had been shopping in quite another place. The football world knew little about El Hadji Diouf and Salif Diao before 31 May 2002 in Seoul, when their unconsidered Senegal side defeated favourites and World Cup holders France in the first match of the tournament. This was a little like a French league side beating the overseas French XI, because most of the Senegal team played in France and most of the French stars played abroad. No matter. The blond-rinsed Diouf looked like his media description of a voodoo magician on the left side, floating past the ageing Frank Leboeuf and deceiving the imperious Marcel Dessailly almost at will. With Zidane injured, meanwhile, Diao outplayed Manny Petit and Patrick Vieira at the heart of the midfield scrap. These African boys really looked like they could play – Gérard Houllier thought so too.

Houllier had actually been tracking Diouf from the beginning of May, and effectively hijacked the African's proposed move from Lens to Valencia by agreeing to sign the winger for £10 million on the very day the World Cup kicked off. He needed to get the deal sealed up quickly. Diouf's show against the French certainly made Houllier look like a good judge and might have started a global auction for the African. The Diao signing seemed minor by comparison and, anyway, the plan was that he would not leave his French club Sedan for Liverpool until January 2003. Expect fireworks: against Denmark in Daegu, the new Liverpool man, a 25-year-old middle-class son of a hotel owner, managed to concede a penalty, score a thrilling goal and then get himself red-carded for an horrendous lunge that had the usually phlegmatic Danes off the bench in unison. Interesting.

Diouf, only 21 and already African Footballer of the Year, comes from north Dakar's tough St Louis neighbourhood and began playing street football for ten pence bets. Like Anelka, he had been involved in a few disciplinary scrapes in France, though this was *not*, we were assured, why he had been nicknamed the 'Serial Killer'. These problems don't seem to have troubled his Senegal coach much, as Diouf casually reported on signing for Liverpool:

> I am aware I won't be able to go for a drink with Gérard Houllier at 4 a.m., as happened with Bruno Metsu, the Senegal coach. If I do go out I will not hide though. I will take care. There is no question of me concealing anything because I know the boss is no gendarme. I believe there is great confidence between me and Gérard Houllier. I hope to show him as soon as possible that he was right to have faith in me. Liverpool were my dream club. They are a team I have followed since I was a kid. I used to watch their European Cup games on TV and I loved their style of play – the way they never gave up.

This declaration of devotion might have caused more early alarm than comfort in the Liverpool ranks. Had Liverpool signed an African Robbie Fowler? For the love of the nightlife, perhaps, but certainly not in terms of his goal-scoring record – in fact, Diouf's 'goals for' column was not that impressive. What Houllier really liked about the young African, however, was his attitude to the game: 'He is a fighter, a warrior,' said the Liverpool boss, approvingly. 'He fears nothing. He's a Liverpool player. He'll prove a great signing.' Diouf's approach to the business side of the sport actually seemed more like that of an English player signing for Bill Shankly in the early 1970s than it did the calculated weighing up of financial rewards of the modern-day footballer. 'Even before I met him,' Houllier said excitedly, 'he came to me on the phone. "Boss," he said, "sign me, you'll never regret it." He never mentioned money. I warned him we had Emile Heskey and Michael Owen, but he wouldn't be put off. He's very confident.' We all liked the sound of this.

Houllier also enthused over Diouf's value-for-money adaptability – something long held by the Frenchman as a key ingredient for the modern-day player – and his capacity for producing the out-of-the-ordinary. This last point would have made more Liverpool fans sit up and listen. We all knew Houllier could build solid football units, but he had been rather less successful in moving away from the functional and reliable towards accommodating real match-breaking flair in his rigid playing systems. Was this new signing the signal for real change at Anfield? He said of the new man:

If he were English he'd be twice the price. It will take time to adapt, but he's four players in one: a forward, an attacking midfielder, or a winger on either side. You need players with scope to their game. Not all English players have that flexibility – I was surprised when I came here by the short-sightedness in the self-expression of some of the English players – but El Hadji does. You need that type of player these days.

This all sounded very positive, but could the new man really deliver this sort of exciting invention at the high pace of the English game in his first season in England? And how, exactly, would this new-found Houllier interest in flair fit in with his well-established devotion to a rather dour and formulaic 4–4–2? For all his attributes, Diouf hardly looked like a goal-scoring English-style striker. In midfield, in Houllier's preferred version of 4–4–2, he would have to learn to defend as well as attack. It was all very intriguing – and potentially exciting. But we still needed convincing.

Also intriguing were two more Liverpool signings – left-sided midfielder Bruno Cheyrou from Lille for £3.7 million and Alou Diarra on a free transfer from Bayern Munich, but immediately loaned for a season to the French club Le Havre. Cheyrou had scored in the Champions League against Manchester United and his arrival seemed to seal the fate of Patrik Berger, injury troubled and on the last year of his contract at Anfield. The new man arrived with some hype, and also showed up well in a pre-season home defeat to Lazio, but like all new arrivals his worth could only be judged after he had been watched closely in the furnace that is the FA Premiership. Markus Babbel also started against Lazio, and this was almost like another new signing as the German was back from the abyss of Guillain Barre syndrome, an inflammatory disorder of the peripheral nerves which renders 10 per cent of sufferers unable to walk unattended more than a year after contracting it, and which kills 10 per cent of its victims. Liverpool had admirably supported Babbel throughout his illness, even extending his contract. We should really have been happy simply that he was alive and walking again but, instead, we were now expecting our quality German defender to play full-on football in the most physically taxing league in the entire world. It seemed a lot to ask.

LEE BOWYER – THE GREAT UNSIGNED

On the basis of these new recruits and the recovering injured, and after Heskey and Owen had both scored for Eriksson in Japan before a flaccid

England collapse against ten-man Brazil sent them home at the quarter-final stage, a number of Liverpool squad players now left the Anfield camp. Nick Barmby, perpetual wanderer, was packed off to Leeds, while time-server Jamie Redknapp, admired by Houllier, but an injury-prone and ultimately flattering midfielder, left for Spurs, saying all the right things about his long stay at Anfield as he departed. Which is more than could be said about the still-neglected Jari Litmanen, who complained that he was now so unloved at Melwood that 'I don't think Liverpool expected me still to be here. They expected every player to turn up for pre-season training except me.' It was the sort of public outburst designed to get Houllier to agree a move – almost anywhere.

There was more local comment, in fact, about the departure of scouser right full-back Stephen Wright, to join Peter Reid at Sunderland. Wright had seemed a reasonable stand-in for Babbel and had even scored the previous season in the Champions League, at home to Dortmund. He had his supporters at Anfield, mainly because of his determination and commitment, and he was also a welcome local boy in a sea of increasingly French-based recruits. But he was limited and sometimes rash in the challenge, second best even to the basic Jamie Carragher and Abel Xavier. And £3 million was way too much cash to turn down for a lad who, let's face it, was no Lillian Thuram in the making. This seemed like good business, and so Houllier took the readies within the gleaming new UEFA transfer window. We would have to wait now until January to do any more trading. So this was the Liverpool summer transfer news. Apart, that is, from the Lee Bowyer affair.

I assume you have not flown in from Mars, so I will take it you have a working knowledge of the Lee Bowyer story. Bowyer is a player who has, as they say, a 'colourful' past. He had previously trashed a London McDonald's while at Charlton, allegedly frustrated at being served by Asian staff. At Leeds he had been acquitted of biting the face of an Asian student Sarfraz Najeib during an ugly drunken late-night attack, for which his United team mate Jonathan Woodgate was convicted of affray. In short, he seemed like a trouble-making boozer of the kind long rejected by Houllier.

On the field, Bowyer was a non-stop goal-scoring midfielder, as well as a combative opponent who could readily dish out the tough stuff. During Liverpool's last visit to Leeds, Bowyer had elbowed Gary McAllister in the face in an off-the-ball incident right in front of the apoplectic Liverpool bench. Now, struggling Leeds, £77 million in debt, wanted to get rid of the player. Bowyer had publicly resisted a club fine of £88,000 for his late-night drinking and public humiliation and Leeds were also now trying to manage their image differently. But who could possibly want this bagload of expensive potential trouble at some mad price? Astonishingly, in July 2002 Liverpool's Gérard Houllier, self-appointed King of Clean Living and Moral Propriety, began transfer negotiations with the same Lee Bowyer. The case divided the city.

Let's be honest, most football fans can forgive almost any moral impropriety by a player as long as it doesn't affect his game. 'Child molester? Fair enough, but has he got a decent left foot?' But Bowyer could be, very publicly, a thoroughly unpleasant customer, both on and off the pitch, and he seemed to stand opposed to all the things Houllier had told us he was trying to achieve at Anfield. Among the fans, these transfer talks were producing plenty of the 'I don't like him – but he *can* play, and he is a decent price' sort of response. In any case, Houllier would surely sort him out and turn him around. Save him. Could Liverpool afford to take the moral high ground here? What if a less squeamish rival came in and snapped Bowyer up? A few of us wished this would happen right now.

Not that Bowyer was going on the cheap. A fee of £9 million was quickly agreed with Leeds, and Houllier offered Bowyer a five-year deal on double his Leeds wages. But Bowyer had a reported £1 million legal costs to pay, with a potential civil case also hanging over him. His advisers wanted more dough. Crucially, they began playing on what seemed to be a preferred move to London to try to raise the Liverpool offer. Houllier immediately pulled the plug, saying the Leeds man had shown insufficient enthusiasm for joining Liverpool. Sighs of relief all round. Bowyer's past, it seemed, could readily be excused at Anfield, but not an open snub of Houllier's Liverpool project. The manager received no high marks among Bowyer watchers in Liverpool and those who had supported his painstaking transformation of Anfield standards. Where was the consistency or trust in this proposed transfer? Bowyer, incidentally, later got his dream of a London move. He ended his season in disgrace at relegated West Ham – in the reserves.

NEW SEASON, NEW PROBLEMS

The Bowyer and Duff sagas involving Liverpool were not, in fact, the biggest transfer stories of the English summer. While Houllier had spent a cool £18.7 million over the break, only a fraction of which he had raised in the football transfer sales, rivals Manchester United eventually fell in for Rio Ferdinand, also from Leeds, paying a staggering £30 million for the England man in a dying transfer market. On transfer cost, this made Ferdinand the sixth-best footballer in the world, when it was unlikely he was even the sixth-best player in Manchester. He would have to deliver – big time. While Rio was coining it at the top, kids were still being abused further down the tree. A judge ruled that Pierre Bolangi, a 17-year-old Charlton Athletic youth player, was killed in a pre-season training exercise organised by the army because inadequate instructions were given about players swimming through a weed-infested pond.

In Italy, meanwhile, it seemed likely that the Serie A season would actually be delayed in starting because of club financial problems and disagreements over the distribution of TV income. In 2001–02 Italian clubs had registered collective losses of £448 million. Someone, clearly, needed to get a grip.

Lack of TV cash was also a big issue in England, where the ITV Digital meltdown had robbed smaller clubs of much-needed income and placed as many as 30 Nationwide League clubs under threat, at least according to some 'experts'. This seemed like scare-mongering, especially when clubs were becoming so adept now at opting for administration and then writing off huge debts, before emerging again leaner and fitter, if not necessarily wiser (Leicester City were the latest club to move towards this version of born-again accountancy). Such practices also tended to undermine the claims of league bosses that the TV companies were 'shafting' clubs by not fulfilling their contracts. After all, this was exactly what sick clubs were now doing to small businesses and their own players all the time.

When league chief executive David Burns recommended allowing Wimbledon to relocate to Milton Keynes, argued for the recruitment of Rangers and Celtic to the Nationwide League and then negotiated a panic replacement TV deal with BSkyB, for a paltry £90 million over four years, his number was already up. But even the European giants were now worried about costs: the G14 clubs agreed an informal salary cap in July to avoid auctions between themselves, and even talked about limiting the number of players each club should have in their first-team squad. Not everyone was convinced: 'I'll believe it when I see it,' said Gordon Taylor, head of Fifpro, the European players' union. 'The clubs that put forward this sort of agreement are usually the first to break it.' He was right, of course.

Also in Europe, UEFA were accused of 'shafting' the G14 clubs – it was a summer for 'shafting' – by planning to cut back the Champions League format from 2003–04 by getting rid of the second group stage. One sensible concern here seemed to be the amount of high-intensity football some top English-based players were now playing. Michael Owen called for the restructuring of the English season, arguing that tiredness had hampered England's World Cup prospects. Gerhard Aigner of UEFA argued that shortfalls in the European TV markets, declining attendances and pressure on players were all reasons to reduce the number of Champions League games. Liverpool's Rick Parry and the rest of the Euro elite were clearly shocked:

> What is the point of having a European Club Forum if the clubs are not going to be consulted over any changes? We are not happy with the process; the views of the clubs when the Champions League was altered have been ignored. We don't find that acceptable, and that will be made clear to UEFA. We think it [the Champions League] should be left as it is.

The clatter of discarded toys could be heard in all the major football cities of Europe, though while club bosses wanted to hold to the current format for financial reasons, it was also well known that managers, such as Ferguson and Houllier, wanted a reduced number of European games. Arsène Wenger envisaged a very different football future – and liked what he saw:

> The best way to go is a European League, which will create interest. The formula we have at the moment does not make all television happy. The only way to keep everyone interested is to keep the countries involved all season. You cannot kill the domestic league: that is compulsory. But you have to create a shorter European League and have bigger squads at bigger clubs. When you organise a competition, people want to see the best teams against the best. You want to see Arsenal against Real Madrid and Manchester United against Barcelona. It will happen or all Europe will collapse.

An apocalyptic vision indeed: the possible collapse of 'all Europe', a model for a European League which seemed to argue for ever larger playing squads, *and* a new league that seems to exclude, in Wenger's vision at least, one very important English club – Liverpool. The Community Shield meeting in Cardiff between Liverpool and Arsenal at least offered Houllier an early chance to match his pretenders against Wenger's European League hopefuls. A 1–0 defeat taught nobody very much about the future, with the Liverpool man arguing that it may take months for his new signings to settle. Liverpool seemed in a perpetual state of transition under the French technician; Arsenal looked strong and settled. This promised to be a long road.

CHAPTER 2

Hoping to Believe

18 AUGUST 2002: ASTON VILLA 0, LIVERPOOL 1

Sunshine; awful new kits; teenage girls with too-orange faces. New hopes. Opening day can catch you painfully undercooked and unawares, but not since Liverpool played Forest, away in 1992 – our first taste of the new All Singing, All Dancing, Sky Sports TV Premiership – has the Anfield team lost on the opening weekend. Bob Paisley used to have the Reds up and running early on, and even under Souness and Roy Evans the Liverpool problems usually stacked up only after the opening exchanges. Gérard Houllier has actually won all of his Liverpool openers, courtesy, mainly, it has to be said, of the Premier League boffins at 11 Connaught Place offering the Reds some tasty home bankers to get us warmed up for the stiffer trials that lie ahead. So travelling on opening day actually comes as something of a mild shock. Not so, however, the temper of these West Midlands manic-depressives, who act as our unwilling early hosts.

Villa are victims, of course, of the new commercial division of labour at the top level. Champions in 1981 and then European Cup winners as recently as 1982, they are now lost in the deep, lower midriff of the FA Premier League with only one League Cup win and an FA Cup final humiliation to show for the past 20 years toil under Chairman Ellis. His name on the stand opposite us today both provokes and also reminds the locals that things only change here over Doug's lifeless corpse. The Holte End would offer plenty of willing volunteers to make the conversion happen.

THE LIVERPOOL WAY

Today's home flags proclaiming 'Ellis out' and asking plaintively 'Where's the ambition gone?' tell you that opening day is not awaited in this corner of the Midlands with even one-tenth of the anticipation or the straining desire that is, possibly misguidedly, crammed into the red-and-white seats in the North Stand to our left. We, as always, it seems, have hopes for the Premiership title.

Promotion this season for local rivals West Brom and the hated Blues, Birmingham City, has quickened up all this claret resentment in Aston, this desperate yearning for success. But the truth is that, like a tiring and careful veteran determined to finish a fun run, Villa are too busy now looking anxiously behind at the chasers rather than up ahead to those contesting the tape. This is also why we are able to field today our expensive new World Cup man Diouf, while Villa offer their own supporters only an ageing ex-Red defender, 'Stan' Staunton, in midfield and a stretched centre-forward, oddly called Crouch, who is the kind of awkward but limited striker that Villa manager Graham Taylor seems to have copyright clearance for wherever he turns up in the manager's Big Office.

So, it is not too stressful here; no thoughts of early pointlessness, not even when Stan himself scuffs a couple against post and bar during a piece of untidy first-half scrambling in the Liverpool box. Instead, Steven Gerrard and Danny Murphy gradually take control of midfield affairs, with new man Diouf positively *pleading* for work on Liverpool's right. And this is what really impresses about the Senegalese today: his surprising determination to battle for the team. You can see immediately why Houllier likes him so much: 'He runs his arse off!' he indelicately tells the press later, apparently less taken by the clever flicks and turns with which the Senegalese is also trying to unlock the Villa defence. Less appealingly, El Hadji also likes the deck: he enjoys a roll about. This means that when he *is* fouled – and Barry and Alpay are soon delivering solidly here – referee D'Urso decides our new recruit deserves no protection, no help at all. This also means a booking – for protesting too much – and, later, the bird for our new man. Houllier feels pressed to deliver a 'calm down' lecture to him during the half-time oranges. He will have some fun this season away from Anfield, our man from Senegal.

After the break, Riise soon gets the decisive goal down the Villa right, and even glaring misses from Michael – including a blasted penalty – fail to inspire a serious home response. Later, as we leave the spartan new Main Stand, we watch a giant Villa man, bedecked in the home kit, take away his delighted young son, who is draped in

Liverpool red. This is a sign of the football times that probably no one here can now reverse. And it signals our first three travelling points, perhaps too easily secured.

THE LEAVING OF LITMANEN

The arrival of so many new players at Liverpool over the summer inevitably means others will either have to move or get used to Saturdays in tracksuits – or worse, collars and ties. Biscan, Berger and even Smicer are at risk for sure, and Jari Litmanen will now struggle even to make the bench here, and he knows the truth. Like the frustrating Christian Ziege before him, he so palpably fails to fit the manager's modest model for the new Liverpool that it makes you wonder why Jari was ever brought to L4 by Houllier. Football managers sometimes seem to shop like you or I would: 'Will I ever need him? Possibly. Who knows? Wrap him up.' Except, at over £2 million a year, this Finn is no obvious bargain – at least not for a handful of appearances a season. Jari has been publicly moaning recently and GH has typically fired back in the press about not being willing to suffer malcontents in the Liverpool camp. So now the little man is finally off, back to Ajax, where they still chant his name, and where his talents might be better valued. Let's hope we don't meet him again later, angry and determined, with a score to settle, in Europe.

24 AUGUST 2002: LIVERPOOL 3, SOUTHAMPTON 0

The Flattie (The Flat Iron pub in Liverpool 4) is host this lunchtime to the red-and-white stripes from the south coast and also to inflated home expectations about this season, which most people here are still too wary to voice. The build-up on Merseyside has also been dominated by Diouf's arrival, which most threatens Emile Heskey, who scored only eight Premier League goals for Liverpool all last term. Typically, the guileless Heskey has been warmest in his welcome for the new man. A generous and kindly guy, Emile lacks real devil, which is also why he's not scoring as he should be. Ironically, Heskey is also one of our few 'big stars' who has publicly stated he wants to stay at L4 for his whole career: 'Why would I want to leave?' He works hard, and is liked by Michael and by the rest of the team. But he also gives reason to the manager's long-ball tactics and he, too soon, loses all confidence near the goal. Houllier is far too cautious to include all three forwards up front, so Emile may well have to adopt the 'Fowler position' of 2000–01: that is, mainly on the bench.

But not today. John Arne Riise has played the full 90 minutes in a Norwegian friendly international in mid-week. So Emile plays in his place, wide on the left. With Markus Babbel still not ready to start (will he ever be?), Xavier and Traore retain the other current 'problem' Liverpool positions, at full-back, with Cheyrou (the 'new Zidane', apparently) still under League wraps. He says he needs to do much more to prepare himself for the physical challenges of the English game. A suited Diao has also arrived early (the 'new Vieira' – oh, yeah?), after playing what good Liverpool judges describe as the worst-ever debut by a Reds player in a pre-season defeat at Chester City. French, you might gather, is increasingly the preferred language in the modern Liverpool dressing-room.

Anfield gleams today, hardly the obvious candidate for replacement by a proposed new 60,000-capacity venue in nearby Stanley Park. But we *will* have to move, of course, compelled to do so by the cramped and dishevelled surroundings and the new economics of the European football elite. The Fellahs in Front – ageing working-class locals and Liverpool fanatics – are in full working order on the Kop, and my footy mates, Steve and Cath, and local football scribe and researcher Rogan Taylor are also primed for another L4 assault on the championship. Rogan is full of news of Everton's new Chinese sponsor and their two Chinese signings, Li Tie and Wei Feng, and, pleasingly, the way they hate each other's guts. To his mandarin mate's disgust, Li Tie is even in the Bluenose first team at Sunderland today; the Premiership menu now has endless variety.

Not so Southampton, who have packed the midfield and, even early on, look neat but toothless. Their plans to frustrate and then threaten Liverpool are soon undone when Heskey stumbles around Telfer on Southampton's right, to cross hard and low for Diouf, the old 'Serial Killer' himself, to bundle in almost on the visitors' goal-line. Stan Collymore, Nigel Clough and plenty of others have all made great starts here in the past and then disappeared down the toilet, so no one wants to look too impressed with this three-minute opener. But it *is* a good start.

And when Heskey heads on a Xavier throw-in early in the second half for Diouf to score again, in front of the Kop, well, most people here would queue to buy the new man a pint. Cheyrou does enough in a late cameo to show us he might be useful – and to earn a penalty, which a starring Danny Murphy powers in, below us. A comfortable 3–0, despite *no* goals from Michael. We have been quietly impressive, defensively secure, as always. Strachan picks out Hyypiä later as having given one of the best centre-back displays he has ever seen – which is a normal Sami showing for us. Heskey has 'made' two goals in his new role, and we even top the embryonic League table. But in the Flattie there is only understated contentment. We know the real tests lie ahead – and that we are in it this time for the long haul.

GROUNDS FOR COMPLAINT

Early season controversy. Glenn Moore, football correspondent of *The Independent*, picks his ten best football grounds in Britain. His list includes Molineux and the Reebok, as well as Highbury, Parkhead, the Millennium Stadium, and some massive place in Manchester. Anfield fails to make the list of ten. Atmosphere? Forget it. History? Not really. A real football ground? Not a bit of it. The next 'ten best' *Independent* feature: on moisturisers. Enough said.

The Observer, meanwhile, argues that the new Ronaldo-packed Real Madrid – which we haven't even seen play yet – is, perhaps, the best European club side ever, and goes on to list past competition. The original multi-Euro champions Real from the 1950s – fair enough. Cruyff's 'total football' Ajax team from 1973. Who could argue? Van Baston's AC Milan from the late 1980s, obviously a great side. Bayern, from 1974, with Maier, Muller and Beckenbauer – hard to resist. But the Liverpool side from 1984? Domestic Treble winners, who won the European Cup for the fourth time in seven years, in Rome *against* Roma? Do they even get a mention? Wake up!

28 AUGUST 2002: BLACKBURN ROVERS 2, LIVERPOOL 2

Blackburn is a preferred visit for many Reds fans from Merseyside: a local trip; a big ticket allocation; good pubs; not mad prices in a new ground; decent bizzies; and only a few local crazies. (Paul Reynolds, a Liverpool fan – and a truly good man – was in charge of policing here, until he died recently. RIP.) Add Souness as the boss here, strikers Yorke and Cole recently of Old Trafford fame, and also the Damien Duff: 'Will he, won't he?' Liverpool transfer saga, and this meeting has all you need to get the early-season football juices working at close to full tilt.

These East Lancs folk were awakened in the early 1990s, of course, from a deep football slumber and slide when a local scrap entrepreneur, Jack Walker, decided he wanted to devote a large wad of his retirement cash to bringing back the title to the decaying Lancashire mill towns. Flowers, Hendry, Shearer and Sutton duly arrived, the builders moved in, and Kenny Dalglish put his Hillsborough woes behind him to shape up the new Blackburn. In these corporate football times, a provincial 'town' club winning the English title had seemed like a thing of the past. But Rovers' 1995 triumph proved, simply, that in the new era big cash wisely spent really can conquer all. I guess, for some Liverpudlians, Kenny toppling United in 1995 was a 'victory' of sorts. Not for me. Not even close.

The blue plaque on a tiny terraced house nearby reminds us tonight that the captain of the 1922 Rovers FA Cup-winning team was actually born and raised right here. He probably drank in the local pubs with other working people, and played in a ground that matched the very modest pretensions of his surroundings. By contrast, today's Ewood Park resembles a giant, redbrick spacecraft that has alighted, but has barely settled, among the homely back-to-backs we are walking through now. Tonight's Rovers squad live in distant mansions and they could buy entire streets in this area if they wanted (to rent out, obviously). Rovers now boast a Turk, an Australian and a Swede to face the multi-national Liverpool. Same place, very different times.

Our own Liverpool pre-match focus tonight is on whom, in the absence of Robbie, the injured Jamie Redknapp, the departed Barmby and the out-of-favour Carragher, the Liverpool bar-room critics will now alight. Smicer is always an easy target, of course, talented but soft-centred and too work-shy for his many doubters. Heskey also provokes, a sometimes clumsy striker without goals in his blood. (Tonight a Liverpool fan says of Heskey, with the sort of darkness – and racism? – only football humour can ride: 'With a touch like that, Emile, in a previous life you must have been a fucking rapist.') Danny Murphy still has his critics, but he is answering them.

Abel Xavier also fails to impress at right-back. His technique is suspect, his positional sense is often poor and he's a ball-watcher. And at Anfield, he is still a Bluenose ball-watcher. Our bleached blond now faces young Duff, a hyperactive and willing dervish, with something to prove. Predictably, it is just too much for him.

So, when Rovers score early on, through Dunn, following fieldwork by Duff on Xavier's watch, it is all pained, knowing looks in our little section of the upper tier at the Darwen End. Up front, Houllier has decided to play Diouf in the centre of the Liverpool attack, but he has also asked him to try to play Emile's role of back-to-goal, holding the ball up. None of this impresses our new man, or the giants who line up at the back for Blackburn. In fact, it is the maligned Xavier and Murphy who combine on Liverpool's right to get us level before the half. For now, the travelling moaners hold their counsel.

We get stronger after the break, especially when Heskey and, yes, Smicer are finally called off the bench and into the action with Owen and Diouf among those who give way. And when Tugay gives the ball away cheaply, following a Liverpool corner, it is Vladdy who carefully floats the loose ball beyond the Blackburn far post to the lurking Riise. And this scoring header, let me tell you, is something special, because Riise not only has to climb high, he also has to power, control and direct this pace-free cross back *over* Brad Friedel and into the only sliver of the Blackburn net he can see. He does all of this – brilliantly – leaving the Reds only 13 miserable minutes to hold out for another three points.

We can't do it. We can't do it because we can't defend on the right. In the closing minutes the Italian Grabbi gets outside Duff and beyond Xavier to cross, too long, from the Rovers' left. But when Traore allows the ball to be returned into the danger area from the *other* flank, only one of the following two players – Grabbi (Blackburn), Xavier (Liverpool) – reacts to the cross. I'll let you guess. The Italian's header arrows past Dudek, for 2–2. The L4 'Xavier Out' lobby, which is bubbling up around us, hurriedly calls its next meeting.

Walking home, as we face the terrible post-match Blackburn traffic jam, we rationalise that a point from here is actually a decent return, that other top visitors to this footballing heritage park will surely struggle. But we also know that losing a late goal like this is deeply unprofessional and a sign of real weakness. Because this is exactly when true championship teams manage to hold together: when they are ahead, late on, away from home and chiselling out a precious win. We are not there, not yet. Houllier, above all, should know this.

2 SEPTEMBER 2002: LIVERPOOL 2, NEWCASTLE UNITED 2

Still they come to Liverpool, these Geordies, flooding the Walton alehouses, desperate for a win, a goal, or even a sign, anything. My Newcastle mates tell me that, inured to the constant taste of defeat at Anfield, the black-and-whites just enjoy the day/night out in weekday Liverpool. These are fellahs who are the morning workers or the self-employed, the fiddlers and the minor local gangsters. They are the guys who never miss, no matter the cost or the pain. And tonight they have their unlikely comeback reward, escaping another drubbing and sharing the Anfield spoils for once. They should thank the England players on show tonight, Owen and Shearer.

Michael has lacked confidence, and possibly fitness, since he returned from his summer England work in Japan. Houllier has talked about tiredness affecting all his World Cup players, but the usual press talk is about Michael already being burned out, lacking mental strength or being endlessly troubled by injury. Most of this is bullshit, of course, though the joyful, free-running force that was Owen, even a couple of years back, seems unlikely ever to return. Michael has worked through better defences than this Newcastle one in his sleep. Tonight, with Smicer in his favourite central role behind the home strikers, Liverpool play with skill and pace for more than an hour – and Owen misses countless chances.

Instead, the impressive Hamann is moved again to pick his old club Newcastle for a rare goal at the start of the second half, before Owen scores from the spot in front of the Kop after Dabizas energetically uses Hyypiä as a penalty box climbing frame. The score, 2–0, reflects well our superiority, and Newcastle's catastrophic defending. But as Smicer tires, Sir Bobby Robson, the Spencer Tracy of football, in an annoyed triple substitution, brings on the returning-from-injury Robert and Bellamy and also the waspish Jenas. Robson's aim is to try to get at the Liverpool defence with serious pace.

And Bellamy soon obliges, pulling a ball back from the Liverpool right for Speed to score easily. When the Frenchman Cheyrou comes on for Liverpool, he looks, by comparison, like a talented boy – frightened, uncertain. And the visiting fans now begin to cease their 'Liverpool slums' dirge and to take a real interest in the proceedings that only seconds before promised their all-too-familiar emptiness. Laurent Robert takes a late corner-kick right in front of them.

Forget the negating England affinities for a moment: most opposing fans really *hate* Alan Shearer. They hate him for his cynicism and moaning; his self-centred ruthlessness and attempted manipulation of officials; and for his enjoyment of the humiliation of opponents. They also hate him for his aloof and boring public persona. 'In Cluedo,' a journalist wrote obscurely of Shearer recently, 'he would not be the revolver but the lead piping.' But, most of all, opposing fans hate him for the goals he delivers, like a knife to a dying opponent's chest. Here he outwits even the towering Hyypiä, gets to the Robert cross first, and threads his header home through tangled Liverpool bodies on the home goal-line. The Newcastle end collapses in disbelieving joy, while streams of angry scousers now buzz around the Anfield exits.

Another lead squandered, another two points carelessly tossed aside. Outside, Newcastle fans are babbling uncontrollably into mobile phones, setting up the next pub rendezvous and wondering whether they can now scrub together enough cash and excuses for a forthcoming Champions League visit to Kiev. In the Flattie, meanwhile, it is only gloom, despite the thrilling style of the first two-thirds of the contest, because playing well for a home draw offers cold comfort. These lost points will cost us. Our competitors, we tell ourselves, will not make the same mistakes.

SINGING THE BLUES

It gets worse before it gets better. Because Vladdy Smicer, at last showing us his real form, now breaks a big toe playing (and scoring) for the Czechs. Against the rough house, promoted Birmingham City in L4, Michael continues to flounder. In the absence of our glue-at-the-back defender Henchoz, another 2–0 home lead is given up, this time to Clinton Morrison, a man ridiculed for his boasting and no-game-to-match with Crystal Palace on his last visit here, a 5–0 League Cup thrashing in 2001. This means **Liverpool 2, Birmingham City** 2 actually stands as a result: a joke one.

14 SEPTEMBER 2002: BOLTON WANDERERS 2, LIVERPOOL 3

At Bolton Wanderers – and by now in need of a win – Houllier decides to change things around. Diouf has looked raw and unconvincing since his early promising start and Michael, certainly, needs a rest from watching his shots and headers pass unerringly high and wide. So Milan Baros comes in for Owen, with Bruno Cheyrou starting for the confused Diouf. Carragher starts too, and Diao also fills in for Henchoz at the back; an inexperienced foreign midfielder asked to play centre-back in the buffeting madness that is the English Premier League. Interesting.

Milan Baros is one of those young continental players who arrived at Anfield on the back of Houllier's work with the junior French Academy. GH saw Baros come on to change the direction of an under-18 international fixture and so followed the later progress of the Czech before stepping in with a £3.6 million bid in December 2001. Plonked in a hotel room, with no useful English, and with reserve-team football as his only reward for changing clubs, the new man failed to impress the club's coaching men – or reserve-team watchers – with his moaning, poor application and a tendency to pile on the pounds. Houllier joked later that his staff must have thought the manager had made a real mistake with the signing. Baros was obviously ambitious and unhappy – and seemingly unwanted at his new club. And they call this player management? But with a full pre-season under his belt and a place cemented in the squad as Fowler and Litmanen both departed, at the ripe old age of 20 Baros's outlook – and game – had suddenly brightened.

Here, he finally shows us something special. By using the good movement and deception in the first half offered by Cheyrou, Baros starts to get behind the Bolton defence on the Liverpool right. The first time this happens, he hits the post. The second, just before the half, he thunders a shot high past the left hand of Jaaskelainen for a deserved Liverpool lead. In the second half Bolton soon equalise in what is already, it seems, an 'equalising' Liverpool season. An uncertain Hyypiä, trying to compensate for Diao's defensive unease, stretches for a ball the African should contest and, instead, deflects a Bolton punt into the path of Gardiner, who scores.

But Liverpool respond well. One of Steven Gerrard's many strengths is his flat, bending cross-field ball into the box from deep on the right and hit to land behind advancing defenders. For maximum benefit, your strikers need to anticipate where this delivery will end up, but they also must *time* their runs to be onside and to be moving forward as defenders are clearing their lines. Heskey, and even Owen, struggle here – but not Baros. He delays his move, instinctively, and meets this driven cross by Gerrard perfectly – and in oceans of space – directing it with his leading right foot beyond Jaaskelainen. Tugging on the badge of his jersey, he now has many willing Liverpool supporters nearby waiting to aid with the wild celebrations.

Now, this *should* be enough for the contenders we claim to be. We should close this game down, take home the spoils. But, late on, defenders lose track of the mad Spaniard, Campo, and from a cross which ought to be cut out much earlier by the Liverpool centre-backs the new Bolton man lashes past Jerzy from five yards. Another 2–2 draw. Our fourth lead lost on the trot, two goals conceded every game. Two more points surrendered. Except that, while the Bolton team and crowd are already mentally in local pubs and restaurants, celebrating a famous come-from-behind draw with Liverpool, Baros, Murphy and Riise combine right from the kick-off, eventually, to squirt a pass through the heart of the home defence. And the guy who bursts into the Bolton box, shrugging off all challenges, before chipping the ball confidently past Jaaskelainen and into the home net for a Liverpool win? Emile Heskey. Damn you, who *ever* doubted him.

DON'T PANIC!

Lloyd Owusu, the Sheffield Wednesday striker, has yet to start a match for his club this season because of recurring panic attacks. A catastrophic short visit to Spain could easily induce the same in L4. 'I told you at the end of last season you'd see a different Liverpool this year, one that would take risks. I can tell you we will go for a win. We have to attack.' This is Houllier, to the press, before the match against Valencia, at a place where a draw is a perfectly good return. If this is the new Plan B, we should find and revert to Plan A. Immediately.

17 SEPTEMBER 2002, CHAMPIONS LEAGUE: VALENCIA 2, LIVERPOOL 0

Houllier has some claims to mitigation. Henchoz, our defensive key, is still missing. Diao, a very square peg, fills in at centre-back. And we don't really attack: we can't get the ball. Perhaps GH actually believed all this British press guff about Valencia starting badly this season, being tight for cash, and struggling to score goals. Coach Benitez has even had problems getting his stars to turn up for training. Valencia are a little like Liverpool – winning, but not always pleasing their fans. But you don't win La Liga (the Spanish Premier League) for the first time since 1971 and play in two Champions League finals, in 2000 and 2001, without some real quality and strength. And we see it all here tonight. In spades.

Diao is shredded by Carew and the talented Aimar. Filleted. Traore fares little better against the clever Rufete. And to start, as Liverpool do in the Mestalla, without either Baros or Owen is just perverse: it is typical Houllier, putting two fingers up to the press and fans and saying: 'I'm the boss; I pick the side.' In fact, only one Reds player, Carragher, survives from the Liverpool team that played here in 1998 under Evans and GH – the occasion when Phil Thompson, then working for radio, met Houllier for the first time. So Diouf starts with Heskey, and plays like an idiot, losing the ball endlessly in midfield. 'Maybe it was too big a match for him,' Houllier muses later, insightful to the last. And the Liverpool midfield – our strong four, in fact, of Murphy, Riise, Hamann and Gerrard – are also completely outgunned here, chasing shadows. They are subjugated, outwitted, by Aimar, Baraja and Vincente. We have come to try to play, to attack, and instead we are only humiliated. Devastated.

After 20 minutes, Albeda, Baraja and then Aimar befuddle the Liverpool left with crisp one-twos for the first Valencia goal. Traore is static, watching on. Fifteen minutes later it is Baraja who is allowed the freedom of the Mestalla, by Hamann and Gerrard, to strike home from 20 yards. The end. Don't be fooled by Liverpool's 'better' showing in the second half because Valencia are just shutting up shop, soaking up the little we can offer. Dudek later complains that Liverpool played 'like girls' in Spain, a damning critique of the Liverpool Ladies' squad. In fact, we look much worse: raw and naive. Pretenders.

RACE ALERT

Sophisticates on the field, the real deal, by contrast sections of the Valencia crowd are patently gobshites off it. Emile and Traore are loudly barracked by the locals for, well, let's see, being black. Elsewhere this week, Thierry Henry, in Eindhoven, and various Fulham players playing in Split get the same treatment. Liverpool's official website is soon to the fore on this, condemning the Spaniards with gusto; as if *my* club is at the heart of some marvellous positive-action work on race in the city – which, of course it isn't.

I met ex-Red Howard Gayle recently, who now works on his own coaching scheme in the Liverpool 8 area. He is, understandably, wary now about contacts with the club, unwilling to risk his kids in the harsh professional football environment, which chews up and discards all but the fortunate few. The Liverpool under-17s and under-19s teams rarely – if ever – have local black kids in the ranks. Ironically, Everton probably have more impact, more presence, in Liverpool 8 than the Reds, while Liverpool FC trawls the globe for young talent from any background. Local racism, cheek by jowl with international cosmopolitanism. Thierry Henry says he will walk off the field next time he is abused. He is a brave and noble young man – and a fantastic footballer. This is also why, of course, he is such a target for abuse. Wenger and Houllier should lead their *whole* team off until this shit is sorted out. It won't happen.

21 SEPTEMBER 2002: LIVERPOOL 2, WEST BROMWICH ALBION 0

This *should* be easier than Spain, because after 17 years away, the Baggies are back in the big time. But West Bromwich Albion arrive here with three solid 1–0 victories on the bounce – the 1–0 scoreline is their parsimonious stock-in-trade – so we expect the visitors to defend with plenty of bodies and confidence. After the humiliation in Spain we, needless to say, are likely to lack the latter. Houllier's team selection today at least begins to make a little more sense. Both Owen and Baros play and Henchoz is fit again. Cheyrou plays behind the home strikers, with Riise at full-back. Albion are shaped around Darren Moore, a defender so large in the arse area his shorts must be specially constructed; Sean Gregan, a quality deep-lying midfield stroller, recently recruited from Preston; and Jason Roberts, a strong and willing handful up front. With this solid core, patience is likely to be required from the home crowd today – but don't expect any.

Houllier says Michael has 'looked sharper' in training this week – a bit of sixth-form psychology which is worth a try – and Owen is soon buzzing around the giant Moore's legs like an excited dog at a pair of chunky brown lamp-posts. Just as we might be beginning to worry about achieving a breakthrough after more than half an hour of this foreplay, confusion at the back for Albion lets the alert Owen in and Hoult, grasping for the bouncing ball, collars Michael instead. Penalty.

Nobody who really understands the game thinks the current ruling on penalties and sendings-off makes any sense. *Nobody*. In this case, Hoult has made an honest attempt to play the ball, but Owen has just been too quick for him. A clear penalty, certainly, but no more. Instead, Hoult is also red-carded by David Elleray for denying our man a scoring opportunity, which is crap. Dismissals should be reserved only for premeditated 'professional' fouls, consciously aimed at stopping a player scoring. This is what the new law was aimed at. Book the guy for a reckless challenge, OK, but this automatic 'last man' law is stupid and unfair; it punishes defenders who are trying to defend and offers an overly harsh double penalty against defensive mistakes. It is spoiling the game.

Not that any of this matters too much to Michael, who is still struggling with his own demons. Incredibly, he has already been asked to play with *five* different forward partners and is now the man chosen by Houllier to take the penalty. Owen's penalty record (six scored, five missed) and his current form are both poor. Very poor. A confident fellah, anywhere in the Kop, might be a safer bet to take this kick right now. Houllier thinks, 'Let Michael score from the spot and it will ignite his season.' We think, 'Murphy will score this kick and, anyway, Michael is not a great penalty taker. Why risk damaging his confidence more?'

So when the great man virtually *passes* the ball into the arms of the substitute keeper – according to today's programme, a rookie who is a *Liverpool* fan – Joe Murphy, we are not that surprised. Crestfallen, sure, but not surprised. Albion, invigorated by their escape, are then, themselves, denied a sure-fire, stick-on penalty in front of the Kop, Hyypiä (what is wrong with him?) flooring Roberts. The Albion manager (and cheeky bastard, ex-Bluenose) Megson jokes grimly later that the last away penalty kick awarded at the Kop end was given just after the war – the Crimean War. At half-time, the score is 0–0.

Thus far, Milan Baros has looked willing but crude, a young, raw talent with lots still to prove, but at least he begins the process now. Gerrard, again, is the provider, a right-wing cross, positively begging the Czech to head it in before the Kop, which he does, with no fuss. For a while, at 1–0, we look safe against the 10 men, passing and keeping the ball, making more chances, with Michael still unable to convert. But only a last-minute goal by Riise – laid on by Murphy and Owen – really quietens the Kop's anxiety and our own complaints that we should be battering this depleted, promoted outfit. It's a win, but not an entirely convincing one.

THE LIVERPOOL WAY

STRIKERS

Milan Baros now has three goals in two games for Liverpool – but he still has work to do. After all, Bolton and West Brom are hardly part of the new European elite. Diouf, meanwhile, suddenly looks anxious and lost, while Emile Heskey still searches for goals and confidence. These three, together, may contribute 20 goals to our cause this season. They will have to. And Owen? 'Worried?' Houllier says later, 'Michael had a good game and his contribution continues to be excellent, so why should I be worried?' He's right, of course. Hansen, Rushie and all the decent judges say the same. Owen *will* score goals again. For Liverpool still to be unbeaten in the League, while trying to accommodate new players and without goals from Owen, suggests there might be better things to come. The way Arsenal have started their own campaign, blasting the opposition, Wenger calling on all-comers, there will need to be.

26 SEPTEMBER 2002, CHAMPIONS LEAGUE: LIVERPOOL 1, BASLE 1

The jackals are already out for Houllier in the red-tops. This infuriates even us, his willing critics. But we have been churning over the same ground in the Flattie this evening: Houllier's post-illness attacking vogue; his recent selection gaffes; and his uncertain summer transfer dealings. Foreign starters across the whole of the FA Premier League last week actually outnumbered home-based players for the first time. A sobering thought. But our own criticisms of recent LFC business emerge out of affectionate concern for GH and his strategies – and for a better Liverpool future. The press jibes are aimed only at stupid radio phone-in cheese-heads and sniggering Mancs disbelievers. So we are justly outraged.

But here, tonight, in the old Main Stand, among the players' dodgy friends and their glossy, blonde girlfriends, there is more depressing evidence for the prosecution.

And it is not that Liverpool play especially badly here, because Baros, Gerrard and Murphy all drive the Reds urgently forward. But it *is* because Michael still can't get it right, and the young Frenchman Cheyrou, playing in the Smicer spot behind the front pairing, has some of the skill, certainly, but not any of the strength of character or the belief to grab a football match at this level by the lapels and demand that it plays his tune.

And there is another troubling theme just beginning to emerge here. Jerzy Dudek, a reliable rock last season, has stopped making saves. After the lively Baros puts Liverpool ahead on the half-hour, and after the home team also hits the frame of the goal *three* times in a swirling first half played almost exclusively at the Anfield Road end, Carragher and Dudek manage to botch the only serious Basle attack, allowing Rossi to equalise from a narrow angle on the left and through the Pole's legs. Jerzy might have done better, that's all I want to say. Despite Steven Gerrard's non-stop honesty and passion in the second half, and scrambles and escapes in front of the Kop, we can't get another goal – and Michael sinks deeper and deeper into the wastes of midfield, away from his true centre of operations, the soft belly of the penalty box of our opponents. A European draw, at home and against opponents we had counted on beating. Only pointless Spartak Moscow now hold us off the bottom of Group B. We have real work to do.

FERGIE: A MAN ALONE

United are desperate, of course, to reach the 2003 Champions League final – it is at Old Trafford, after all. But Alan Hansen argues that turning around the apparently floundering and Keane-free Manchester United of this 2002–03 season is Alex Ferguson's biggest test. 'My greatest challenge is not what's happening at the moment,' says the great man in red-faced reply during a press briefing. 'My greatest challenge was knocking Liverpool right off their fucking perch. And you can print that.' No wonder they love him, the Glams fans. As we all do.

28 SEPTEMBER 2002: MANCHESTER CITY 0, LIVERPOOL 3

And we are also supposed to love dear old Manchester City, a homely local counter to the global corporation next door, with gritty supporters who cherish their 'we are so bad, we're good' public persona. They now adore Kevin Keegan, a manager so immune to defensive strategy he would rather perish gloriously in a 3–4 than hang on to a saving point in a dull 0–0. Even the 'new' Houllier is not *this* insane. But this is hard to warm to, this parody of the cheerful losers they are supposed to represent. Keegan has also spent big money to keep City in the big time. They deserve our respect today, not our roll-eyed sympathy. Truth is, we fear defeat.

It is also our last time at Maine Road, nestling as it is in the vaguely menacing Moss Side. The old Main Stand here still gives off a real whiff of exotica, with its Far Eastern curves and pretty sky-blue mosaics. On the Kippax side of the ground, however, Maine Road still looks more like a claret Stalag, a dreadful enclosure which is fearful of the world outside. This outer wall now guards the new Kippax Stand, which has tumbled out of some architect's kit and is a truly grotesque construction even to the untutored eye – of which there will be many here this afternoon. Some of these are already engaged in steely battle, we hear later, in a pub across the city, even though our common enmity with United tends to dampen down a little of the traditional north-west tribal rites at this fixture. The shadow of Old Trafford never quite disappears from the consciousness of those who wear the pale blue of Manchester's 'other' football club.

Team news: Hamann replaces Cheyrou for Liverpool, a sensible defensive precaution, but Traore also replaces the injured Henchoz – a risk. 'It is adapt or die if you want to make your mark in the Premiership,' says *Le Boss*. This is why it is still a mystery that City's Ali Benarbia, an Algerian specialist midfield conductor of the exact type Liverpool need, is someone Houllier would never contemplate signing. Mercifully, magical Ali is suspended for City today. Anelka plays, however, keen, no doubt, to show GH the recent error of his ways. Owen also starts, and in the opening minutes the City defence *gifts* Michael a goal, allowing a corner to ricochet to his feet inside the six-yard box. Even in his current trough, Owen greedily accepts this chance, a break at last. Already, you get the feeling this is not the sort of gimme any team can afford to give our previously shot-shy hero. But after all the loose Houllier talk about attacking hard and winning matches, this post-Valencia Liverpool now retreat into a familiar mode, allowing City the ball, inviting attacks. The moping Anelka is alone up front for City, Huckerby in a familiar doze. After half-time it is more of the same, Liverpool defending, with City's Benarbia-free attacks lacking penetration and direction.

Until, with just over an hour gone, Steven Gerrard makes his first real contribution to the afternoon by putting Michael clear down the centre, with the home defence by now playing way too high. Last week – yesterday, even – Owen would have ballooned this chance, or might even have been caught by chasing defenders. Today, he races away and his early right-foot shot glances off Schmeichel's left shoulder – and skids into the bottom corner. Later Owen characteristically dips his left shoulder at the retreating Sun Jihai – and scores again. Really, 3–0 is a joke result. We have looked nothing like the rampant Arsenal, for example, and have struggled for any sort of grip today for more than an hour. But, in the right mood, Michael Owen can do this: he can make a mess of reason.

FOOTBALL MANAGERS: A DOCTOR WRITES

Elsewhere in the FA Premier League there are already worries aplenty. Glenn Roeder is under pressure at stuttering West Ham, Graham Taylor is in early trouble at Villa, and the peppery Strachan is also struggling, early doors, at Southampton. Liverpool fan Peter Reid has built Sunderland into a hard team of alehouse battlers, tagged to Kevin Phillips' life-giving goals. But suddenly the Roker men – including ex-Reds Phil Babb and Steven Wright – look spent and uncompetitive at this level, out of their depth. Unforgivably, they fold in the first north-east derby, with Newcastle. Alarm bells. The media, and Reid's football-commentator drinking buddies, are aghast that Wearside supporters now want him out: 'Have they forgotten what Reid has done for the club?' But the truth is that Reid has hit his own personal football-management wall and he probably has to go. Real Sunderland supporters – rather than, say, Radio Five 606 telephone monkeys – have a right to demand it. Sentiment, or even justice, will play no part in this decision, though the transfer window also means that any new appointee will have to work with the straw Reid has assembled, at least until January. This unattractive package may delay the inevitable but, by then, a £30 million relegation loss may be nigh on unavoidable. It will soon be over for him at Sunderland.

2 OCTOBER 2002, CHAMPIONS LEAGUE: LIVERPOOL 5, SPARTAK MOSCOW 0

It is tempting, I know, to see this scoreline and think the 'new' attacking Liverpool is now truly with us – but don't go there. We do OK tonight, but this is really a sad tale of the near-terminal decline of the Russian game. Ten years ago to the day, Spartak beat a callow Liverpool, home and away, in the Cup-Winners' Cup. They also have recent European wins at Villa, Blackburn and Highbury to look back on with pride. But in the past decade the Russian economy has gone belly up and the new international football order has relegated the Eastern Europeans – including some former European Cup winners – to the status of also-rans.

Spartak, the 'patriot's team', can no longer hold on to their best prospects. Young Sychev, a real teenage talent, is actually on strike at the moment, seeking a move to improve on his £39,000-a-year salary. We have guys sitting in the stands who 'earn' this in a week. With hooligan problems at home, no wins in 13 in Europe, the usual mafia tales of corruption, and the presence of teenagers and also second-rate Brazilians and Portuguese in the Spartak side, coach Romantsev has worries enough. Houllier, by contrast, can afford to leave out Baros (for a struggling Cheyrou) and can reunite Heskey with Owen.

And from the start, although Spartak play neat, measured football, we can see their defence has that 'just in time' look of imminent collapse. It takes only 14 minutes to kill the game: Heskey through a hole in the visitors' back-line the size of the Russian national debt, and then Cheyrou to get his first goal for Liverpool, from Murphy's pass. Danishevskiy, the Spartak captain, is already berating his withering colleagues and hiding on the right wing, claiming all of this has no connection at all with him. Hyppiä's header near the half-hour confirms that our guests may have some skill, but they have no heart and little defensive coordination.

We don't get the expected second-half landslide, the Kop regularly standing and then returning, disappointed, to their seats like the bristles of a giant hairbrush realigning. In front of us the bench boys, Berger and Biscan, warm up and chat. A wag behind wonders what Patrik is saying: 'Who's more crap – me or you?' Berger was injured last season but has now been overtaken and is expected to leave. Igor is nowhere, the disappeared, and a subject of gentle crowd ridicule. Markus Babbel is cheered to the rafters, of course, but for our own forgotten men from Central Europe it is now only the usual casual cruelty of supporters.

Salif Diao does make it on – and scores, from Heskey's cross – before Emile finishes things off with the fifth goal. This win puts us back on track in the group because Valencia have whacked Basle tonight. Second place is now within Liverpool's grasp once more. Michael, meanwhile, is in his latest striking crisis: one match without a goal. For Spartak, third only in the Russian League and strapped for cash, the Champions League may soon become only a memory from better days before the crooks, and the football money-men, stepped in.

REFEREES – FOR EVER?

Football referees are required to retire at 48, while those officiating in European and international matches have to pack in this little bonus at 45. Say goodbye to the Russian gift clocks. The pace of the game today means that few refs over 50 could handle the slog – though some of the current crop barely seem to get out of the centre-circle. The European Union is now investigating whether this compulsory retirement age is actually illegal. This makes sense: match officials should be judged on their fitness not on their age. Or, perhaps, they ought to be judged on their fitness *to referee*. If this ever became the norm we would struggle to keep many Brits on board. Durkin perhaps. Scottish referees are now sponsored by Specsavers, an optician. You couldn't make it up. Some of the continental refs are pretty good: Collina, though hyped; most of the Scandinavians; and also the Germans. But it only gets harder to referee as the managers and players get better at deception. It's the modern way.

5 OCTOBER 2002: LIVERPOOL 1, CHELSEA 0

'Unlovable' and 'charmless': two words used in the press this week to describe Chelsea. Or was it Ken Bates? Chelsea fans were saying worse a few days ago after yet another collapse against European rookies, this time to Viking Stavanger, not even the best side in Norway – or, possibly, in Stavanger. This sort of surrender does not help the housekeeping: Chelsea are a reported £97 million in debt. Liverpool are still utterly inept at Stamford Bridge, while the Boys from the Bridge have won only once in L4 since George V wore the top hat. So this is a home banker.

If Henchoz is fit, Houllier has only one decision to make today: pick Bruno Cheyrou and the European midfield 'diamond', or a 4–4–2, with Baros up top and Heskey playing left-side of midfield. Rotation seems to have gone out of the Melwood window this season: is the manager as unsure as we are about his recent signings? *Le Boss* opts to give Cheyrou his chance, a big challenge. And it is not a complete success, to be honest not even close. As usual Chelsea, with good technique and something owed to their fans due to the European disgrace, dominate possession and make Liverpool look as crude and ideas-free as any opponents can. 'Nothing much for Sky in this game,' mutters Rogan, showing mock concern for the national TV audience. 'Fuck Sky!' immediately from the Fellahs in Front, angry and frustrated.

The second half brightens – slightly – and at least Cudicini is given a little more serious arm-stretching exercise, by Gerrard and Hyypiä. But it is only with Baros off the bench, finally ending Cheyrou's misery – and why did *this* take so long – that the visitors are really discomforted by some Reds pep and pace. Diao's late appearance (for Murphy) is important too, in forcing through a post-90-minute prod to Heskey on the left, who shoves defenders aside before forcing Cudicini to push his shot on to the far post.

This rebound could now fall to any grateful defender because the Chelsea box is full of friendly blue shirts. But you just know it will fall to just one enemy red one. After all his recent troubles, Michael is now destined to score even when he is otherwise anonymous. Petit, Le Saux and Gallas all throw themselves to the ground at this injury-time injustice, while Dessailly angrily clobbers the ball over the Main Stand. The Chelsea fans are silent for the first time today. On the Kop we are celebrating shamelessly. 'We don't deserve it,' I squeak to the Fellahs in Front, mid-hug. 'I know,' says a beaming Barcelona Bob, 'but who fuckin' cares?' A home banker, for sure. Stolen gold.

KING SVEN AND ROONEY TUNES

The early-season international break now kicks in, with the FA Premier League, generous to a fault, wondering exactly *why* it should allow its expensive stars free passage to play for Team England, which is rapidly being turned into a greedy cash cow by the smooth ex-Saatchi man Crozier. There is nothing smooth about Sven's England in Slovakia – or at home to Macedonia. Steven Gerrard looks lost, as he has already been too often for Liverpool.

After the international interlude, a grim three points from **Leeds United 0, Liverpool 1** falls on the anniversary of Gérard Houllier's illness. One year on, GH looks strong and determined, his Liverpool as grinding and functional as ever. 'Once the season starts,' he says, 'it's a battle every day.' He looks fit enough for the test. Diao's name on the scoresheet for the first time is overshadowed by an impressive Leeds pre-match anti-racism crowd display (there's a few words you might be surprised at seeing in the same sentence) and a knowing Liverpool 'One racist bastard' chant to home hero Bowyer. Not everything, you see, is solved by clever crowd mosaics.

Over at Goodison, meanwhile, Bluenose hearts are finally lifted by a snotty 16-year-old butcher's boy from Croxteth, who has already been seen playing street 'shots in' this season with the local scallies. Earning a respectful £80 a week, Wayne Rooney shoots down Arsenal to have Wenger gagging on his 'We'll lose no games this season' prediction – to put his grateful Red pals from across Stanley Park top of the Premiership. Moyes is doing a good job at Goodison, where village idiots are already comparing this young Croxteth 'Micky' to the Red Boy Wonder. No question, the first derby game is already eagerly anticipated in these parts.

26 OCTOBER 2002: LIVERPOOL 2, TOTTENHAM 1

Before that spicy little local dish there is more European fare and north–south scores to settle. In the Champions League, Spartak offer more in Moscow than in L4 – but not that much more. After conceding early on and looking shaky for fully the first half-hour, the Reds slowly take over, Michael weighing in with a first-half header. A second-half Hyypiä-inspired goal-line scramble further feeds Owen's goal craving, so you know that with a European hat-trick in the offing, and against mediocre and fading opponents, Michael is not readily going to stop at two. Murphy provides the chance in the last minute for **Spartak Moscow 1, Liverpool 3**. 'I just feel I'm on the Earth to be a footballer,' says Michael later, moving dangerously into David Icke territory. No English club had ever won in Moscow.

Tottenham, on the other hand, are the only club to beat Liverpool now in 27 League matches, but in those 27 unbeaten games you would struggle to identify one complete performance, one utterly controlled and dominant, free-flowing Liverpool victory. But there is a real determination here not to lose, and today's game is another hard-fought, but deserved, win against improving opponents who lay third in the early table this morning.

Gerrard, Diao and Hamann all start, a robust and physically committed midfield, if one lacking in real lock-picking guile. Up front, with Heskey injured, Diouf partners Owen, but to no great effect. He needs time, maybe. But Diao's strength and purpose already seem much more suited to the pacy biff-bang of the English game than does Diouf's head-down trickery. The latter bounces off Dean Richards today and lacks control and vision. 'He plays in training like in the final of the World Cup,' Houllier says of Diouf. Maybe this is the problem. He's still young and raw – but he also has a £10 million price tag, a hefty burden. Today, it is only after Poyet has twice gone close in front of the Kop, and when Baros and the returning Smicer replace Diouf and a struggling Gerrard for the last half-hour, that Liverpool really begin to get at the Spurs back-line. Danny Murphy finally gets the goal, setting himself for a favourite 'free kick' in open play, which he brilliantly bends around Richards and Parry and beyond Keller.

Tottenham have shown so little in attack that this feels like it should be enough, but Richards sets up Acimovic on the Liverpool right before lumbering into the box to meet the cross with a scoring header. Hyypiä is visibly furious with this lapse, angry at his own impotence (again). In the distance, the Tottenham end boils over with predictable joy. And a home team that does not really believe in itself will now settle for this hard-won sharing of the spoils, especially after a punishing trip in mid-week. But not a team with Michael Owen back in the scoring groove.

With minutes left, Owen drags the ball away from a returning Jamie Redknapp and sets off once more down the Spurs right. He, first, squares up Perry, and then nutmegs him into the box, while already eyeing up Carr's approaching tackle. Michael computes that a spurt to the ball will send Carr clattering into him: simple football physics tells him as much. So he plays for the penalty, and Carr sits forlornly on the Anfield turf in front of his own fans, having been suckered into obliging. Murphy offers to step up, but Owen wants to exorcise his spot-kick demons. The Kop has wavering faith: 10,000 pairs of eyes force themselves to watch. And in the flattening distance, one point magically becomes three: 2–1. Four points clear at the top.

AT HOME AND IN EUROPE

'The Champions League is so big and so important financially to the club. But the one I want to win is the League,' said Michael at the start of the season. 'I'd love to win the League. *Love* to win it.' Kevin Keegan revisited. We sometimes pick up vibes that Michael sees Europe or the England project as more important than his domestic Liverpool work. Maybe we're harsh. 'Me and Stevie Gerrard, we have been there for 10 or 12 years now so no one can doubt our commitment to the club and it's a nice feeling to know you are part of a select band that's represented the club through thick and thin,' Michael said recently. 'I hope the fans can see that through all the comings and goings that there have been loyal players who have gone through the good and the bad times.' We hear you, Michael. It is still early days, sure, and we don't yet convince, but we are beginning to think this could be our time.

30 OCTOBER 2002, CHAMPIONS LEAGUE: LIVERPOOL 0, VALENCIA 1

Our time? Our time? Not in the Champions League in 2002–03, not after this harsh football lesson. We have scraped and battled our way to the top of the Premiership, but en route we have seen nothing even close to the quality that this Valencia have to offer tonight. As a result, we look like schoolboys in comparison, with only Hamann and the young Traore at the back offering the sort of steely belief *all* your players must have to succeed at the very pinnacle of European club football these days.

Baraja and Albeda in the Spanish midfield have power, strength and skill and also the sort of intelligence and maturity still painfully lacking even in Steven Gerrard at this level. Aimar is elusive and clever and plays at a pace that Danny Murphy, for one who has been so impressive in the English game recently, simply struggles to achieve. Curro Torres reminds only what a willing, but severely limited, option Carragher is at right-back. Rufete and Kily Gonzales, meanwhile, offer the sort of width and trickery for the Spaniards that has long been confined by Houllier to the 'not needed' pile in L4. As soon as the former strikes, close to the half-hour, we know in our Red hearts that the game is up. And they do not lack for cynicism or violence, these Spaniards; they are happy to put a foot in, if invited. Valencia have all you need, and more.

CLOWNS OR CONTENDERS?

Later, Houllier will say we have to 'learn' from such defeats, but Liverpool are not even reading from the same texts, studying the same notes. Under GH we still think power and teamwork, allied to athleticism, is enough.

Valencia have all of these, but they also prize intricate possession passing, cerebral skill and deep thought. It is hard to avoid the conclusion that it is not a difference in experience or ability that divides us from the Valencias and the Reals: it is, in fact, a difference in culture and *philosophy*, one which makes GH's calm talk of Liverpool 'catching up' with Europe seem absurd. Technically, we are still nowhere; little further on, in fact, from when Houllier first took over. This may seem harsh, but it is also true.

In the League Liverpool are already more than one-quarter of the way to unlikely glory: unbeaten and top. We have had easy fixtures and yet, apart from one hour at home against Newcastle, we have barely performed, certainly not how we would like to. Is this a show of real championship grit while we find our true form? Or else is it the summit of our capabilities, winning in this ugly and pragmatic style? Who knows? After blasting off and looking unstoppable, Wenger's Arsenal have now lost two on the bounce and United, short of strikers and with Keane injured and suspended, have won only one away. But look no further: these two are the true title opposition, even if neither of them look really secure.

At the bottom, meanwhile, the predicted relegation scum is already foaming around the Premier League plughole: Bolton; Baggies; Sunderland. West Ham are at risk, but Everton, young Rooney to the fore, are floating clear. Leeds, under Venables, look unsure; Keegan has already reined in his attacking plans at City, while the Mackems have hired Sgt Wilko to save them, as a drowning man might claw at a dropping stone. Leicester City were relegated last season – and, as a result, went bankrupt. All clubs in the same spot this season look down at Leicester's current plight and try to look only upwards – to safety and thus financial rectitude.

Our new men will ring home with very different tales. Diouf, briefly, started brilliantly, but now looks callow and inexperienced. Cheyrou is lightweight but talented, while Diao is already a model of limited Houllier midfield strength and work-rate. Baros has done enough to suggest that releasing Anelka might yet be excusable transfer work. Jimmy Traore is now stronger and more composed at the back, despite his European exposure: we hope a budding French Phil Thompson, complete with stick legs. Perhaps not. All will play their part in the months ahead, but we still have no guiding light, no organiser or poet. This manager, as always, wants to compose everyone's lines. And they all know, as I do – as every Red does – that our dreams at home and abroad also ultimately rest on just one man's form and fitness. Can he (Michael, of course) really row our struggling boat ashore?

THE LIVERPOOL WAY

FA PREMIER LEAGUE TABLE AT 31 OCTOBER 2002

	P	W	D	L	F	A	GD	Pts
LIVERPOOL	11	8	3	0	22	9	13	27
ARSENAL	11	7	2	2	26	13	13	23
CHELSEA	11	5	4	2	20	12	8	19
MAN. UNITED	11	5	4	2	14	8	6	19
TOTTENHAM	11	6	4	1	17	16	1	19
MIDDLESBRO.	11	5	3	3	15	8	7	18
BLACKBURN R.	11	5	3	3	18	13	5	18
EVERTON	11	5	2	4	14	15	-1	17
NEWCASTLE U.	10	5	1	4	16	15	1	16
SOUTHAMPTON	11	4	4	3	11	10	1	16
FULHAM	11	4	3	4	16	14	2	15
LEEDS	11	4	2	5	13	12	1	14
BIRMINGHAM C.	11	3	3	5	11	14	-3	12
ASTON VILLA	11	3	2	6	7	11	-4	11
WEST HAM	11	3	2	6	10	17	-7	11
MAN. CITY	11	3	2	6	9	17	-8	11
CHARLTON	11	3	1	7	9	16	-7	10
WEST BROM.	11	3	1	7	8	18	-10	10
SUNDERLAND	11	2	3	6	5	15	-10	9
BOLTON W.	10	2	2	6	10	18	-8	8

CHAPTER 3

And if you Know your History . . .

EARLY DAYS

Two powerful football clubs in the same northern city with no obvious or strong spatial or sectarian divisions, and which even divide families in their footballing allegiances, are bound to throw up some difficult cross-club loyalties in local player profiles. Perhaps because of Liverpool's longer spell of playing success in the 1970s and 1980s it has been mainly Everton supporters recently who have been faced in derby games by players who were once young Blues, now turned cruelly blood Red. Battling Peter Reid was certainly a staunch Liverpool fan, a Kopite, who ended up on the other side, but in recent Liverpool ranks Ian Rush, and later Robbie Fowler, Steve McManaman and Jamie Carragher, were all born as Blues. Michael Owen's father even coached at Goodison. This makes Wayne Rooney's royal blue blood all the more important today to the Everton School of Science.

These sorts of club exchanges should not really surprise. Most fans know that Liverpool's origins actually lie inside Everton Football Club. When the Sunday school of St Domingo's was sited on Breckfield Road North in May 1870 and the adjacent Methodist chapel was formally consecrated in July 1871, it signalled the beginning of not one but two north-west professional football clubs. Football actually came rather late to Liverpool, perhaps because of the unique industrial structure of Merseyside, centring as it did on sea trade, rather than on manufacturing, and producing a large semi-skilled and non-unionised casual workforce.

THE LIVERPOOL WAY

The late arrival of the Saturday half-day holiday for Liverpool's casual workers especially inhibited the growth of *playing* football in the city, so that in 1879–80 the Birmingham press recorded 811 football matches in the second city, while in Liverpool the local press noted only 2. So right at the very start, there was some catching up to do on Merseyside.

The nineteenth-century Christians who first spread organised sport among the Liverpool urban poor began their work using the gentleman's sport of cricket and American-imported baseball (still played in Liverpool today). But the lively young men from the Everton and Anfield districts of Liverpool soon demanded more physically robust team games for the winter months. By 1878 a football club, St Domingo's, had been established, growing out of the summer's cricketing activities around the church, and one year later it became Everton Football Club, locating its headquarters in a pub in Everton village, the Queen's Head. Everton played its first game – which was won – against nearby St Peter's on 23 December 1879.

By 1880 Everton were already playing in the Lancashire League, using public land on Stanley Park for home matches. However, a league ruling in 1882 required that the new club find an enclosed ground for its home fixtures. At a club meeting, hosted in his own Sandon Hotel in Anfield, by John Houlding, an Irishman, a football follower and errand-boy-made-good as a self-made brewer and notable local Conservative politician, it was decided to rent a roped-off pitch near Priory Road. But following complaints about noise from the site, another venue was soon found for rent, at Anfield Road, where Everton first played on 28 September 1884, beating Earlstown 5–0.

In the years that followed, the new club prospered and ashes and wooden terraces and small stands were erected at the new ground at Anfield Road to accommodate paying crowds. These now sometimes numbered thousands and had been needed to support professional players from 1885. In 1888 a sea change occurred. The small businessmen and solicitors who ran 12 of the larger football clubs in Lancashire and the Midlands, including Everton, agreed to establish a regular fixture list under the auspices of a new organisation, the Football League. Ironically, the more established neighbours Bootle FC were omitted from the League. They were riled at being overlooked by the new body, claiming, with some reason, to have a better ground and larger crowds than the upstarts at Anfield.

With a regular list of fixtures and with dockworkers winning the right to half-day Saturdays in 1890, crowds continued to grow at Anfield Road, which also hosted an England v. Ireland international match in 1889. However, a rift was growing between the powerful Houlding and his colleagues at Everton. Houlding not only owned part of the land at Anfield Road but he also acted as the agent for the landlord for the rest. As the Everton club's profitability grew, Houlding decided to increase the Anfield Road rent, from £100 to £250. By 1891 Houlding had also formed a new limited company with a view to buying the Anfield ground and nearby land. Everton members were disgruntled. On 15 September 1891 the *Liverpool Echo* reported that feelings ran high as an Everton member had told a shareholders' meeting that: 'it seemed to him that they could expect nothing but the policy of Shylock from Mr Houlding. He was determined to have his pound of flesh, or intimidate the club into acceptance of his scheme.' Something had to give.

When Everton's 279 members rejected the new rent proposals, in October 1891, Houlding served notice for his own club to leave the land he now partly owned. In February 1892, Everton were set to quit Anfield, as four club shareholders agreed to contribute £1,000 each towards the £8,000 cost of a new ground, at nearby Goodison Park on the north side of Stanley Park. Evertonians must wish a new ground was as easy to come by today. On 12 March 1892 a meeting of Everton members overwhelmingly voted Houlding out of office, and the move across the park was cemented. Later, Houlding claimed that it was the 'teetotal fanaticism' of Everton's Methodist members which had forced him into his actions and which had produced the rancorous split. To his credit, Houlding resisted the temptation to then sell his Anfield Road site for housing development and, instead, he set about 'reinventing' Everton. He had actually invented Liverpool FC.

OUT OF THE BLUE . . .

Houlding wanted to keep the name Everton for his new football club, but the FA ruled in 1892 that the name should stay with the relocating majority group. Although a rugby union club called Liverpool Football Club already existed in the city, on 15 March 1892 Houlding formed the rather grandly named Liverpool Football Club and Athletic Grounds Company Limited to play at Anfield Road. He charged the new club just £100 in rent and immediately donated £500 to its coffers. Houlding viewed the ground from his Stanley House home, which still stands on Anfield Road today, opposite the Centenary Gates. The club's application in the same year to join the Football League was rejected, however, on the grounds that 'they did not comply to regulations' and that Liverpool had refused to join any division other than the First. But Everton's opposition to their upstart neighbour's bid for League membership was presumed by many to be the crucial factor in Liverpool's rejection. At this time, it was Everton who played in ruby shirts while the new Liverpool club played in Everton's original blue-and-white quartered shirts, a kit they kept until 1896–97, when it was finally exchanged for the more familiar red and white.

Forced to join the Lancashire League, instead of the more prestigious Football League, Liverpool's first fixture, a friendly against Rotherham Town at Anfield on 1 September 1892, drew only a handful of spectators and could not even cover the Yorkshire club's financial guarantee. Early Liverpool matches in the Lancashire League – like the first, a local 'derby', at home to Higher Walton – rarely attracted more than 200 fans. But on the day Liverpool defeated Stockton to go top of the regional league, a reported 3,000 turned up at Anfield to see the win. Liverpool went on to win the Lancashire League title and the Liverpool District Cup in 1892–93, but both trophies were immediately stolen, costing the club a painful £130 in replacements.

The Anfield Road ground in the 1890s could already accommodate up to 20,000 spectators, 4,000 of them on an exposed bank of wooden terraces at the Anfield Road end of the ground. At the Oakfield Road end a smaller stand stood in front of open fields, an area which would eventually house the new standing Kop. The original south end at Anfield was recalled by one early fan as: 'a very old wooden stand with newspapers on the floor. I often used to wonder how it didn't catch fire, with people throwing their cigarettes down.' On the west (Main Stand) side of the ground stood a modest pavilion and paddock, while the narrow, Kemlyn Road enclosure was squeezed between the near touchline and the tight, terraced housing of the Kemlyn Road itself.

'Honest John' McKenna, an Irish-Catholic rugby devotee who had been converted to football by his early Everton involvement, and a man who had taken Houlding's side during the great split of 1892, was now a key figure in the new Liverpool club. McKenna, from County Monaghan, was a grocer's boy who became a vaccinations officer in the West Derby district of the city. He lived modestly all his life in a terraced house near the Anfield ground. McKenna effectively became Liverpool's first manager and was soon famous for his legendary player-scouting trips to Scotland, which resulted in the famous 'Seven Macs' Liverpool team of the 1890s – including one English 'Mac', goalkeeper McOwen. (Eerie, isn't it?) McKenna had quickly recognised the tactical advantages of the passing game that was then popular in Scotland. It was a lesson that would stand Liverpool managers in good stead throughout the following century.

LOSING MY RELIGION

McKenna and Houlding, new partners in the shaping of the new Liverpool club, along with the administrative brains, William Barclay, were both prominent Liverpool Freemasons and Conservatives, while McKenna was also a Catholic. Houlding was a well-known Orangeman with strong links to the Protestant-inclined Conservative Working Men's Associations. This fact, the large Irish-Catholic community in Liverpool, and the strong early recruitment of Scottish Protestants as players by Liverpool, all probably fuelled the early view that Everton's was the Catholic football heritage, while Liverpool had a more Protestant base. However, there seems no strong evidence for this. Both clubs had a tradition of contributing evenly to Catholic and Protestant 'good causes' in the city, and there is no pattern of fan or player recruitment by the clubs that indicates any obvious sectarian divisions between them.

As early as 1927 the teams from the city emerged on the field together for derby matches and, unlike the situation in Glasgow, for example, there are plenty of historical accounts from Liverpool of cross-religion divided family loyalties and even city-wide support for whichever of the local clubs was left playing in important cup ties or cup finals. This suggests a strong Liverpool footballing tradition around the two clubs of both separation *and* togetherness, a tradition that does little to support notions of a divisive football sectarianism in the city. By the mid-1930s, in fact, a social survey of Merseyside commented that: 'The intense religious antagonism which undoubtedly exists – and which from time to time breaks out into more than verbal strife – is also peculiar to Liverpool, but it should be added that this has declined in recent years.'

Nevertheless, popular sentiments about the alleged religious leanings of the two clubs lingered well into the post-Second World War period, sentiments that remained important for some of the clubs' supporters in a city where education, for example, continued for many years to be delivered along religious lines. Indeed, strong religious divisions in housing areas persisted in Liverpool until the city slum–clearance programmes of the 1950s and 1960s, and employment practices on the docks and elsewhere in the city in the 1930s and 1940s could also be shaped by religious background. Popular memory also suggests that the two football clubs were 'unofficially' recruiting youngsters from the Liverpool Boys' teams largely along the lines of religious denomination well into the 1950s. This may have suited the rival clubs, of course, avoiding as it did unnecessary competition for local talent. The supposed Protestant-Irish roots of Liverpool FC are probably seen to strongest effect today in Dublin or Belfast, rather than in Liverpool itself, especially in the staunchly Protestant Shankill Road area of Belfast, which has been insulated a little from the global push of 'Catholic' Manchester United, as well as from Everton.

Much later, of course, Kenny Dalglish – a Rangers-supporting Protestant who went on to become a cult hero at both 'Catholic' Glasgow Celtic and 'Protestant' Liverpool – became a useful marker for understanding the real mix of modern sentiments involved in football allegiances in the city. Liverpool FC's recent strong connections with Glasgow Celtic, in fact, probably go back to 1966 when supporters of the two clubs joined forces for Liverpool's Cup-Winner's Cup final defeat against Borussia Dortmund in Glasgow. Twenty years later, a Liverpool side managed by Liverpool and Celtic hero Dalglish played in Glasgow for Jock Stein's testimonial, and the clubs met again following the Hillsborough disaster in 1989. Today – as was shown in the 2003 UEFA Cup clashes – Liverpool and Celtic fans happily share the famous Kop anthem, 'You'll Never Walk Alone'. So there were no surprises in a survey conducted among fans of the two larger Merseyside clubs in the mid-1990s: when asked which Scottish club they supported, Everton fans strongly favoured Celtic, while Liverpool supporters were split, almost exactly, between both Rangers and Celtic.

FOOTBALL LEAGUE PROSPECTS

In 1893, and unknown to other club officials who were quite happy to see Liverpool slowly find its own level in the local leagues, John McKenna applied for the club to join the newly expanded Second Division of the Football League. Local neighbours Bootle FC had fallen on hard times, and out of the Football League, allowing scope for Liverpool's opportunist application. When the club was duly elected into the League, McKenna travelled to London to arrange the new fixture list in good company: he arrived with representatives from Woolwich Arsenal, Middlesbrough Ironopolis, Newcastle United and Rotherham United, all clubs elected into the League in the same year. By 1902 the gregarious and popular McKenna, a man of even temperament who was reckoned to speak with the lowly and the elite on equal terms, was elected to the League Management Committee. In 1910 he became the third President of the Football League, a position he held until his death in 1936, when he was 81 years old. He stayed on the Liverpool board until 1922, only then fully devoting himself to his work with the Football League.

On 9 September 1893 Liverpool FC played its first home Football League fixture at Anfield, against Lincoln City, in front of a reported

5,000 fans. A 4–0 win signalled a first-season promotion drive – 26 wins out of 28 matches – via the end-of-season test match system played against the bottom three clubs in the First Division. Satisfyingly, Liverpool succeeded in relegating Newton Heath, later to become regional rivals Manchester United. Once Liverpool were in the First Division, Anfield gates rose quickly, initially to 20,000, showing the obvious hunger for football in a city that was already, uniquely, supporting two of the top sixteen clubs in England. Liverpool's attendances more than doubled between 1895–96 and 1896–97, to just over 12,000 fans, and by the early 1900s Liverpool crowds had pretty much caught up those across the park, marking out the city as an authentic footballing hotbed of the north.

On 13 October 1894, a Blue and Red Riband day, the city rivals met for the first time at Goodison Park, in front of 44,000 fans, the Lord Mayor and other local dignitaries. Both teams had already embraced the new, 'modern' approach to match preparation, and were even using hotel retreats – Liverpool's was in Hightown – to prepare for major fixtures such as these. Alas, Everton's superior strength and experience produced a 3–0 home victory. Nearly 30,000 spectators watched the return match at Anfield a few weeks later, this time a 2–2 draw, and early rivalry was predictably fierce. 'Local rivalry keeps the game alive,' one spectator memorably remarked. 'It is never so much alive as when Liverpool and Everton meet. Then, the wonder is that instead of everybody being alive, everybody is not killed dead, as an Irishman would say.' Not *that* much changes in football.

The step up to the top level had severely tested the Anfield club's still embryonic resources and support, and relegation looked increasingly inevitable for Liverpool, despite the efforts of the clever forward Jimmy Ross. Ross had scored eight goals for Preston in the 26–0 record FA Cup demolition of Hyde, and had signed for Liverpool in 1894, but was reluctant to play for the club after his footballing brother Nick asked him on his deathbed not to desert North End. Liverpool insisted on the transfer, however, and Ross was a key member of the team that gained promotion again in 1896, scoring 23 times in only 25 games. A year later the versatile forward Harry Bradshaw became Liverpool's first England international, but something of a one-cap wonder when he was dropped after playing his part in a 6–0 defeat of the Irish! Bradshaw later moved on to Spurs and Thames Ironworks, before he died, mysteriously, on Christmas Day 1899 at just 26, a promising career unfulfilled.

In 1895 the barrel-roofed Liverpool Main Stand was built, with its famous curved mock-Tudor gable to cover 3,000 seated fans with an enclosed standing paddock area below. The stand would survive as a landmark of English football ground development for the next 75 years. However, one Anfield observer around this time reported that even under the astute stewardship of new Secretary-Manager Tom Watson – who had been recruited by McKenna from Sunderland in 1896, and was reputedly 'the most popular man in all football' – at some Liverpool home matches, 'there were not enough spectators to go around the field'. The Liverpool police might have complained at this, because the Chief Constable of Liverpool seemed to approve of football in the city. He told the Royal Commission on the Liquor Licensing Laws in 1898: 'I think that now when there is a match on the Everton or Liverpool grounds, a great number of working men . . . rush off home as quickly as they can, get a wash and a change, leave their wages with their wives, and are off to see the football, and I think that has led to a great decrease in drunkenness.' Wishful thinking, perhaps?

TITLE-WINNERS – AND THE PEOPLE'S KOP

Despite these early relegation setbacks, with McKenna's enthusiastic backing and the recruitment of more quality players, these early 'yo-yo' years at Liverpool soon gave way, albeit briefly, to real success. In 1901 the club won its first Football League title, with a team built round the aggressive Scottish defender Alec Raisbeck – described by a writer of the day as 'an intelligent automaton . . . pulsating to his fingertips with the joy of life' – and the prolific English centre-forward Sam Raybould, dramatically clinching the Championship in the last match of the season at West Bromwich. On returning to Central Station in Liverpool at midnight on that mild Monday evening of 29 April 1901, the players were met by thousands of Liverpool fans and even a drum-and-fife band. It made little difference that most players in the victorious team were not raised in Liverpool. Like today, it was clearly the territory of the *crowd*, not that of the players, which really mattered. Players with no organic ties to the place of their clubs were charged then, as now, with offering reflected glory, social cohesion, shape and meaning to the lives of working men in the hard industrial cities of the north. Liverpool was not unusual here: even as early as 1910 over half of *all* League players in England were born outside the region in which they played.

There was no doubting it, Liverpool FC, under McKenna had, in a very short time, become a well-supported and also a highly 'commercialised' and wealthy football club, with little thought for aiding its weaker rivals. The Liverpool board resisted proposals to share match income between rival clubs, especially as gate money had already been spent on improving Anfield. 'Clubs which had provided covered accommodation . . . should reap the rewards,' a Liverpool director told the Football League AGM in 1901. 'Why should they be called upon to divide with, say, Bury, who had little or no covered accommodation?' So it is no surprise that Liverpool also opposed the maximum players' wage of £4, introduced in April 1901 by the public-school orientated and London-based Football Association, which was still troubled by what it saw as the pernicious effects of football professionalism. Key members of the first League Championship team at Anfield were reputed to be earning as much as £10 per man, but Liverpool still recorded a profit for every season between 1900 and 1915. Why should there be a maximum wage? McKenna complained bitterly – as Rick Parry might do today – about those FA 'amateurs' being involved in the business decisions of professionals.

By 1910, when the FA handed over to the Football League and its members control of professional clubs' financial affairs, objections to the maximum wage among the clubs had rather died. McKenna himself had changed his views, he told *Athletic News*, in the light of the 'exorbitant demands of players' that made it difficult to see 'how free trade can be allowed'. Poorer clubs, of course, actually *liked* the imposed wage ceiling; it offered welcome opportunities to keep down costs, provided strict regulation and control of players, and offered opportunities for the least well-off clubs to compete more equally with the rich city giants. But clubs like Liverpool were hardly inconvenienced. Like their main rivals, they got around the ruling by inventing additional 'jobs' for top players or simply by paying them under the counter. The maximum wage ceiling at this time also helped release funds for limited work on grounds. With Liverpool back in the Second Division, in 1903 a roof was finally built at the Anfield Road end, a barrel-shaped corrugated-iron construction, perhaps in fond hope that more goals might now be scored at home games at this lower level, and a third barrel-roofed stand was built on the Kemlyn Road side.

Self-interest was what determined McKenna's attitude to wages and income – as it did other football administrators. Everyone – except the Player's Union and the players who were not paid illegally – was 'happy' with retain and transfer arrangements, though the canny McKenna also accepted a vice-presidency of the Players' Union, and he showed later that he knew well enough the importance of the strong helping to support the weak in the League structure. Although Liverpool threatened to break away in 1916, with other League clubs rather than pool wartime gate receipts, it was actually Liverpool's McKenna who, in 1920, devised the Football League scheme for 20 per cent of the home club's net gate to be paid to visitors, thus ensuring that smaller clubs benefited from larger crowds elsewhere. He, and Everton's William Cuff, were hugely influential figures in the early years of the development of the Football League and its policies.

Right up until the Second World War the Liverpool board, initially under McKenna, was a very stable one, made up mainly of brewery managers, local merchants, solicitors and, for a time, an undertaker and even a schoolteacher. These were by no means the wealthiest or most influential people in Liverpool; they were, above all, comfortable and respectable local citizens who knew how to tend to local business and to local 'community' interests. The early directors were carefully selected by John Houlding, of course, in order to ensure a large measure of personal control over the club, especially given his earlier problems at Everton. Brewers were especially prominent in football clubs, charging rent for ground use and selling their products at matches. Carlsberg's Liverpool sponsorship today actually continues a tradition started many years ago, though without its local roots. Despite early talk in the city of the need for 'democratic' involvement of fans in their clubs, it was clear that this did not include even ordinary shareholders – mainly clerks, managers and bookkeepers – never mind the modest sixpenny spectator. Working people might have soon colonised the professional game in England, but they have never controlled it.

In 1905–06 Liverpool won the League Championship again, just one year after another promotion, and Everton won the FA Cup. The city of Liverpool was certainly the national centre of football excellence, with an aggregate average attendance of 34,400 fans, higher than any English city outside London. A survey in 1907 also revealed that nearly 80,000 football pools coupons were collected in a single week in Liverpool, home to the football betting industry. Some Liverpool fans also already travelled to away matches; around 1,000 Liverpudlians were reported to have made the trip for a vital match at Bolton in 1906. In the same year, the club's directors, encouraged by the gate returns from the second League Championship season, and perhaps anticipating more new support and better prospects for increasing gate receipts, entered into the second phase of major ground development at Anfield.

For this new work, Archibald Leitch, the celebrated Scottish engineer, was called in. According to a suitably buoyant *Liverpool Echo* on 25 August 1906: 'The entire scheme is modelled on a new departure from what football grounds are generally supposed to be. The stands . . . are as safe as skill and good workmanship can make them.' The Anfield pitch was raised five feet and the ground was, for the first time, totally enclosed, reportedly by 'fancy brick walls' and with turnstiles on all four sides. But even the impressive 1903 Leitch Main Stand was dwarfed by the huge cinder-and-wood support banking which was rising out of the fields behind the old open terrace at the (Oakfield) Walton Breck Road end of the ground. Known originally, if rather inaccurately, as the Oakfield Road bank, the new standing area was not the first major bank of terracing at an English football ground, but with 132 treads from top to bottom it was quite probably the tallest. From the back of the open Kop, supporters could see across Stanley Park and down to Goodison. Apparently, Arsenal had already used the term 'Kop' to describe football terracing in north London, but a local journalist, Ernest Edwards, of the *Liverpool Daily Post and Echo*, is accredited with christening Liverpool's new terracing 'Spion Kop', after a hill in Natal District, upon which many young infantrymen from local regiments had perished in a losing battle in January 1900 during the Boer War.

With a capacity for 28,000 fans, the Kop attracted visitors, too; in 1907 Blackburn Rovers supporters on the Kop were reported to have 'waved their colours to a set motion and sent forth a weird, unearthly cry' when the teams appeared for a League match. Goal celebrations on the early Kop seem to include ranks of mainly male fans joyously throwing their flat caps and hats in the air, and chancing on getting their own headgear returned. Local betting syndicates were also rife among Kopites, as they were at most other major football grounds of the time. Betting coups might replace lost wages, because attendance at football frequently drew workers away from their jobs, much to the consternation of local employers.

Women fans were, clearly, prominent at Anfield, too, but some men saw little in the new Kop to further attract members of the fairer sex. In the *Liverpool Echo*, a local male fan complained, soon after its opening, about the narrowness of the Kop turnstiles, which meant that if the club directors thought that, 'any gentleman would ask a lady to squeeze through such an aperture, to the destruction of her dress, they are mistaken'. It could also be very cold and wet on the Kop, and tough on the field, too. In April 1914, for example, a survey of the top 1,701 professional players in England and Scotland found that only 61 had survived the season without missing a match through injury.

In 1913–14 Liverpool reached the FA Cup final for the first time. It was an all-northern affair, against Lancashire rivals Burnley, and the first to be played in the presence of the King. It was an occasion on which to parade, ritualistically, the distinctiveness and hard-headedness of northern cultures compared to those of the 'soft' south – the final was held at Crystal Palace. But the Cup final was also growing at that time into a properly national event, rich in the symbolism of community and country. Despite this, northern fans were determined to resist the sophistication – and exploitation – of the Metropolitan area, a common feature for complaints, of course, about Wembley FA Cup final trips that followed. Spectators for the 1914 final, for example, had to pay a shilling (5p) admission to the pleasure grounds before gaining access, for an additional payment, to the football stadium. This was, naturally, frowned upon by the Liverpudlians who had gone 'down' for the Cup. Liverpool lost the final. It would take another 51 years' hard graft finally to secure a Liverpool FA Cup final victory.

LIVERPOOL BETWEEN THE WARS

After 19 years in charge as Liverpool's secretary-manager, the mercurial Tom Watson finally died in 1915. Watson was briefly followed into the manager's chair at Liverpool in 1920 by David Ashworth, an ex-referee who won the title, Liverpool's third, in 1921–22 before, incredibly, giving up another title to Matt McQueen in 1923. An ex-Liverpool player who had first arrived at the club in 1892. McQueen had also tried his hand at refereeing and as a Liverpool director, and he had a leg amputated in 1924. No matter – he managed Liverpool for four more years after his surgery, before being forced to retire by ill health in 1928, when he was replaced by George Patterson.

These were halcyon days for the Liverpool football club, with Elisha Scott supreme in goal, England captain Ephraim Longworth, the 'prince' of right-backs, and Tommy Bromilow, the slim and sophisticated brains of the double championship team of the '20s at left-half. But Scott was the star, surely the greatest-ever Liverpool goalkeeper, perhaps Liverpool's greatest ever player. Scott was rejected by Everton as a 17-year-old – as too young and too small – and Tom Watson immediately turned down a £1,000 bid from Newcastle United for the young keeper in 1913. The wily Watson knew what he had: 'the eye of an eagle, the swift movement of a panther when flinging himself at a shot', as a journalist once described Scott in full flow. After one especially memorable Elisha save against Blackburn in 1924, a Liverpool fan even got on the field and kissed his hero. When Scott addressed Liverpool fans at his last match at Anfield in 1934 after 467 appearances for the club, tears were openly shed in the crowd. Everton now wanted him, but Liverpool fans' protests about his proposed move across the park sent Elisha back, instead, to his native Ulster, where he won the last of his 31 Northern Ireland caps at almost 42 years of age. A Liverpool great; no question.

By 1921 the Kemlyn Road enclosures at Anfield were fully covered, but it was not until 1928 that a local architect, Joseph Watson Cabre, was asked to place a roof on the great standing Kop. This meant that Anfield now had cover on all four sides for the first time, a capacity of 68,000 fans, and scope for 45,000 Reds shilling spectators, most of whom were under cover. The acoustics produced by the new Kop roof offered encouragement to working-class standing supporters who wanted to get more 'involved' with their heroes on the pitch. The singing of club songs and popular tunes seems already to have been established at some other football clubs by the late 1920s. At Liverpool, fans chanted, rather than sung, especially for Scott: 'Lisha, Lisha'. One Kopite from these days recalls the devotion to the Liverpool keeper – and also the class relations within the Anfield crowd:

> He was idolised by the Kop . . . When the players came out on to the pitch they would run down to the Kop end, just as they do now, and Lisha would wave to us. He also used to give us a wave when he left the pitch. He was a great favourite . . . The opposition fans would be there as well [on the Kop] but there were never any problems . . . It was a very working-class crowd on the Kop, mainly dockers and the like. The 'toffs' were in the Paddock and the stands. We called them 'the mob' or the 'toffs'.

In the 1920s, and for the whole of the interwar period, it was still possible to walk all the way around inside Anfield, and some fans used to 'follow' their clubs at half-time by changing ends, bringing plenty of visitors on to the Kop to join the locals. Links established with visiting supporters at home could even be used to set up future away trips. The football camaraderie is very clear in accounts of football support at this time, but rival fans could also fall out at football. Life on the football terraces was not always sweetness and light, though the police were seldom called in to sort out disputes in the crowd. Fans would, typically, take care of them themselves.

On the popular (Kemlyn Road) side of the ground in the 1920s, young lads between the ages of six and ten years were allowed to sit between the hoardings and the touchline, while their parents watched behind. The supposed absolute sanctity of the pitch was not always observed by fans. In 1933 Liverpool signed the Rangers centre-forward Sam English. When the feisty English tangled soon afterwards with a rival defender in front of the home supporters, a Liverpool fan standing with

Kopite Billy O'Donnell also dived in – to his cost: 'Well, my mate jumped up, "I won't be long, Billy," he says. He jumps over the barrier and he gets mixed up in it. This [police] Inspector grabs him, and he lets fly at the Inspector. I never saw him for six months after that. "I won't be long," he says. He got six months.'

Football spectators of the time were mainly working-class men of working age who were generally young enough to endure what was often a long walk to the ground and two hours standing, in often pretty terrible conditions, at the match. Although football crowds were aggressively partisan, on the whole they were also largely self-policing, discriminating and restrained. In 1914–15, as the War took hold, average crowds at Everton had fallen from 25,250 in 1913–14 to 18,530, and at Liverpool from 24,315 to 16,805. In the 'War season' of 1914–15, scandal enveloped Anfield: four Liverpool and four Manchester United players were suspended by the FA *sine die* after allegations about match-fixing, following the Good Friday fixture between the two relegation-threatened clubs at Old Trafford. But it seemed to have little effect on fan enthusiasm. Both Liverpool and Everton averaged almost 30,000 fans at home games in the season immediately after the War, enjoying, as did other football clubs, a renewed hunger for leisure and sport in Britain after the carnage of battle – even with minimum admission charges raised from 9d to one shilling.

Trams and bicycles were now the favoured forms of transport to Liverpool matches; tram drivers often used to park up near kick-off time and watch the games, and those riding bikes contributed to the local informal economy around Anfield by paying for them to be minded in nearby gardens and yards. But droves of fans would also grab a bag of chips and walk home after games, even to the South End of the city. Kids would be deposited by Kopites in the boys' pen, which took up a section of the terraced area of the Kemlyn Road side of the ground in the 1930s, to be collected again after the match. For the rest of the decade, average crowds at Anfield stayed in the high 20,000s to low 30,000s, as the club struggled for consistency on the field. Average attendances in the First Division as a whole increased from just over 23,100 in 1913–14 to 30,700 in 1938–39.

Football attendances, generally, fell in the north, including Liverpool, in the recession years from the mid-1920s, and neither of the Liverpool clubs ever averaged home gates of 40,000 or more in any season during this period – a figure consistently exceeded by dominant Arsenal in the Herbert Chapman years in the 1930s, for example. But, in 1920–21, aggregate football crowds in the city averaged a period high of just over

72,600, and for the whole interwar period, despite crippling economic depression, combined crowds at Liverpool and Everton only once dipped below 50,000, in 1932–33, as crowds elsewhere in the north fell much more dramatically. In 34 seasons from 1900 Liverpool had 10 top-5 League finishes, Everton 11. Only Sunderland (with 15) clearly outstripped the Merseyside clubs. The city of Liverpool was, unarguably, the centre for northern football support – and success – in England in the interwar period.

Football players of this time also remained culturally and economically connected to the people who supported them – and profoundly the property of the club. This was certainly true at Anfield, where Ted Savage, a Liverpool right-half between the wars, was tracked down one night by a club director's son and had to appear before the club committee because of his relationship with a professional dance teacher. Liverpool expected their men to make the right kind of match – one that had to be approved by the club. Savage's wife remembered much later the Liverpool regime with young players in the 1930s:

> [Liverpool] were very, very strict. They had them like boys, like tiny little boys. Every move they made, every move. They couldn't move a finger without *them* having to know where they were and what they were doing. They [the players] were a lot of children, and I think that's why they transferred Ted to Manchester United. I think it was the money. Once they bought a man they wanted their pound of flesh, and I think they also thought he played better if he went to bed and didn't associate with women. I can't understand why they were so strict. The footballers had a hard time, I suppose.

Contrasts elsewhere were striking. Everton's Dixie Dean was once offered a reported £25 a week to play soccer in the USA, and he also complained bitterly that he had been paid only £50 from a cigarette firm for a lifetime use of his image. In 1930 the American baseball star Babe Ruth visited Liverpool and met Dean. Both men had recently scored a record 60 goals/home runs in their respective sports. Dean was earning £8 per week and was astonished to learn that Ruth earned £300. Average weekly manufacturing earnings in Britain were £3 a week at the time.

Despite these disparities and the growing size of football crowds, the effects of the national economic depression in England and the weak bargaining position of players kept most footballers 'contented'. A £9 maximum wage was agreed for players after 1945, with a bonus for a win (£2) and a draw (£1). By 1952 the maximum football wage had been raised to £15 and £12 in the off-season. The average professional player, however, earned only around £8, compared to the £10 average industrial wage, a fact which encouraged player unrest and corruption and which led to many clubs continuing to make under-the-counter payments. Liverpool even championed foreign football stars when they were little known in England, claiming six South Africans on their books in the early 1930s.

Cost clearly limited football attendances in Liverpool in the 1930s, as it did elsewhere, especially in the north. From almost the earliest days at Anfield, people who couldn't afford to attend matches would simply stand outside the ground and, on hearing a roar inside, would collectively ask, 'Who scored?', to be quickly answered from within. The perimeter gates at matches in the city would be opened at three-quarter time to allow for early departures and opportunities for those outside to watch the last 20 minutes of games. That the general enthusiasm for football in the city in the entire period up until the Second World War remained high cannot be doubted. When the Pilgrim Trust reported on unemployment in Liverpool in 1938, it noted that unemployed men who could not afford the shilling entrance fee still used to turn up on Saturday afternoon just to watch the crowds going to the match.

A DIFFERENT PEOPLE?

After the Second World War, football attendances in England soared to record levels. In 1946 Entertainment Duty, first levied in 1916, was reduced for theatre and sports, and the Chancellor specifically requested football clubs to reduce the minimum admission price from 1s 6d to 1s 3d. Football was not alone in flourishing in Britain in the post-war glow: 45 million fans watched greyhound racing in 1947; 3 million went to cricket; and 300,000 a week to speedway. Cinema attendances topped a record 1 billion entrants.

In 5 years, between 1947 and 1952, football club revenues in England increased, on average, by 20 per cent. In 1946–47 Liverpool's fifth League Championship win drew average crowds of 45,732, bettered only by the 49,379 average at Newcastle United. Liverpool had, of course, signed a new star just after the war, centre-forward Albert Stubbins from Newcastle, for a record fee of £12,500. Everton had bid the same sum for Stubbins, who tossed a coin to decide which club to talk to first: it came up 'heads' for Liverpool. Inside-forward Jack Balmer scored three consecutive hat-tricks in the 1947 Liverpool championship season – a feat never repeated. With Stubbins and a young tyro called Billy Liddell at hand, Liverpool tore up defences in 1946–47 under manager George Kay, a man renowned for his 'deep thinking' about the sport, who had shrewdly taken his Liverpool team to the USA to build up on their frugal post-war diet for the successful campaign. The first Liverpool manager, perhaps, to be concerned about player diets?

Aggregate average football crowds in Liverpool came close to 90,000 for the first time in 1948–49, when attendance figures in England also reached an all-time peak of 41.27 million admissions. In September 1948, the record football crowd for the city of Liverpool, 78,299, was shoehorned into Goodison Park to watch the 1–1 draw in the 'derby' match. By February 1952, when Liverpool had its own record home gate of 61,905 for an FA Cup tie against Wolves at Anfield, minimum League admission prices had already been raised to 1s 9d. They were raised again, in 1960, to 2s 6d. Nationally, and perhaps unsurprisingly, English football attendances dropped in that one season, at the start of the 1960s, by 3.9 million. The post-war football boom was deemed to be over, though many football clubs, Liverpool among them, were actually destined to enjoy their own best average attendance figures in the 1970s.

In the 1940s and early 1950s football remained the ruling passion of working men without television and cars, whose world still revolved around the communal influences of the works, the pub and the match. Rising living standards, growing levels of car and television ownership, and an increasingly 'privatised' and domestic focus for personal consumption are generally blamed for declining football attendances in England in the 1950s and 1960s. The working week also was gradually shortened to five days, so the early industrial link with football diminished. Football started to become the province of the die-hard fan rather than the natural recreation of the working man.

The growing attractions of staying home on Saturdays, for DIY, gardening and for other home entertainments – including more and more Saturday afternoon TV sport – began the long decline of mass active working-class support for local football clubs as a central part of the way skilled working men, in particular, connected to their towns and cities, and also defined themselves. Later, the impact of hooliganism would make fast this initial loss of 'respectable' working-class club support. Ironically, of course, later still it would be television, car travel and a new emphasis on the sport as a focus for conspicuous consumption that actually boosted football crowds once again in the Sky TV era.

On the Kop, and in the rest of Anfield, life was also slowly changing for spectators. The old boys' pen, later quite brilliantly captured in all its terrifying glory by Liverpool fan and writer Alan Edge in his book *Faith of our Fathers*, had now been moved into the Kop, and it was the first sign of the later, more informal, segregation by age which was to become such a defining feature of the terrace 'ends' in Britain from the early 1960s. For big matches in the early 1950s it was not unusual even for adults to climb into the pen on the Kop to escape the crush on the main terrace. It was astounding, in fact, that stadium disasters around this time were largely confined to individual tragedies and to the Burndon Park catastrophe of 6 March 1946, in which 33 people died and 500 were injured when an exit gate was opened by a man leaving the ground, thus allowing thousands more spectators inside.

Floodlit football finally came to Anfield under manager Phil Taylor in 1957, though it had been tried in England 25 years earlier – a move which also stayed the mass absenteeism on the docks and in other local industries when mid-week games had been staged in the city in daylight. The very rhythms of football in England were now beginning to change, especially as English clubs began to take their first, tentative steps into Europe. On the administrative side of affairs, even following promotion to the top level in 1961–62, the Liverpool club remained pretty crude in its approach. Most fans simply queued and paid their money at the gate; neither the segregation of rival fans, nor fan safety, seems a major concern of the time.

But singing among the crowd seems finally to have arrived at Anfield in the early 1950s. A visit to Anfield by Wembley's own Arthur Kagan, the man who conducted the community singing before Wembley FA Cup finals, seems to have been the key. Kagan toured Football League grounds in the 1950s, and at Anfield, before a match against Blackpool, Kagan arrived, complete with a brass band, in order to 'conduct' the home end. Things did not go as planned. As Kagan and his band went hard at one popular tune, the Kop, to its own collective amusement – and probably surprise – piped up with quite another song, wilfully refusing to follow the frustrated Kagan's lead. Others who have since tried, officially, to guide the Kop's singing, especially from the pitch, suffered similar fates.

The career end for the great 1950s hero of the Kop, and of other Liverpool fans, Billy Liddell, a flying Scottish winger, but a modest man and a devout Christian, a player who used to retreat to the toilet before kick-off to pray for the well-being of all the players involved, probably symbolised the end of an era at Anfield – and in English football. Liddell played in every part of the Liverpool team, except in goal, and every new Liverpool signing in the 1940s and 1950s was ritually photographed on arrival shaking the great man's hand for the benefit of the local press and fans. Liddell, like most other highly localised top football players of the 1950s, was an authentic sporting hero rather than a celebrity. He, and other top footballers of his day, neither suffered, nor would have enjoyed, the sort of massive public exposure that awaited most top sportsmen in the approaching television age for sport. He seldom appeared on TV and his image was only really available to local kids in Liverpool on cigarette cards and, to men, in articles in the local press and football magazines such as *Football Monthly*. Few fans would have easily recognised Liddell out of his very specific context of Anfield and the red of Liverpool.

All of this would soon change, of course. As football players became more recognisable, they would also become more socially and economically distant from many fans. Soon, few players would travel on the tram or bus anymore, or live among even affluent working-class supporters, as had been common in the 1950s. Instead, after the football maximum wage was finally abolished in 1961, we were on the brink of the emergence of very new lifestyles and identities for top footballers in England. This would increasingly stress media coverage, image management and cash as central, defining components that would define star identities in the new era.

Liddell, like many players of his day, also worked in another job while he had been a professional player – he was an accountant, and later went on to be a JP. His retirement from Liverpool in 1960 after 22 years at the club and a, then, record 536 appearances, signalled the emergence of a quite new set of social and economic relationships in English football, as well as the effective end of a long-established set of quite specific supporter traditions in the sport. Above all, it signalled the beginning of the redefinition of football as a television show, whose moral categories were altogether less distinct. In just a few years, as the new Liverpool took off under the charismatic Bill Shankly, Liddell and other loyal club servants – essentially gentle and 'ordinary' sons of their clubs, but men blessed with quite extraordinary gifts – would seem increasingly anachronistic figures as the effects of the lifting of the maximum wage and the rise of youth cultures and the 'new commercialism' in football in the 1960s kicked in. English football – and football culture in Liverpool – was about to change, dramatically so.

CHAPTER 4

(Not) Staying on Track

3 NOVEMBER 2002: LIVERPOOL 2, WEST HAM 0

'He's good, Hamann, but he's too fuckin' one-dimensional.' Half-time toilet-talk today, from my left, in the steaming lower Kemlyn bogs. 'One fuckin' dimensional!' spits an outraged mate of this guy, a Didi fan, his laughter fired right across where I'm pissing. 'How many fuckin' dimensions do you want?' A football philosophy master class.

Only one dimension is needed today, provided, of course, by Michael. In pouring rain Liverpool refuse to allow a poor, Di Canio-free West Ham to settle and with Smicer prompting from just behind Owen – and offering real passes, for once – we see the sort of movement and guile which has not been a feature of Owen's play for some time. He glides through tackles for the first goal, squirting his finish over the advancing James. Fellahs in the lower Kemlyn are captured in the press pictures later stretching out to touch him, a saint once more, as Michael jogs, square-jawed and smiling, back to the sodden centre-spot.

The second-half clincher, scored on the break, is made by Smicer's oblique pass and Owen's crippling pace around James, but the ball only slowly aquaplanes into the empty Hammers' Kop goal, followed in by a slithering *pas de deux* of Smicer and Dailly. 'Keep it tight, Sally,' now implores a scouse voice from behind: the powerful Salif Diao is, seemingly, already on his way to being 'one of us'. But not much more is needed today, in a performance which is both a convincing response after the humiliation of Valencia, but also one which simply highlights the chasm between the English Premier League and La Liga, rather than pointing to a resolution of Liverpool's European problems. 'He has got terrific belief, yet he always keeps it under control,' says a deflated Glenn Roeder of Michael later. 'There is not an ounce of arrogance in him.' Joe Cole? Did he start? 'So flawed, and yet so far ahead of most of the rest of the Premiership,' a journalist says of Houllier's team, reflecting on contrasting outcomes this week in Europe and at home. Liverpool, briefly, are seven League points clear.

RUSSIAN ROULETTE

In the Champions League it is Spartak Moscow 0, Basle 2. So now we have to *win* in Switzerland to advance. Shit.

'Our strengths aren't Arsenal's strengths; our strengths are keep it tight, make sure we are defensively right. But we have tried to create more width this season. We have played more courageous football, having a go at teams more, creating more chances than I can remember.' This is Danny Murphy talking.

Houllier agrees: 'We've developed a strength over the last few seasons, but I wanted us to open up a bit more to make our game richer. We have a stability and continuity to our play, to which we've added a fluidity.' They think they can fool us, these football professionals, but we know what we can see. We *do* know the game. Sheer managerial gutlessness costs us any chance of League points in the north-east – and our unbeaten record.

9 NOVEMBER 2002: MIDDLESBROUGH 1, LIVERPOOL 0

Lifted by Man. City's lunchtime demolition of a vapid United, and now walking through the Sovietised student quarter of Teeside, and then past the proud constructivist statues of local football heroes Hardwicke and Mannion, we happy, travelling Liverpool fans still have no idea of quite how we are about to be betrayed today. The Riverside Stadium, no more than a shoddy dockside container, already feels old and overtaken by the new generation of English grounds – and with dreadful facilities to match. Visiting fans are still wading through half-time piss in garbage toilets and the away-end 'concourses' feel like a stifling underground pen. But this isn't the real problem, the true source of our misery today. And not even the brainless pre-match music that produces a stupefied and Orwellian response from the home punters, or its idiotic replaying after the Boro goal, hurts quite like the managerial cowardice we have to endure this afternoon from our own quarter.

OK, we have a poor record at Boro, but we should be buoyant and confident; we are undefeated in the League and a virtual reserve-team Liverpool home League Cup win (3–1) against Southampton this week has lifted the whole club. We have just one League loss in 29. So do we come here even to *try* to win today? You judge. Houllier fills the Liverpool midfield with quality 'water-carriers' – Hamann, Diao, Gerrard and Heskey – and also plays Murphy in the hole behind a solitary attacker, Owen. This means we have *one* proven goal-scorer in the side, a flyer who is supposed to be 'supported' from deep by probably the slowest player in the entire club. A clueless Heskey on the left makes no dents at all in rookie Boro full-back Parnaby, while Steven Gerrard still lacks confidence and guile out of position, wide right. Strangled by defensive duties, no other Liverpool midfielder ever gets ahead of the ball or beyond the isolated Owen. And the manager changes nothing. Michael spends his entire afternoon alone, chasing aimless punts from Dudek or our full-backs, and is surrounded by three or four Boro defenders. It's crap football, it really is. Visionless and shameful.

Late on, Dudek drops a harmless cross against Hyypiä's leg and Gareth Southgate, of all people, bumbles the loose ball into Liverpool's net. We are now treated to *eight* whole minutes of attacking from Liverpool. Eight minutes. Through all the pain and the disappointment of this impending first loss we now want to shout over to Thommo and the prowling Houllier: 'There! Are you happy now?' Because we simply get what we deserved from this witless, defensive surrender, as if we have learned nothing at all from similar 'tactical' defeats at places like Leicester, Southampton and Spurs – and, year after year, here in Middlesbrough. Fluidity? Courageous football? Don't make me cry. This is stuff of the madhouse. And this utter abdication makes us all ask, suicidally, on the long, long drive home: does our leader really have the balls to win the title for Liverpool? I wonder.

FOREIGN INVESTMENT REQUIRED

Is another famous British institution to be salvaged by revolutionary foreign investment? The Libyan Arab Foreign Investment Company, which Colonel Gaddafi's son Saadi advises on football investments, has already claimed a stake in Italian giants Juventus and, according to the British quality press, Saadi now has his eyes on Liverpool FC. 'Maybe we make a deal to market their merchandise or we invest in their new stadium,' he says. 'When I meet the management of Liverpool, I will discuss this with them.' He has hopes. But Gaddafi also plays for the Libyan national team, and if he is an athletic, defensive midfielder he has every chance of making GH's current squad. G. Zola, on the other hand, need not apply.

THE LIVERPOOL WAY

11 OCTOBER 2002, CHAMPIONS LEAGUE: FC BASLE 3, LIVERPOOL 3

FC Basle – FCB – have a stadium at St Jacob Park nicknamed Joggeli, 'the little imbecile', built by the same architects who converted London's Bankside power station into the Tate Modern. It glows red during matches: 'The idea is that the energy of the people and the players surges outwards,' says Jacques Herzog, one of the men responsible. A strange notion this for a football stadium, which should, surely, intensify and focus internally both its noise and light. But then Basle are also managed by Christian Gross, an Uncle Fester doppelgänger, under whom Spurs once suffered both an energy and ideas evacuation for 292 excruciating days. Gross is now after revenge on his many English critics. FCB have never lost a European match at the new Joggeli, and Houllier, cutely, tells a Swiss press conference that Liverpool have come here as the underdogs. This night in Switzerland is already a defining moment in our season. Can *Le Boss*, the unchallenged master of repressed control, actually find it in himself to release and attack?

Smicer plays in 'the hole' behind Owen, with Heskey shackled again on the left. This means that in a match we must win we still have only one player in this team we can rely on to score goals. Stevie G. is selected – but surely only on reputation. Truly abysmal at Boro, he has looked supine, troubled, for weeks. The Carling Opta statistics – usually useless media guff – reveal that SG has made *three* tackles in the whole of October and November. He looks lost, or else betrayed. The nervous-looking Dudek also starts, when Kirkland, so impressive last season in Turkey, actually deserves his go. Hakan Yakin, Basle's playmaker, shows that the concept of 'the creative' in midfield is now so utterly alien to the men who run L4 that no one seems to have been deputed to pick him up. The Red selection – more hope than reason – and Liverpool's tactics, for the most important match of the season so far, smack of unprofessionalism. Soon, Yakin is played into the familiar 'European hole' on the Liverpool right behind Carragher, while a dozing Riise trails in the wake of Rossi, who meets the low cross and scores easily at the far post. The clock shows 87 seconds.

This game is already dangerously loose, stretched, and both Smicer and Heskey have chances to score before Basle get a second, after 21 minutes. Yakin again: this time he simply plays in Jiminez down the middle-left while the rookie Traore, crucially, turns away to his right, thus allowing the Argentinian precious extra time for his strike. Dudek's blind rush from goal helpfully makes up the forward's mind. But even at 0–2 we have seen enough of Basle to think we could get back into this match.

They lack quality and pace at the back and will get nervous, for sure, if we even threaten a recovery. Except we have to recover not from 0–2, but from a fatal 0–3, courtesy of Jerzy. His pantomime save from a Yakin (him again) free kick weakly palms the ball out – instead of away – and directly to Atouba, who scores. So after 29 minutes' play the team ranked 64th of the top 64 teams in Europe and 32nd of the 32 left in the Champions League lead Houllier's fancied Liverpool by three goals. We are already undone.

A man on death row will risk anything to escape his fate: what does he have to lose? But Houllier has not yet seen the noose. So his beaten, bedraggled side is allowed to play out the vital 15 minutes to half-time without alteration. Even now this might be a dreadful error. Because Diao, for Gerrard, actually gives Liverpool a little more drive and solidity in the second period and the new man is involved, with Smicer, in setting up Murphy's goal on the hour. Only now is Baros introduced, for the impotent Heskey. And *he* makes a goal for Smicer almost immediately: 2–3. Incredibly, Carragher and all his defensive mates are still left on by Houllier, even as we are positively swarming now all over an exhausted Basle. When Michael is hacked down in the box with five minutes left, it is even possible to dream of a crazy Liverpool victory. But yet more unprofessionalism intervenes: Michael, an inveterate misser, hashes the kick – and has to scramble in the rebound. But it is still not enough: manager Gross has his English revenge.

GÉRARD – ON GERRARD

A 3–3 draw, and out of Europe. Only four victories out of 14 Champions League matches. The brave Liverpool comeback tonight has changed the media story, but it cannot hide our deeper failings. We lack potency and poise; the truth is we are a team full of quite ordinary players when placed alongside top continental technique, creativity and movement. We have a suspect goalkeeper and a rigid manager, who may not be able to move us on to the next level. On *Radio Merseyside* tonight there will be something of a first: with Liverpool sitting top of the FA Premier League, above Arsenal, well clear of United, and defeated only *once* in the League, it is argued that Houllier, the architect of our triumphant League form, winner of five trophies, should go. Calls flood in pledging support.

Successful football clubs are like sealed vacuums against this sort of psychological pollution, the kind which can so easily seep in from enemies and supporters, and especially from the press outside. At the best of times they are unreal places in which any even reasonable criticism can sap the spirit, destroy the collective energy and belief which are the threads that can bind together a winning run of football matches. The great managers almost *never* reveal their negative inner thoughts on players to the world outside. Indeed, any sign of this happening is usually an indicator of the wheels coming off, the collective will disintegrating – of managerial desperation. So when Houllier turns on Steven Gerrard after Basle, publicly accusing him of believing his own headlines, we all suck in our cheeks – and wonder. And this is really strong stuff, a casual remark turned by the press into a humiliating public bollocking for an established international. Is Houllier simply deflecting blame from himself, from his own recent tactical and motivational failures? The back cover of the Liverpool *TTW&R* fanzine carries a knowing picture of the LFC coaching staff with a bubble from Houllier saying: 'I'm great, you're all crap,' hinting that GH is not one to admit publicly to his own failings or to underestimate his strengths. He sees admissions of doubt as a sign of weakness.

The public dressing-down of Gerrard must also be seen as a sign of total managerial exasperation with the player, a signal that nothing else has worked. Steven has looked poor for weeks, a shadow of the driving, combative midfielder he used to be. Maybe he *does* now want only to hit raking 50-yard passes without first earning, in the tough football boiler-house of the centre-circle, the right to play them. Someone needs to persuade him otherwise. Urgently. Gerrard is 'punished' for his truculence by being left on the bench for Sunderland (H). Like all professional players who are omitted from first-team action, part of him will have enjoyed **Liverpool 0, relegation candidates and battered Sunderland 0**. Markus Babbel starts for the first time for Liverpool but Howard Wilkinson takes home his point, which he owes to a defence of 11 players, especially goalkeeper Macho – and barrels of luck.

Liverpool are drawn to play lowly Vitesse Arnham in the UEFA Cup, and are installed as unlikely favourites to win the thing again. But compare 2001 with 2002–03. In midfield in 2001 McAllister and Litmanen offered variety and class and Barmby and Fowler options up front. Gerrard (2001) provided quality and fire in midfield and Heskey (2001) was scoring goals. Today, Riise and Diao give us mainly hard running, and Cheyrou and Baros have yet to be truly tested. Gerrard (2002) looks vapid, and Heskey (2002) seems to have signed non-scoring papers. Dudek looks increasingly like the flaky Westerveld. I wouldn't clear space in the present trophy cabinet, would you?

23 NOVEMBER 2002: FULHAM 3, LIVERPOOL 2

O'Neill's Bar, Shepherd's Bush Green: Man. United and Newcastle share eight lunchtime goals on the big screen, sadly five for the homeboys. I'm with Dave Hill, author of *Out of His Skin*, the seminal book about John Barnes and Merseyside racism. He's now writing a 'parenting novel' for big money to jump on the Nick Hornby and Tony Parsons literary gravy train. Good luck to him. Today he's interested in the Reds' mini-crisis, no wins in three and out of the big Euro League. Fulham are miserable tenants and also on the slide, so we can at least hope for some help today.

Ground-free Fulham are using QPR's tight little B&Q of a stadium, in which Mark Wright scored the winner for Liverpool during our last League visit, against Rangers. Apparently, England's summer World Cup jaunt has added 3 per cent foreign tourist trade to Britain from the Far East and today's home crowd seem to prove the point. The Japanese are out in force for Fulham's Inamoto, but their man has only made it to the bench. When he performs his warm-up runs, his devotees can almost touch him. Gerrard remains on the bench for Liverpool. Babbel keeps his place, with Heskey and Owen up front and Riise back in midfield.

Behind us, in the School End lower tier (no sky, all standing), we have an obvious Irvine Welsh acolyte, a master of the autistic verb-free swear fest: 'Knob! Cunt! Hole! Fuck!' His gasping frustration at what he sees before us – and, no doubt, quarts of ale – utterly impairs sentence formation. Actually, Heskey starts with unusual determination, as if fearing *he* will get the next public verbal rocket from his manager. (He would probably burst into tears.) But Jean Tigana has also done a bit of homework and soon has his men firing in long-range shots at the dodgy Dudek. The pale Sean Davis tries one from fully 35 yards.

This is more of a gently bouncing bomb, the sort of shot park goalkeepers absent-mindedly sweep away to safety. Jerzy has no such plans. Instead, he offers it to the arriving Sava, who gratefully accepts the gift. When Fulham get a deflected second, off Sava's arse, this 'contest' already looks over. Owen has had no service; the forlorn Riise looks clueless in midfield, as does the water carrier Diao. The experienced and usually calm Reds fan extraordinaire Paul Hyland, standing next to us, even launches into a wild tirade against the mild Heskey, who is fading as usual and showing familiar penalty-area phobia. Gerrard and Baros warm up during half-time, with Sammy Lee doing stupid little games with them on the pitch. Babbel and Diao are the visiting fall guys.

There are still no signs of an away goal: none. So when the erratic Hamann lines up a free kick wide on the Liverpool left, I might be the only clown shouting out: 'What are we doing? Don't let Hamann take it!' but I can tell you most Reds fans are thinking the same. Naturally, his shot fairly screams into the top right-hand corner – and I get loads of delighted stick. Thanks, Didi. But, at least we can now fight our way back into this game, 'The Fields of Anfield Road' at last bouncing off this old, low tin roof. Until, that is, Traore gets muscled out by Davis, and Sava slams in the loose ball at Dudek's near post. This all happens right in front of us. Three long Fulham shots, three goals, Dudek (and others) culpable. Steven Gerrard gestures angrily to the pair of crestfallen Liverpool defenders, thankful he is no longer officially to blame for another approaching defeat.

There is still time here for Goma to get his marching orders for hacking Owen and even for Baros to score. But this simply means the home fans can also preen themselves on surviving Liverpool with only 10 men, a perfect day. We never look like getting level. Never. Irvine Welsh and his mates, behind, had already left at 3–1, no doubt in search of more ale and, perhaps, a vocabulary. Dave Hill thinks this Liverpool 'lacks something': a clue for us to work on. Arsenal have, at least, lost at Southampton, but Everton have won again, no goals conceded, and are now a nose-bleed third. We, by contrast, are in a familiar November slide. Next weekend already looms: United visit L4. It's stand-up time.

HOULLIER, THE RATTLESNAKE MAN

Houllier decides to go on a media offensive before the United match – and there are worrying signs. A **1–0 v. Vitesse Arnhem** away win (Owen) in the UEFA Cup offers no convincing evidence that our game has returned, though Henchoz is a welcome sight at centre-back and is a big part of the reason for the home no-score. GH has a couple of nagging themes for his mid-week discussion with the press. One is that he would rather die than give up managing, that he is 'addicted' to the sport. Maybe he actually *needs* to get some critical distance from football and become a little more reflective. Maybe then he could see more of what we see. The second is his obsession with responding, with facts and figures, to the press 'Liverpool are boring' charges. He stresses the number of shots on goal Liverpool have had this season (203) compared with United (195) and Arsenal (168), as if this is definitive proof of anything. This brings a chilling thought: this may actually be how Houllier reads the game – through the suffocating straightjacket of statistical analysis. This is self-deception of the starkest kind. But there is worse.

Most football managers would find a host of successful Brazilian teams to admire before arriving at the depressingly functional side that won in USA 1994 on penalties. But this 1994 Brazil – a positive offence to the sport's aesthetes – is Houllier's model. This is why the 2002 Liverpool now begins to make more sense:

They had Romario and Bebeto up front, who were not the quickest, so they relied on what became known as the rattlesnake strategy. They would go forward and back, forward and back, and then suddenly they'd strike . . . The ideal is to play the two types of attacking football, knowing that the breaks will bring goals, but also that the ones that come from build-up – what I call positional attack – are also important too.

This 'rattlesnake' metaphor is familiar Houllier territory, but it can only work in a team designed to keep the ball for long periods – and one with the talent to make occasional killer passes. In these interviews Houllier also returns, time and again, to descriptions of his relations to players as that of a father to his sons. Initially, this caring, nurturing image was rather comforting, especially when used with younger players. But it also describes a preferred relationship of dependency: it suggests that Houllier likes best to work with younger players, whom he can shape and whose gratitude he can enjoy, rather than with fully formed, experienced internationals, who have their own agendas and ambitions. How hard it is, after all, for a father to give up his sons and to let them grow and live their own lives. Am I too harsh here, simply jumping on the Houllier-knocking bandwagon? Perhaps. This may be cod psychology, but it does seem to make a lot of sense.

1 DECEMBER 2002: LIVERPOOL 1, MANCHESTER UNITED 2

'The best team always wins. The rest is just gossip.'

Jimmy Sirrell

The Bluenose Flattie landlord – the soft get – now has a picture of himself and the snotty Goodison poacher Rooney up behind the bar. It's almost enough to drive me to shop him to the bizzies for selling early-morning Sunday ale. Almost. Because, another midday Mancs Sabbath kick-off has the pub heaving behind drawn curtains, and doors unbolted only to a strategic, secret knock. Those Reds inside all know there is more than just three points at stake this lunchtime. Defeat is unthinkable.

Goalkeepers suffer more than they deserve. Their basic skills go unpraised, their minor mistakes are accentuated, pored over and dissected in hours of forensic TV analysis. Their split-second judgement is the heartbeat of the team. Get it wrong and the patient dies. Moacyr Barbosa, the great Brazilian, was voted the best keeper of the 1950 World Cup finals, but his alleged error of judgement in the 1950 final handed the match to Uruguay. In 1993 he visited the Brazilian training camp to offer encouragement before a World Cup qualifier. The authorities wouldn't let him in. 'For 43 years,' he complained, 'I've been paying for a crime I did not commit.' A goalkeeper's life.

In October, Houllier had been enraged by press suggestions that Liverpool had agreed a new four-year deal with goalkeeper Jerzy Dudek worth an unlikely £15 million. 'The figures are total fiction,' he said. 'Even if you divide that by two, you're not at the figure. I think it is an attempt to destabilise the player and the club. He's been extremely influential in our success.' For most of last season Jerzy was worth all this cash – and more. This season his confidence has been shredded by costly mistakes, which actually go right back to the end of the last League campaign and the World Cup finals in the summer. He has looked flaky for months. The previously solid Dudek has utterly lost his positive energy. What are the coaches and their psychological team doing at Liverpool to earn their own tasty salaries? Not enough.

So the 'tragic' sporting picture of this weekend has an intensely concentrating Jerzy, half-kneeling, left leg splayed, clutching a non-existent football in the Anfield sunshine, when the real object of his attention is actually already past him, squirting gently between his legs. A friendly Carragher header completely missed. A disbelieving Forlan, up until now a goalless freak at OT, has the simplest of goal-scoring tasks in front of his visiting friends. 'Jerzy Dudek is a Manc. He hates scousers!' sing the gleeful baggy unwashed in the away sections of the Anfield Road. The Kop is silent as Dudek paces the 18-yard line: he is a man lost among 40,000 doleful others.

In a tight, messy match this first goal early in the second half effectively defines the contest, so when Forlan scores again three minutes later as a cap-less Jerzy – in true Jack Johnson fashion – shades his eyes against the low sun, it only confirms what we had feared. That currently we cannot beat even a weakened United team, one without Beckham, Keane, Ferdinand, Veron and Butt. Hyypiä's late goal offers no comfort. At the end, as the Kop rapidly escapes into the humming discontent of the streets of Anfield, a tear-stained Dudek runs off the pitch into the silence of the dressing-room, his life changed, now an open wound. His very career is suddenly at stake.

HOULLIER UNDER FIRE

Rogan Taylor (and others) repeats his mantra now about the sterility of this 'boring' Liverpool team and about how Houllier needs to be 'kicked upstairs' to be replaced by another, a more forceful, more imaginative, coach. The fanzine boys, meanwhile, recycle stories about Steven Gerrard's alleged local shagging exploits as if this is an explanation for another vapid midfield performance. Typical boy-zone football-trash talk – but what else do we have? Houllier, meanwhile, points out that the squad rallied later around the stricken keeper – 'He was very tearful in the dressing-room afterwards' – and also that Dudek's mistake had ended the match. 'We tried not to talk to him about football,' says Smicer, helpfully. So, what *was* discussed? Art? Politics? Fame Academy? Kirkland will now play for the foreseeable future says GH – too fucking late.

7 DECEMBER 2002: CHARLTON ATHLETIC 2, LIVERPOOL 0

More game-playing from the manager, by now a past master. 'Chris [Kirkland] will play against Ipswich,' he says. 'After that, we'll see what happens, but Jerzy is going through a difficult period at the moment.' So who is really surprised when, in the League Cup in mid-week against the Tractor Boys, Dudek starts in what is virtually a reserves outfit captained by Steven Gerrard? Kirkland obviously is: he is spotted just before the game in L4 kicking lumps out of his Jeep, no doubt imagining Houllier's French mug gleaming out from the hubcaps. Liverpool sneak past Ipswich.

Despite this (uncertain) League Cup progress (5–4 on penalties), travelling to Charlton today is not a great idea. With Charlton chasing four consecutive Premiership wins, this is also the ten-year anniversary of the Addicks' return to the Valley – a mere £5 for today's commemorative programme – so there is a dizzy, upbeat feel about the hosts in the south London gloom, while their downtrodden guests would settle for any scrappy kind of win. Or a draw. Or, let's face it, any positive signs at all. 'There are clubs like Port Vale in despair, but their fans should look at us and see what can be done,' says manager Curbishley. *We* are also in despair. These decent Greenwich folk know they follow a good club in heady times: they deserve their success.

Kirkland finally plays, while the unconvincing Traore holds his place, so there is still no Riise. Diouf starts with Owen, and Heskey remains on the left, Houllier still oblivious to a nation's doubts. If Michael doesn't score in this line-up, then who will? After *60 seconds*, I swear, Heskey is limping, a record even for a man with his fragile limbs. He lasts for 36 disabled minutes and departs (for Riise). But not before Liverpool are already undone down his left flank, with Traore also culpable. Euell should score from the cross with a header four yards out, but picks up the rebound anyway, off a flailing Henchoz. Only Kirkland prevents a second goal, with Hyypiä exposed by Lisbie's pace. Another disturbing, *losing* 45 minutes.

THE LIVERPOOL WAY

For the first 25 minutes in the second half we really have a go, our best show for some time, with Danny Murphy in the van and even Stevie G. showing some welcome energy. Michael, starved of service and with confidence low, misses a sitter, trying with his right foot when the left is needed. So, too, does Baros, on for Traore. And on this sort of run, missed chances usually signal reprisals at the other end: a Konchesky lob over a stranded Kirkland with 12 minutes left. After this second home goal goes in, Reds fans already start to stream home. They know London Bridge station is a welcome haven from this pain and that Liverpool's last five League games now read: LLLDL. 'I trust my players,' says Houllier later. To do what? 'Houllier is running out of time,' says Tony Cascarino in the *Independent* on Monday. If he wasn't such a non-scoring ex-Millwall striker, you might even take him seriously.

CUP COMFORTS?

Liverpool play modest Arnhem at home next in the UEFA (1–0, Owen), but what we really need now is two easy domestic cup draws, something to help with the confidence levels, to get us back on track at home. We need some *help*. Instead, in the last eight in the League Cup we get Villa – away. First teams will play, and it is Villa's only chance of winning something – perhaps ours. In the FA Cup Third Round – and when the Soho Square pot is full of the likes of Macclesfield and Darlington, Exeter City and Farnborough Town, and John Barnes is drawing the balls out, for God's sake – we miss the also-rans and are lined up to face Keegan and Nic Anelka at Maine Road instead. Another telly, one o'clock Saturday start, laced with danger, a real Cup trap-door. Thanks, Barnsey – for nothing.

15 DECEMBER 2002: SUNDERLAND 2, LIVERPOOL 1

Although Leeds United fans might quibble, currently the two worst teams in the FA Premier League meet at the £23 million Stadium of Light. Sgt Wilkinson has already produced a team and a style that even these inveterate fans of the ale-house vernacular find objectionable, not least because the points – and goals – have dried up for Sunderland. Liverpool, nevertheless, travel with their collective arses hanging out: no confidence and less shape. The sensible thing to do now is to get back to a familiar pattern with your best players and dig in, tough it out. But the manager and players seem to have lost sight of any pattern or strategy. Worse, Houllier seems to take this losing run as a personal challenge, a puzzle to solve in his own perverse way.

So in a ground offering rows of empty seats – so much for the unswerving support in this football 'hotbed' in the north-east – Houllier produces another unwelcome surprise in a season in which they are already beginning to stack up. Hyypiä, our defensive cornerstone, who has, admittedly, shown signs of recent stress, is 'rested'. One of Sami's problems this season has been full-backs – notably the dozy and inexperienced Traore – who have failed to cover around the back, thus exposing the Finn's obvious lack of pace. We, the fans, would still play Sami today because we need his strength and experience and Sunderland have no strikers with speed. In fact, at the moment, Sunderland seem to have *no* strikers at all. More than five hours without scoring for the home team makes this an away banker, surely, if we can only keep our nerve. But we can't.

Instead, Houllier selects Biscan for his first-ever first-team League start at centre-back on a typically foul and windy English winter afternoon, when we need stability and continuity above all else. Only Henchoz and Carragher now remain from our previously near-impregnable back five. With Heskey also out injured and Owen sulking, we look weak at the back and unconvincing up front. Steve Gerrard has now been made captain by Houllier, but Stevie G. is still a mysterious shadow. Ex-Red Paul Walsh said this week that the Sunderland manager genius Wilko once 'roused' the England under-21s before a meeting with Norway by reminding the players of the looting and raping by the Vikings in England! God knows what he's saying now, but I do know which dressing-room I would rather be in today: the one that contains no rookie Croatian centre-back, and no conversational French.

An ugly, messy match betrays the lack of guile and confidence on both sides, and when Sunderland score after 36 minutes it is a goal made out of mistakes by both Carragher and Gerrard. McCann, the scrapping Evertonian, the scorer, is emerging as the key player in the contest, especially after the early departure, with injury, of Hamann. Meanwhile, Traore is busy wasting crossing space, and Owen is already hanging out on the left, dispirited by his lack of synergy with the similarly self-obsessed Baros. At least the Czech is testing Macho in goal, and Murphy is working hard as always. But at half-time it is 1–0, the home fans now starting to believe.

The second period has the same (lack of) shape and it looks all over for a truly terrible Liverpool when Sunderland are awarded a penalty for a high ball, which is actually 'faced' away by the distraught Carragher. Kirkland saves, and momentarily this fillip seems to have turned the contest because after too, too many misses, Baros scores for Liverpool, following Carragher's precise pass. Incomplete and unsatisfactory as this all is, Liverpool are at least now bossing this poor contest, with Murphy switched to the centre and controlling matters: our best player for weeks. With chance after chance, we even dream, briefly, of an inglorious win. But this is before Houllier intervenes, determined as ever to play his part, to use his full quota of substitutes and, seemingly, now settling for a scruffy, inconsequential point when Sunderland have so clearly lost their way. This means Diao replaces Smicer – and Murphy is relegated to the solitude of the right flank. Liverpool suddenly look a hopeless, shapeless mess once more, with Gerrard and Owen virtual passengers, and Diao a new Senegalese in the rainy battlefield of the English north-east, unsurprisingly struggling to get a toe-hold. We totally lose our way.

Proctor, a late Sunderland replacement – a north-east kid – even has time to wave his foot at a cross from the left before beating all of Henchoz, Kirkland and Carragher and slithering the ball home in the dying seconds. The travelling Liverpool fans, singing to the last, deserve none of this, another largely self-inflicted wound. Houllier looks lost and impotent on the bench and wonders later: 'Why on earth are we leaving this stadium with nothing?' Now we have to face more of the 'Houllier must go' and 'Liverpool in crisis' radio phone-ins. But we are all beginning to wonder.

COMETH THE HOUR?

Gérard Houllier has brilliantly reconstructed Liverpool football club, but in 33 of the last 34 Premiership matches when we have gone behind, Liverpool have failed to recover to win. This is a sobering statistic. It suggests a lack of flexibility and even spirit in this Liverpool team, but especially its stunning incapacity to think on its feet. Have the team been 'programmed' by GH and his staff only with a Plan A? Do we have no other possibilities when the strategy of pressuring rivals high up the pitch has failed? Houllier hints later that he will stay at Anfield at least until 2005 and he rejects accusations that he has signed too many young players: 'I bought players who will get better, not players who will get worse.' He sweeps press criticism aside with more than a touch of *Le Eric*: 'The wolves always come out when they think the flesh is ready to be eaten.' He says he has great visions for this club, real ambition. We need to see it now: some courage and real leadership. Without it, we will be lost.

18 DECEMBER 2002, LEAGUE CUP QUARTER-FINAL: ASTON VILLA 3, LIVERPOOL 4

We have even found a pub for Villa, a post-apocalyptic little number, the Armada, a piece of proud Hispanic kitsch sited right underneath spaghetti junction. We lack only a Ken Loach film crew for a 'bombsite Britain' feature. From here at least it is an acceptable trudge through the back streets of Aston for a match that suddenly carries far too much weight for Liverpool and their manager in a competition we are no longer supposed to care about. Apart from our own desperate need for a lift, the Worthington Cup has also had something of a surprise resurrection this season, mainly because Ferguson seems to have taken fright that United might end up trophy-less for a second successive season and so has planned on having silverware wrapped up early on to assuage the frustrations of the north-west prawn-sandwich eaters. So, after dumping an equally committed Chelsea, the Mancs now wait in an impressive semi-finals line-up, along with holders Blackburn Rovers and Sheffield United.

Problems. Because of the vagaries of the Christmas post, the Ticketmaster agency has told 4,000 fans to pick up credit-card tickets before the match. Did Villa even know this? Given this is a 7.45 p.m. start in the middle of the worst traffic bottleneck in the country, this effectively means around 4,000 fans sorting themselves out in, say, 40 pre-match minutes? You work it out: 100 fans a minute. You might sooner get a smile out of Michael Owen. As we queue – at just *two* disorganised windows – the proposed kick-off time disappears into the distance. The words 'brewery' and 'piss-up' come immediately to mind. Surprisingly, not the words 'shafted customers'.

The crowd is actually incredibly patient: in Italy or Spain, on this sort of freezing night with no play imminent, punters would have found other ways of entertaining themselves, rather than standing and shivering in this poxy away end – such as ripping the seats out. Instead, we get a few boos and cat-calls while some angry Villa geek tells us over and over on the PA that it is *not* his fault and that these are definitely 'CIRCUMSTANCES BEYOND OUR CONTROL'. Charmless to the last. We eventually kick off at 9.05 p.m., an unprecedented *80* minutes late. Houllier says the Reds' players have been joking and laughing in the dressing-room to pass the time. Presumably, he had circulated the team sheet. The last train back to Liverpool remains helpfully fixed at 10.18 p.m., or just after half-time. Shafted, once more. Not that too many here will be going home to Liverpool. The Reds' Asian branch is well represented tonight, in what is a favourite Midlands spot.

THE LIVERPOOL WAY

The 'big' Liverpool team news is that Babbel plays instead of Carragher, Diao fills in for Hamann and Riise plays left midfield. Hyypiä returns and Baros keeps Heskey on the bench. For Villa, Johnsen is crocked in the extended warm-up, so young Samuel will have to play centre-back. Good. Liverpool play in white rather than the new grey pyjamas the sponsors have dreamed up, but still begin under pressure, much of it aimed by Vassell at Markus Babbel's right-back zone. The German already looks in trouble. Just as we start thinking we might even survive this early onslaught, Villa take the lead, Traore clumsily fouling Hendrie after more incisions down the Liverpool right. Vassell scores from the spot, filling the central gap left by Kirklands' collapsing frame.

But we get back quickly. We have to. Steven Gerrard is at the heart of it – as he will be all night – nicking the ball off Barry and feeding Baros, who has a typically direct head-down surge illegally halted by Leonhardsen on the right edge of the Villa box: Danny Murphy country. Sod Beckham, Murphy does this better than pretty much anyone now and he gently curls the kick over the wall and miles beyond Enckelman. There is still time for Houllier to sub Markus after 39 minutes, the German stalking straight down the tunnel, shirt akimbo. It's 1–1 at half-time.

Suddenly, for 20 minutes or so after the interval, we begin to see again what this Liverpool can really do, we are reminded why we actually *go* to watch rather than slope round to a pub for ale and Sky Sports. Steven Gerrard, a man transformed from recent weeks, is absolutely immense now and, supported by Murphy, Riise and Baros, we begin to get at the provisional Villa back four. First, Stevie G. volleys a sumptuous pass to Riise, who forces his way inside past De la Cruz on the left before finding Baros. Using the overlapping Carragher as a decoy, our new Czech carefully slides his shot the other way, through Samuel, and beyond Enckelman. The Liverpool crowd celebrates wildly, weeks of painful despair suddenly eased. Our mate, Chris – daft bastard – continues to argue that Baros *should* have passed to JC rather than take on the strike! Michael Owen, face fixed grimly, gives Milan a perfunctory pat before returning to the halfway line.

2–1 is soon 3–1, Gerrard actually getting *beyond* the front two with a surging burst down the right – am I dreaming this? – before picking up the bits from another chaotic Baros run and screwing his shot beyond the keeper's right hand. He now struts towards us, chest puffed in mock domination, before disappearing beneath more Liverpool white. How we have missed him. There are 25 minutes still left. It is a measure of our uncertainty that, when the celebrations die down, no one in the

Liverpool end assumes this is over. *No one.* We fall back, too deep, and within five minutes Hitzlsperger hammers in a low left-footed drive from Diao's clearance, which skips over Kirkland's horizontal left hand. Dread and doubt begin to invade once more as Villa pour forward. When Dublin scores a late equaliser, deflected off Henchoz, I have to sit down (we are all standing). Few teams can lose a 3–1 lead and then come back to win in extra time, against the crowd, especially a team whose confidence has been as fragile as Liverpool's has this past month. We need to hold on, be brave. One last attack.

It is Gerrard again: in all three Liverpool goals he has been crucial. Now he's driving down the right once more, outside and beyond the tiring Samuel, to pick up from Murphy, and he forces himself past the falling defender, looking to pick out a Liverpool player outside the crowded area. Stevie's cutback catches the heel of the retreating Mellberg, which sets the ball rolling slowly, slowly towards the right foot of the arriving Murphy, and Danny Boy seems to take an absolute age to line up his shot through the scrum of connecting bodies. We are all gob-opened, watching, waiting.

And as the Villa net extends to accept this arrow at exactly 10.57 p.m., close to 4,000 Liverpool supporters, including hundreds who have no idea if or how they might get home tonight, positively howl with near-bestial delight at this final, final act. The Liverpool players make an exhausted, celebratory human mountain right in front of us – but no one cares about them right now. This is *our* victory, a private party, a small payback for all the shit we have watched recently. A magnificent reply. The Villa sections drain immediately, as if a claret-and-blue plug has been yanked out from below. It has.

CARDIFF CALLING

Later, as we are returning to subterranean motorway nowhere-land, exhausted and elated, Paul H. rings to tell us that Liverpool have drawn Sheffield United in the semis. Out of nothing – out of a black hole – another Cardiff Cup final trip now looks likely for Liverpool and we can even think more positively about little Mickey Rooney's visit to Anfield on Sunday. This changes none of the fundamentals, of course – unless Stevie G.'s awesome bombing-on is suddenly a central part of Houllier's new way. But a win like this really lifts the supporters and the club and replenishes the confidence tank. It *feels* better. A whole lot better.

THE LIVERPOOL WAY

22 DECEMBER 2002: LIVERPOOL 0, EVERTON 0

'Send for the Boy.' An Evertonian on the *Red All Over the Land*
web forum

Liverpool's recent slump in the League means that Everton, the 'People's
Club', as manager Moyes has cheekily labelled our near neighbours –
complete, note, with their global Chinese shirt sponsorship and multi-
million-pound King's Dock expansion plans – are above Liverpool in the
table at this stage in the season for the first time since the mid-1980s. So
the press coverage this week has been all about the Red 'crisis' and the
Blue 'revival' on Merseyside for the season's first derby game: never has
this fixture taken place closer to Christmas or later in the League season.
It might still be too early for us.

Attention has also focused on Michael Owen's relative slump at
Anfield while the young Croxteth Bluenose Rooney has had good
judges marking him down as a new local star in the making. Better than
Owen, some say. *The Times* today has an eerie photo of Rooney as the
gangly, big-eared Everton club mascot standing between Dave Watson
and John Barnes at the derby game back in 1996. He is already generating
his own myths, young Wayne, the latest one being that he was allegedly
chased out of Chelsea estate-agent offices with fellow track-suited
scouser Alan Stubbs. These rich footballing scousers – who looked more
like typical urchins – were suspected of 'casing' some monster west
London houses when they were actually filling in some time before a
recent Bluenose fixture at Stamford Bridge. As a kid, Rooney had been
seen by the Anfield coaching gurus; he turned up defiantly for Liverpool
FC trials in his Everton kit.

We want to crush this Blue resurgence before it rises to embarrass us,
before we are engulfed. So Liverpool begins with the team that
eventually suppressed Villa: Traore and Diao hold their places, Heskey and
Smicer are again on the bench. Rooney is only a sub for Everton, who
soon lay out their plans to defend and play on the break. The first half is
scrappy and inconclusive, Graveson dominating Gerrard and Rooney
drawing 'fat bastard' catcalls for the Kop in his warm-up runs. Abuse is
the new respect in football. Traore is troubled, disorganised, on the right,
while Diao is almost entirely destructive in the Liverpool midfield –
glaringly so. Riise tests Wright from distance from a Murphy corner but,
in truth, no football is played here: it is a dull, cancelling half, showing all
the, by now, familiar Liverpool failings.

Only after Smicer and Heskey replace the awful Traore and Diao and

Rooney comes on for Radzinski – to wild applause from the Bluenose garrisons – do we get any signs of a derby-day goal. Heskey misses a header right away and Smicer adds shades of the midfield pace and invention which is looking quite beyond the limited Diao. Rooney, on the other hand, looks both solid and deadly, the giant Kirkland bouncing off the little man as they arrive simultaneously at an upfield Everton punt. Rooney then gets Hyypiä to turn and positively thumps a shot, which loops off Henchoz and on to the Liverpool bar – and over. This five-second piece of action marks everybody's card: this porky 17-year-old, who can barely communicate his own name, offers a more serious goal threat than any seasoned international on show. Emile just blinks, oblivious to this disturbing message. Soon he is tentatively prodding at the ball in the Everton box, a (very) distant relation to the guy who shredded the Blues in his first derby just two years ago. Heskey still has one League goal to his name this season: this is our 19th fixture.

It ends goalless, but not before Steven Gerrard has jumped, two-footed, all over Naysmith on the Main Stand touchline, studs on show, a 'tackle' which is missed by both referee and linesman, but one which sends Kevin Campbell into on-field hysterics and soon has the national football phone-in lines fizzing with Bluenose calls for the return of public stonings. Gerrard is likely to get slaughtered by the FA, because he has some previous experience in this direction. Just what we (don't) need. The muted boos from the red sections of Anfield contrast with the singing that comes later from the visitors' dressing-room, as Houllier faces the usual press questions. Evertonians will enjoy their Christmas turkey one League place above Liverpool. But every Liverpudlian secretly fears that there might be a much bigger message here: that the Merseyside Blues are truly on the rise once more as *Le Boss*' Liverpool slide quietly out of contention.

MARABOU(T) REDS' NIGHTMARE

A Senegalese witch doctor – a marabout – claims to have been hired last year by El Hadji Diouf to make him a star and is now claiming payment, threatening to take away the powers of the Liverpool man if no cash materialises. Diouf scoffs – but respectfully so: 'Of course, I believe in marabouts; they are an integral part of Senegalese culture. But there is no such thing as a marabout who does evil things; they cannot kill or cast an evil spell on someone.' This means one theory to explain his recent form is out the window. Diouf has a strong mother, whom he alludes to in almost every interview and he also identifies Senegal coach Bruno Metsu, tellingly, as 'a father, a brother, he was everything to me'. Now

Houllier has stepped in. Diouf says he wants to become 'the best player in the world' at Liverpool. Challenging the best at Melwood would be a good start. At the moment he is a £10 million misfit – but one still with time on his side.

A Boxing Day **Liverpool 1, Blackburn Rovers 1** does not improve his local standing and means a 59-year non-winning Anfield League record. Our new signings – Diouf, Diao and Cheyrou – have added too little so far, and we have missed the harder qualities and experience of Fowler, Barmby, Anelka and Litmanen, the guys who made way. Already there is talk of more Reds' spending action during the January transfer window, even though, only a month ago, Houllier had said he was 'happy' with his squad. This was the first of three tough Christmas matches, so we badly need the points before travelling to Arsenal and Newcastle in the League and then to Maine Road in the FA Cup. The next four matches in 11 punishing days could determine our entire season.

Houllier later says on TV that he thought this might have been the 'crappy 1–0 win we have been looking for'. He meant 'scrappy', of course, but crappy actually does the job much better. At least Gerrard's game is returning and Riise proves that he *can* still score at the Kop end in the first half – with a helpful deflection – and our hopes are briefly raised about this elusive win until nerves begin to set in once again for the second period. By this time Kirkland has already made some ready saves and the home manager has, bafflingly, replaced Smicer with Biscan – a poor centre-back asked to play right midfield, a sure sign that we are now trying, only, to hold on. Cole scores the deserved Blackburn equaliser with 13 minutes left, a looping volley from distance, but two late missing 'Michael moments' really sum up our current state. 'It's frustrating,' Houllier says later. (You think?) 'It's a team that is young, but we have to be patient.' (There it is again, the 'youth' defence.) 'When you go through a period like this you either get stronger or you sink.' (Now he is Nietzsche, no less: whatever does not kill me makes me stronger.) We, the fans, can no longer tell whether we are swimming or drowning, but on the Kop, I can tell you, we do frequently now taste bitter salt water in our mouths.

DEATH OF A CHAMPION

Albert Stubbins has died at 82. He was chased by 18 clubs when Liverpool signed him in 1946. As a young Bob Paisley was trying to urge more scientific approaches to the treatment and preparation of players at Anfield, Stubbins recalled that at Newcastle in the early 1940s the captain usually passed a whisky bottle round the players in the dressing-room five minutes before kick-off 'for luck' and that injuries on the field were also treated at St James' Park with a strategic drop of the hard stuff. Stubbins and Paisley were neighbours in Liverpool club houses at Bowring Park just after the Second World War. Paisley once told Stubbins that he fancied taking on a fruit and veg business or a pub after his playing days were done. Stubbins thought Paisley had more to offer football. He was right, of course. Albert's career was split by the War and he won only one England cap; a scandal. For my father's generation, Stubbins was – and is – a Liverpool great.

29 DECEMBER 2002: ARSENAL 1, LIVERPOOL 1

As a Liverpool fan at the moment, you really have to work hard to drag yourself to this one. OK, it is Highbury, one of the great English football venues. Liverpool also have a decent record here, and Arsenal are not quite the invincible proposition they were proclaimed to be in the early part of the season. This fixture is also one you really look out for when the summer starts to drift by. But in the sort of form we are currently in and with Arsenal clear at the top and on a gloomy Sunday, rain lashing down, in the middle of the holidays when we could easily watch this (let's face it, probable defeat) on the box, this is a visit based largely on a fan's blind commitment. Even the emergency evacuation alert we suffer at King's Cross en route today seems to suggest only further trouble lies ahead. So these are just some of the reasons why there are hundreds of empty Liverpool seats behind us in the Clock End, as this usually sold-out heavyweight meeting gets underway.

Riise replaces Traore today, but Cheyrou's surprise return on the left – Smicer is omitted – is the real Liverpool selection story. Can he compete and defend properly in the rain on this narrow pitch when we will need to do both today? Hamann is still out. Baros and Owen start again, with Heskey injured once more. Not that Michael lasts too long: he soon claims a hamstring twinge (a possible convenient exit line from this torture?) and is replaced by Diouf. Arsenal are surprisingly deliberate, even cautious, and lack ideas – beyond, that is, exploiting the Liverpool left side, and also trying to pick out Campbell (against the confused Diao) at corner-kicks. Carragher is doing well against both Pires and Henry on the right and Kirkland is solid, confident – Dudek may find it hard to return at all. Arsenal fans chant: 'Liv-er-pool, HOOF the ball'. We smile uneasily at this hurtful charge – the uncouth Carragher is a particular target. We also grin at the announcer's half-time message that the big screens will soon show the first-half highlights. Highlights? We are glad, nevertheless, to be level at this tough school.

THE LIVERPOOL WAY

The second half offers more hope. Perhaps we are ashamed of our own inadequacies, spurred on by the public ridicule from the Arsenal ranks? This Liverpool 'revival' is shaped around the industry of Gerrard and Murphy, naturally, but also around the welcome thirst for the ball and the verve and running of both Baros and Diouf. We even start to press, winning corners, forcing goal-line clearances. Arsenal, collectively, are starting to doubt. So when Baros fastens on to a Gerrard pass and forces Campbell into a rash penalty-area challenge right in front of us, we are hollering for justice with the rest of the Reds fans who have been drawn here expecting grisly last rites. Referee Winter – a mile or more behind the play – relies on the old 'arm across the chest' masonic-like sign from his assistant for confirmation and we are, indeed, in spot-kick business.

How do you respond to a penalty award, which is, after all, only a cheque not yet honoured? Unbridled joy soon gives way to sensible foreboding – have we celebrated too soon and too much? At least Michael is off the roster, but the reliable Murphy has to prise the ball from both Baros and Diouf before settling on the spot to beat Seaman high to the goalkeeper's right. Even now our wild celebrations soon give way to an overly intense concentration on the Highbury digital clock, a measure too far in these circumstances. Who can watch the play when there is such fascination in seeing just how slowly 20 minutes of a fan's life can pass? Coming out of a historic slump with a win at Arsenal is beyond our dreams, but now we have to contemplate it: at least we do for nine, whole, minutes.

Jeff Winter is widely known in the game for never understating his own importance. He is thought by most fans to be dangerously inconsistent. By now both Bergkamp and the urchin Jeffers have decamped from the bench for Arsenal, who have finally gotten the wake-up call. This trio – Dennis, Jeffers and Winter – now decide the outcome of our visit. These days, cute defenders instinctively drag their arms around and across attackers in order to slow their progress, put them off their penalty-area stride. Officials rarely pick this up, seeing this tangling as part of the normal weft and weave of penalty-box play. A clever flick by Bergkamp, through to the hatchet-faced Jeffers, now induces this familiar, slowing tactic from Riise. A full stride *later* and the ex-Bluenose crumbles, as if poleaxed. His reward for this blatant deceit – the punishment for Riise's casual impediment – is an assistant flagging in the sort of controversial semaphore Mr Winter relishes. Penalty.

Henry does the needful, setting up a gut-wrenching last ten minutes, which Liverpool barely survive. We should be happy with 1–1, would have taken it greedily before the start. But waiting in the away end after the final whistle to watch, on the big screen, Jeffers 'earn' his kick is too much, as Arsenal fans next door gleefully mime the saving dive. Wenger says Jeffers has 'no choice' but to go down, as if he was faced by some weighty moral dilemma. GH is furious that the officials have been 'conned' by Jeffers and that Riise, not the diving Franny, has been yellow-carded. There was no card of any colour, of course, for the earlier scything Campbell. The only satisfaction which now awaits us in the cold and drizzle is loud scouse talk in the Piccadilly-line queues about that 'cheating cunt' Jeffers and how woeful Wenger's Arsenal really are. Woeful enough to be five points clear of the pack and nine in front of an ailing Liverpool with just 17 games left.

A WINTER'S TALE

How do we stand at this year's end, over halfway through the League campaign? Two months ago Liverpool stood clear at the top before visiting Middlesbrough. Since then we have also fallen to poor opposition in the Champions League and have also lost, unforgivably, at Fulham, Sunderland and Charlton, points effortlessly thrown away. Liverpool took 27 points out of 33 before November; since, it has been a miserly 7 out of 30. On occasions, we have looked lost and forlorn, at home and abroad.

Our confidence has been shot and four key players, Dudek, Hyypiä, Gerrard and Owen, have all suffered crippling losses in form, while the new Liverpool recruits have done little to justify the near £20 million spent by Houllier in the summer. Our squad looks large but inexperienced and lacking in real quality. The manager also seems flaky, distracted, blaming the World Cup for player form loss – what about at Arsenal? – and making, at times, quite inexplicable selection decisions. His system and very philosophy also seem critically flawed. As a result, the Championship now seems further away from L4 than it did a year ago, even though we started this campaign with such high hopes and promise. Worse, Everton now head their near neighbours in the League rankings.

And yet, despite the gloom, which has produced no League wins for fully two months, Liverpool still look on target for another Cardiff final visit and are still in touch with the top group of clubs. Just. Ferguson said recently that 78 points might even win the League this year. If we can find our form – or anything approaching it – domestic trophies and a Champions League berth are still a reachable goal. This is not enough, of course, and some Kopites still talk of winning the title in 2003. But surely that is all it is: wild, wonderful talk. Isn't it?

THE LIVERPOOL WAY

FA PREMIER LEAGUE TABLE AT 29 DECEMBER 2002

	P	W	D	L	F	A	GD	Pts
ARSENAL	21	13	4	4	42	22	20	43
CHELSEA	21	10	8	3	34	17	17	38
MAN. UNITED	21	11	5	5	33	21	12	38
NEWCASTLE U.	20	11	2	7	34	29	5	35
EVERTON	21	10	5	6	23	22	1	35
LIVERPOOL	**21**	**9**	**7**	**5**	**31**	**22**	**9**	**34**
SOUTHAMPTON	21	8	8	5	24	20	4	32
TOTTENHAM	21	9	5	7	30	30	0	32
MAN. CITY	21	9	3	9	28	29	-1	30
MIDDLESBRO.	21	8	8	5	25	20	5	29
BLACKBURN R.	21	7	8	6	28	25	3	29
CHARLTON	21	8	5	8	24	25	-1	29
LEEDS U.	21	8	3	10	28	27	1	27
ASTON VILLA	21	7	4	10	19	23	-4	25
BIRMINGHAM C.	21	6	7	8	19	25	-6	25
FULHAM	21	6	5	10	23	27	-4	23
BOLTON W.	21	4	7	10	23	35	-12	19
SUNDERLAND	21	4	6	11	14	30	-16	18
WEST BROM.	21	4	4	13	16	32	-16	16
WEST HAM	21	3	7	11	21	38	-17	16

CHAPTER 5

Servants and Stars:
Big Ron and Little Bamber

SHANKLY, SHANKLY

Promotion from the Second Division under Bill Shankly in 1961–62 brought Liverpool crashing into the new post-maximum-wage era, in which they would pursue European football adventures for the first time, and the club would remain – for many, very different, reasons – right in the centre of public debate about the very future of football in England. There were four very different decades ahead here. In the early 1960s Liverpool FC were slowly becoming a focus for international attention for the first time, mainly because of the synergy between music and football in the city and the increasing cultural inventiveness of its football fans. In the 1970s the spotlight fell on Liverpool because of the excellence and dominance of the club's football team and its shrewd management. In the 1980s it was more footballing brilliance, from Anfield, but also an altogether much harsher glare following Heysel and the terrible crowd disaster at Hillsborough. By the 1990s the focus was on the prospects for reviving the club's football status in a new, global era; first, under Souness and Roy Evans and, finally, in a new departure but one rooted in Liverpool values, under the Frenchman Gérard Houllier.

When Bill Shankly arrived at Liverpool in the winter of 1959 he bullied the club's board into modernisation, sweeping out players from the old maximum-wage austerity era of the 1950s, and bringing in the backbone of a new, young, dynamic side for a very new footballing age. At Shankly's insistence, the old training ground at Melwood was transformed in 1960, and the names in the Liverpool team under Shankly also changed dramatically over just four years. In 1959–60 among the first-team core were still John Molyneux, Ronnie Moran, Dick White and also a young Roger Hunt. By 1960–61 Byrne, Milne and winger Lewis began to figure much more strongly. In 1961–62, in the Liverpool promotion year, there was another slew of new younger names – Ian St John, Ian Callaghan and a new captain, the giant Ron Yeats. In 1962–63, and facing the challenge of the First Division, the names of Lawrence, Lawler, Stevenson, Arrowsmith and Tommy Smith appear for the first time. The manager was ruthless in discarding players who had helped the club gain promotion but were now found wanting: White, Leishman, A'Court and Furnell were soon out of the team or gone altogether. This was now Shankly's side, already heading for a first Liverpool League title in the modern era, in 1963–64. The signs that the Scotsman had new ideas and big ambitions were there right from the moment he arrived in Liverpool. Just as Gérard Houllier later promised to update the Liverpool approach, returning the club to the central tenets of 'the Liverpool Way' by looking abroad for inspiration and new direction, so Shankly was already laying down the blueprint for the modern era by applying lessons learned from the global game. The *Liverpool Echo* reported as early as 14 December 1959 that:

> Shankly is a disciple of the game as played by the continentals. The man out of possession, he believes, is just as important as the man with the ball at his feet. Continental football is not the lazy man's way of playing soccer. Shankly will aim at incisive forward moves by which Continentals streak through a defence when it is 'closed up' by British standards. He will make his players learn to kill a ball and move it all in the same action . . . he will make them practise complete mastery of the ball.

Shankly and his coaching staff, especially Joe Fagan and Bob Paisley, quickly introduced what were then regarded as 'modern' methods of training and preparation at Liverpool. One immediate change made by the new manager was to increase the number of club apprentices – who had previously trained for just one day a week – and to start integrating them with the full-time professionals. Two youngsters, Tommy Smith and Chris Lawler, both 15, suddenly got chances in the reserves. These were also the days of the famous Thursday morning Anfield five-a-sides, when

Shankly and his coaching staff would tell the trainees working inside the ground to 'put it down, boys' and set up a match on the stadium car park against passing Liverpool Corporation bin men. Shankly, reputedly, also used the willing bin men as football scouts in the city, urging them to keep tabs on any likely youngsters they saw playing on the street in the course of their rounds.

Shankly also wanted modernisation of the crumbling Anfield, which he described as an eyesore. It was hard to disagree. No major work had been done on the ground since 1928. Now, in 1963, a new daringly modern cantilevered stand for 6,700 fans was built to replace the old barrel-roofed version on the Kemlyn Road. John Houlding's modest old stadium was coming into the modern age at last, and maybe it inspired Yeats and his young men, because the League title duly arrived at Anfield one year later and, for the first time in the club's history, the FA Cup was finally claimed in 1965. Using the Cup final profits, the Anfield Road end of the ground was also re-roofed. Anfield was slowly being transformed to meet the new demands of an increasingly European football age.

THREE SCOTS IN A SIDE

All great football teams have their key players, their totemic figures. Usually – though not always – these are defenders, because most football managers worth their salt choose to build their new creations on solid foundations. Liverpool had just missed promotion in 1961 – but had conceded 58 goals in the process. They needed to tighten up at the back. The old adage in the years of the WM formation was to aim, above all, for a strong central spine: goalkeeper, centre-half and centre-forward. Not much has changed since. Tommy Lawrence, a burly Scot, had actually been at Liverpool since 1957, but after he finally broke into the Shankly team in October 1962 he missed only four games in the Liverpool goal in the next six seasons. He was an intimidating sight for opposing forwards: he filled his goal, and the solid Tommy was also more than happy to charge off his line to confront the opposition on the ground. Few strikers dared try to pass him, this first authentic goalkeeping sweeper, who looked like he might double up as a part-time wrestler. He was Shankly's stopper, a goalkeeper to both respect and fear.

Centre-forward Ian St John, another Scot and a record £35,000 Liverpool buy, was no traditional bustling English-style centre-forward of the 1950s. At only 5 ft 7 in. he was compact but good in the air and, crucially, a player strong and inventive enough to come deep and hold the ball up as Liverpool attacks took shape. He was part of the new European game, rather than the old British one – and a fighter who sometimes punched above his weight and frequently fell foul of officialdom. St John, like most young Scottish players coming to England at the time, also straddled the work/football era. At 18 he had the solid grounding of working in the local steelworks among Motherwell fans, while also playing for the club's first team and even internationally for Scotland.

From £16 a week at Motherwell, St John went on to a basic £30 at Liverpool, which, topped up with bonuses for points and winning matches and a top six £2 bonus for every 1,000 fans over 28,000 drawn to home games, meant a weekly wage of around £100. It was the sort of performance-related contract top clubs were starting to consider once again in the inflationary season of 2002–03. Shankly insisted, however, that all his players were paid the same wage, and it was pretty clear top managers in England worked together to keep players' wages down to these manageable levels. The club could also lay down the law when it was required. The volcanic Tommy Smith had it out publicly with secretary Peter Robinson when there were no crowd bonuses for the players after the 1965 FA Cup final played in front of 100,000 fans. The final was played on a neutral venue, argued Robinson, so the bonus scheme did not apply.

At Liverpool, Ian St John immediately noticed a difference in training compared to Scotland – a much greater professionalism and a planning for activities – as well as an involvement with fans, the dreaded Liverpool 'sweat box', and a clear link back to Bill Shankly's own early experiences of street football in Scotland:

> Shankly had this great rapport with the fans – wonderful – and the doors would be open at [Melwood] and people would come and watch us at training. It was fantastic: they could be three or four deep, right round the training ground. The training at Liverpool was devised by Bill Shankly, and I think he went back to his roots of schoolboy and youth football [in Scotland], kicking a ball around the streets, because we'd never seen it before in a club. We had little shooting boards; we had large ones, full size; we had goals shooting boards. And we had what they called the sweat box: four goals in a square. If he was going to punish us in any way, we went in the sweat box. But it was terrific practice: you'd go in as a pair, and one guy would hit it and it would come back off the board and the second guy would hit it. You could volley it sideways, let it go past you, volley it behind, hit it maybe straight on . . . With Shankly we used to play headed games as well, little

two-a-side heading games. It was just wonderful; it was your own
boyhood games again – but you were playing with the big boys.

This was not like the life of a Scottish 'part-time' professional player,
where youngsters had to wait to do ball work while the trainer read the
paper or went for a cup of tea. The opinionated St John – later one of
Gérard Houllier's fiercest critics concerning the alleged banality of the
'new' Liverpool – thought training for the Scotland national team at this
time was no better than 'a shambles'. Liverpool was another world.

The bullish Shankly insisted that his more lightweight players ate
steaks, even for lunch before games, reasoning that anything good enough
for building up the stamina of his favourite boxer, Joe Louis, was certainly
good enough for his own athletes. Boxers and US gangsters – and Tom
Finney – were Shankly's intriguing heroes. He also used some early native
sports psychology at Liverpool, including some chicanery at pre-match
meals. Tommy Smith found out much later that Fagin and Paisley used to
instruct the hotel staff to serve certain players the wrong food before
games, so that the problems caused would wind these players up, leaving
them in an especially foul and mean mood before kick-off. A defender
like Smith, in a temper, was an awesome opponent:

> By the time you left the hotel you would have torn the head off
> the soddin' waiter. So, I mean, they were working on us 24 hours a
> day, which is quite interesting when you think about all this
> psychological stuff now. They knew who to pick on, who to get
> going, who to work up into a frenzy. They used to say by the time
> the team got to the ground, they'd be ready to go through a brick
> wall.

Shankly also informed Ian St John on his arrival at Anfield that every good
team needed three Scottish players – but no more than three – because
Scots provided the iron will to win and the 'dig' necessary for any successful
club. But more than three Scots in the ranks and you were asking for
trouble: a clannish 'them and us' feeling can set in, argued Shankly, dividing
the Scots from the rest of the squad. St John, himself, was a crucial Scottish
signing for Liverpool, playing 425 times and scoring 118 goals. Save for
injuries at the beginning and end of the 1964–65 season, he barely missed
a game and, lion-hearted, he even returned to score the winning goal for
Liverpool against Leeds United at Wembley in 1965.

But the Liverpool manager didn't always follow his own advice on
Scots – he actually had *four* in his first championship team – Lawrence,

THE LIVERPOOL WAY

Willie Stevenson – an elegant, loping, left-half recruited from the Rangers reserve team – St John, and Ron Yeats. 'Big Ron' or 'Rowdy' Yeats, named after an improbably imposing TV cowboy of the time, provided the platform for all the Liverpool teams of the 1960s. Just as Sami Hyypiä has been central to laying the defensive groundwork for the Houllier era 40 years later, so Ron Yeats was probably the crucial early Shankly buy for Liverpool, at least up until Keegan and Ray Clemence joined the club from Scunthorpe United more than a decade later. He really started off the modern Liverpool story.

BIG RON: 'JUST WALK AROUND HIM, BOYS'

Big Ron Yeats is one of the few people who has seen the Shankly era first hand and who has experience, too, of Liverpool under the current Houllier regime. He was a player at Liverpool between 1961 and 1971, clocking up 451 appearances, and has worked at the club as a chief scout since 1985. Only now is he about to retire from his Liverpool service as both a player and back-room man. Another who fits this description as someone who links the Shankly and Houllier dynasties is the university-educated Brian Hall – 'Little Bamber' to Steve Heighway's 'Big Bamber' – the club's current community officer and an ex-player from a very different sort of background to the working-class roots of Ron Yeats. Hall was just becoming established in the Liverpool first team around the time that a declining Yeats was beginning to be challenged for his first-team place. These two men *know* Liverpool football club.

*

Ron Yeats today has a twinkle in his eye and a winning grin, which slices through the remnants of his transatlantic stubble, when I meet him at Melwood. He has just returned from a Liverpool supporters' event in Vancouver and is full of how beautiful the Canadian city is and how kind and enthusiastic his reception has been. They still remember 'Big Ron' around the globe in Liverpool FC enclaves. He still looks impossibly young and fit for a man approaching his mid-60s, barely an ounce of excess wrapped around the 6 ft 2 in. frame that so thrilled Bill Shankly when they first met in an Edinburgh hotel 42 years ago. Shankly later invited journalists to 'walk around' his new handsome jet-black-haired centre-back as if he was a new building, or a brick tower, a structure perhaps brought in to supplement the new developments already going up at Anfield. When I remark later to Liverpool club staff how genial and charming the big man is today, Brian Hall tells me that, as a player, Yeats had a wicked temper, which, once ignited, could consume anyone who ventured too close. Above all, Yeats was a winner and a leader for Liverpool football club.

*

SERVANTS AND STARS: BIG RON AND LITTLE BAMBER

Yeats, an Aberdonian but a Rangers fan, first played football for the junior teams in the Lads' Club in the north-east Scottish city, the same amateur club that produced the weedy, but deadly, Denis Law. Yeats started out as a loping, hard-tackling midfield player. But, at 14 years old, he was asked to fill in at centre-half. Although initially he still liked to step out from the back – 'I used to be a centre-back that came forward – a little bit like Alan Hansen' – he gradually accepted that he lacked the pace to play higher up the pitch and he concentrated his energies on defence. Given his size, even as a late-teenager, and his fearlessness and quiet determination and steely will to win, Yeats was identified early on as a born football captain in the traditional British mode. Everywhere he played, he also captained:

> I wasn't a shouter. I was more a motivator than a shouter. I think I was one of these players who played the same way, week in, week out. I was very consistent and this was obviously what they were looking for. I was big and strong. If I did say something to somebody they took notice, y'know.

He was also hardened by his working experiences, from the age of 15, as a slaughterman in Aberdeen. When he began to play adult football he already knew plenty of tough working men as colleagues and teammates and he had gained their respect from a young age. At 19 he was well established as captain of the adult Lads' Club team, when Dundee United offered him the chance to play in the Second Division of the Scottish League. In November 1957 he received a telegram informing him that he would make his debut on New Year's Day against St Johnstone at Perth – as captain. He was 19 and had been training for 'a whole month' with his new teammates.

Yeats was big and strong, all right, but he wasn't at all starry-eyed about the chance to become a pro player. After all, he could earn more – £10 a week – from his day job:

> I wasn't born with a silver spoon in my mouth. I was a slaughter man from 15 year old. I got up at half past two in the morning, started at 3 a.m., and you finished early, at 10 or 11 o'clock, giving you time to train. I was quite enjoying the job – I was a good slaughterman. People didn't believe me that I'd been working in the morning before playing football. On match days, y'see, I'd start at half past two and finish at nine o' clock in the morning. Then I'd go home, get maybe three hours' sleep, and then play.

THE LIVERPOOL WAY

The new man continued to live in Aberdeen after signing for United – he made 28 appearances in all for the Dundee club – but was then called up for national service. His army days were taken up pretty much by captaining the British Army football team – 'I must have been the only guy who enjoyed his British Army career' – which was made up of other football professionals, including Tottenham's Dave Mackay and Alec Young, the later Everton centre-forward. The army side played professional clubs in England and Scotland, and although Yeats had already caught Bill Shankly's eye playing in Scotland, it was his performance for the Army against Liverpool that swung the deal. Yeats received another telegram from his club, this time recalling him to Edinburgh because 'an English club wants to sign you'. On the train journey north, his imagination ran wild – but not to Merseyside. He was dreaming of Spurs or Arsenal or Manchester United. He knew nothing of Bill Shankly or Second Division Liverpool. Absolutely nothing.

Although Liverpool had barely featured in Yeats's thoughts, Bill Shankly made an immediate impression on the young man, who had still barely ever been out of the north-east of Scotland. Shankly was not only a Scot himself – a vital factor in his signing, according to Yeats – but he also carried the healthy sheen of professional, even corporate, success. Shankly's sharp dress sense was partly down to his admiration of the US crime mobs, and the Liverpool manager was certainly like no one Yeats had ever encountered before. His managers at Dundee United had been short term and barely one step up from the grime of the dressing-room. This guy was both dapper and familiar – a near film star in appearance, and a real football enthusiast:

> The thing that made up my mind was meeting Bill Shankly for the first time. I went into this station hotel and I could see my manager and I also could see this man with him that I didn't recognise. I'll always remember this: he was a lovely dresser, this other fellah – lovely suit and tie, and white, white teeth. That really impressed me. And then he's walking round me; I can hear him at the back of me and he says: 'Jesus Christ, son, you must be about seven feet tall!' and when he comes back to the front I said: 'No, I'm only six foot two' and he said: 'That's near enough fucking seven foot for me.' I thought, there and then, 'I like this man.' The fact that he was Scottish was very important too. You can imagine, I was very, very Scottish, from Aberdeen in the north-east of Scotland. You didn't meet many managers and I was very impressed with him – and I have stayed impressed ever since.

Like Gérard Houllier much later – who shopped in his native France in the same way that Shankly was doing in his home base of Scotland – the Liverpool boss was determined that the young players he signed around this time to help transform his club should share the same vision he had for the future. Like Houllier, he wanted to emphasise that players were signing up for a very new style of Liverpool project; one, he believed, that was quite unlike anything the English game had yet seen. Neither Yeats nor Shankly spoke about cash at the meeting, and the player had no advisers present, beyond his own manager at United – who was keen, of course, to get his hands on the large £30,000 fee Liverpool had agreed to pay. The young Scot knew he wanted to be part of this adventure south of the border and, like many players of his era, he questions whether similar motives really exist among football players today:

> He [Shankly] was talking in the car about signing this player and that player and what a good club Liverpool was. I think they'd been third or fourth the year before, and he said signing me would mean getting promotion. I was very impressed with the ideas he had, because I had never had a good manager, I must admit. Dundee United had had three managers in the two years I was there and none of them really impressed me. He knew exactly what he wanted to do for Liverpool football club. I thought: 'I want to be a part of this.' Money didn't bother me. We knew if we were successful we would get the money. I couldn't give a damn about money. I didn't really know what anyone else was earning. In 1965 I earned £4,000. In ten or eleven years here I never spoke about a raise. Today, it's different. I'm not sure whether players want to play for the club first or whether they want money first. I can't fathom some of them these days.

'YOU MUST BE HIDING SOMETHING'

Yeats became Liverpool captain right away and soon felt at home with the Liverpool coaching staff, including another Aberdonian, hard-man trainer Reuben Bennett. He moved his family into West Derby, very near Melwood, but after the Liverpool promotion success of 1961–62 prying fans and rising income encouraged him to move out to Formby, north of the city. Yeats was an enthusiastic trainer, a player who enjoyed the hard, physical work of the Liverpool sessions. He was surprised that Liverpool did so little on the technical side of the sport or on rehearsing set pieces. In fact, Tommy Smith and other Reds players of the time claim never to have practised a free kick, corner-kick or penalty during their entire period at the club. Liverpool relied on the quality of their players and a focus on the basics to get them through. Tom Saunders, who later became the first-ever Youth Development Officer at any club when he took up his post at Liverpool in 1970, recalled later that many coaches turned up to Liverpool training in the 1960s for an 'insight' into the club's success – only to be rudely disappointed:

> They had some wonderful people here [at Liverpool], who recognised the quality of good players, and they had a simple application of allowing those players to express themselves freely during the game. You would never see, for example, a player coming anywhere near the bench, looking for instruction of any sort. They were the top men, and once the game started they got on with it, and they were not restricted. Many people came down to Melwood thinking there was some particular kind of magic here, and we'd allow them to watch the training session, and they would feel as though they had been cheated. They would say: 'You mustn't be showing us all of it. You must be hiding something from us.' But the secret was the whole method was simple, but it was based on good rapport with management, good management, good players and the freedom to express themselves.

Bill Shankly's main contribution to training was actually as a motivator and guide – and as an enthusiastic and competitive player – while Bob Paisley made up for what he lacked in communication skills with his football shrewdness and a native knowledge of the game. Shankly *always* turned up for training; if he was absent, it was to make a new signing, setting the rumours and banter off among the players about who was likely for the chop. Ron Yeats is also intrigued today by what he thinks is the relative lack of physical work in training under the current Liverpool regime:

> All the Liverpool staff had qualities of some sort, to say that not one of them had a coaching badge. But they were all ex-players. Shanks would do the talking – it could be half an hour, it could be three hours. And in that time he hadn't even mentioned the opposition! He was a great talker, a great motivator. Before games he used to come around saying: 'You won't give this fellah a kick.' 'Roger [Hunt], you'll probably score three goals.' It was just the way he talked that got you going. What you wanted was to win for him, more than anything. Then, of course, he put it over to the supporters.

SERVANTS AND STARS: BIG RON AND LITTLE BAMBER

At training it was great; we had a good team, a good bunch of lads, and we got on well together. I really enjoyed training. And the banter was unbelievable. The Saint and Smithy were good at the banter. Roger was a good lad too. Most of us became good friends. I just don't see that now. When I watch training here now, there was a lot more running, back in the '60s, under Shankly, a lot more running. A lot more exercises, physical exercises, and we always, no matter what the time, we always finished off with five-a-sides. And they were competitive! The coaches had a team of their own, and they all had whistles. It was impossible to win a game.

Big Ron is openly surprised that Roy Evans later became a Liverpool manager – 'Decent guy, decent coach, one of the lads. And Roy *knew* players. But he was not really a manager' – and at Bob Paisley's incredible success as manager of Liverpool. Like all the Liverpool players of the 1960s, he respected Paisley, especially for his judgement of the qualities and weaknesses of players. But Bob also seemed to lack the charisma – or even the basic communication skills – to make a top football manager:

I just can't believe Bob [Paisley] won 21 trophies for us, I must admit. A lovely guy, but he just couldn't talk! It was all 'Thingies' and 'doins', and you had to think: 'Well, whose "thingies" and whose "doins"?' That's how he spoke. But he was sharp – and he knew a player. But Bob was always just a trainer with us. Occasionally he would put a couple of words in, but that was all.

Not that tactics and talk were unimportant at Liverpool, far from it. Tommy Smith, St John and Yeats all claim that it was Shankly and Paisley's Liverpool of the early 1960s that first adopted the modern 4–4–2 tactical approach in England, well before Alf Ramsey was credited with introducing the system during the 1966 World Cup finals. Smith was the key here. He made his debut in August 1964 wearing Ian St John's number 9 shirt and then the number 10, but actually slotted in alongside Yeats in the middle at the back, with Peter Thompson and Ian Callaghan acting as positive wide midfielders, and Hunt and St John as the two Liverpool forwards. No one in England had ever seen a number 9 or 10 shirt in a defensive position on the field in the early 1960s. It hinted at the kind of necessary flexibility the club's management was probably picking up from Liverpool's football travel abroad.

Even in the early years in Europe, Liverpool were clearly already learning from continental opposition. Tommy Smith recalls how new little techniques would appear in training at Melwood after early matches abroad – a new goalkeeping exercise, perhaps, or a more sophisticated warm-up routine. A back four, rather than the usual British three, was actually cemented in Shankly's mind following a Liverpool European Cup tie with Anderlecht in 1964. Ian St John also remembers Bob Paisley commenting on the capacity of foreign players to keep the ball much better than players could in England. This would mean a very different response from Liverpool in the 1960s was required towards keeping the ball – and towards getting it back:

> I always remember Bob saying after we'd been in Europe a couple of years, what we've got to pick up from these fellahs is that we can't go and win the ball individually, we have to win the ball collectively. So you couldn't go chasing in there, expecting to get the ball, because these fellahs would just knock it around, kill you off and move on. So we never, ever went for the ball individually, we would always go on instruction from the back-up lads. Say, OK, get them to push this way or that way and we would crowd around the ball to try to stop them. We also learned to keep the ball more. We used to be very direct, but we learned to be patient through European football, don't give it away, knock it around, kill the crowd. That's why Liverpool teams have been so successful.

Towards the end of the 1960s, and as Shankly's first great Liverpool team was starting to age, Yeats began suffering the effects of a slipped disc. He made something of a comeback at Liverpool in 1971, but by that time Larry Lloyd had already been signed and Liverpool were moving towards more flexible and mobile partnerships at centre-back, especially to cope with the new challenges in Europe. A coltish and competitive Phil Thompson was already waiting in the wings.

The club offered Big Ron a place on the back-room staff, but the injury recovered enough for him to play on for a while, initially for Tranmere Rovers and then also in the USA. He enjoyed his time abroad and, like most players, he wanted to play for as long as he could. But he later regretted not retiring as a player at Anfield and then moving directly into the Liverpool coaching team, although he also struggles to come to terms with the fact that some players in the contemporary game apparently *choose* to sit on the bench and pick up their wages rather than move elsewhere, where the prospects of playing are greater. He also, perhaps predictably, has problems with today's huge cash incentives and the attitudes of players to them:

> When I came to this club as a player I didn't want cash, I wanted medals, and that's a big difference today, I think. I was happy with the wage the club gave me. Shanks got it through to his players that if we were successful the money would come. It seems to have gone the other way now: if you get £50,000 you're a success, even if you're not winning anything. I think the whole thing has gone upsidedown.

SCOUTING – FOR LIVERPOOL

Yeats remained outside the English game until 1985, during which time he suffered a number of business setbacks through the activities of unscrupulous partners. When he turned back to football for work, he used his old Liverpool contacts, naturally, and wrote first to Graeme Souness at Rangers for a way back into the game at the club he had supported as a boy. But suddenly another friend, Kenny Dalglish, was in line for the manager's job at Liverpool, and Geoff Twentyman was also retiring as the club's then chief scout. It looked like perfect timing, and so it was Dalglish who brought Big Ron back into the game, and also back to Anfield. This was the Liverpool Way, of course: bringing in an old colleague, relying on a trusted ex-player, on someone who knew the ropes at the club. This would change under Houllier, as football as a business changed. But, even by this time, Liverpool's reach for young players was becoming more global, something which made the scouting job even more of an inexact science than it used to be. For Ron Yeats, the Liverpool scout, it made some of the decisions about who to recommend to the club hierarchy more and more difficult to make:

> What you look for in a player is pace, size and how he plays. You also look for different things depending where the player is playing – defence, midfield, attack. If you see two-thirds of the things you're looking for, then you mark that player down. That's not to say that you'll ever sign him. This club will watch a player five or six times. But what you *must* have in a player, that you can't really tell about until you get him at the club, is something useful up here, in the head. How does he think? Does he really want to play? Is he a winner? You can't tell what he's like off the field, or what he does in training. I wasn't a great player, but when I got on that field I wanted to win more than anything. And you never

really know about that until you get them into the club. And then you see players maybe playing in France or Germany, where the opposition will let you play in your own half, but you get to their last third and they start closing you down. This is where you have to be at your best. When they come to your club, in the Premier League, they are getting pressurised in their own 18-yard box, so they don't look the same player. They say this league is not as good as the Spanish or the Italian leagues, but I'll tell you what, it's a hard league to play in. Nobody here gives you space or time. No time to think at all.

Scouting for Liverpool is also very different, in other ways now, from how it used to be in the 1960s or 1970s. Then, Liverpool could sign players of the quality of Yeats and Ian St John, virtually unopposed, and could later snap up Phil Neal, Emlyn Hughes, Larry Lloyd, Kevin Keegan and Ray Clemence from the English lower divisions, who all became top servants for Liverpool. An Ireland scout for the club, Noel McCabe, claimed recently that he had alerted Liverpool early on to the talents of Damien Duff, John O'Shea and Robbie Keane, and that the club had rejected all three players as young teenagers: £30 million worth of talent, lost. You wonder exactly how staff performance is reviewed in this area. But perhaps Houllier and his coaches now have other markets for players that they look at more closely? Certainly, it *feels* as if being French, rather than Irish or Scottish, gives you a better chance of making it at Liverpool today. The quality gap between the Premiership and the rest of British football has also widened, which means finding high-quality players here is much more competitive today, as Big Ron attests. It is a crowded market: too many scouts, too few quality players:

As the years have gone on, everybody's watching the same players, which means to me there are not so many players around now. Wherever there is a decent player, in the First, Second or Third Division, there must be at least ten Premier League clubs looking in the same place. You can't now get a player that nobody has seen. There are no secrets anymore. I've had many, many players I have recommended to the club, many examples, who go on to make it somewhere else, unfortunately. Maybe the club has signed someone else, instead. Agents have come in now and they recommend players directly to the club. But if we haven't seen a player who is supposed to be top class, I'll be surprised if he makes it, because we see them all these days. A lot of it is money, as well.

> I don't get involved in the money side. The club may make
> inquiries – in 90 per cent of cases we might – but if the money
> they want is ludicrous, stupid money, they won't sign them.

Ron Yeats is today in charge of match reports and of sending scouts to watch players and opponents, but members of the Liverpool Academy staff often go to watch very young British players, and the manager and his coaches will often attend the major youth tournaments. The new Liverpool Director of Scouting and UEFA-qualified coach, another Scot, Alex Miller, watches the club's opponents the week before Liverpool play them and also has the main international brief for scouting. He only sees the Liverpool first team play live about six times a season – but has to inform Houllier on how to combat opponents and to find players who can fit into the Liverpool Way. It seems a daunting task. And spotting young players is a long way from signing them: the South Americans Aimar, Saviola and Riquelme and the Czech Tomas Rosicky were all noted as youngsters by Liverpool, and all have gone on to become big stars elsewhere. So what is it that top players really need today? Miller has no doubts: 'Speed is a big, big priority.' You heard it here first.

LITTLE BAMBER – THE RELUCTANT PROFESSIONAL

Unlike Big Ron Yeats, Brian Hall, 'Little Bamber', is a bit of an oxymoron in England; a professional football player who is also a university graduate. The question of why English football players seem to be a little lacking, sometimes, in the intellectual department, compared to those abroad, is actually partially answered by the fact that the English manage to support *two* major winter team sports – rugby union and football – sports that are divided, fundamentally, by barriers of social class. Most other football nations have only the round-ball game to contend with. If Johnny Wilkinson, say, had been born in Italy, Germany or Spain, he would be a professional footballer – and a star – not a footballer making a living playing rugby, as he is here. England without rugby union would also produce a few more football-playing university men – and perhaps a football sporting culture that depended a little more on intellect and a little less on courage or strength. But that's another story.

★

I interview Brian Hall in his office on Anfield Road, just opposite the ground. His room is stuffed full of 'community' materials, including bag-upon-black-bin-liner-bag of numbered Liverpool shirts. On the walls are photos and posters of the great Liverpool players and teams of the 1970s, Hall's era as a player. But he has been here at the club pretty much ever since, seen nearly all the managerial changes that have followed. We get various interruptions during the interview around the routine corporate and community work of Liverpool FC in 2003: 'Brian, Big Ron has rung about that golf day in Ireland. Have you got Gary Gillespie's number?' Steven Done, from the club museum, comes in to collect some Liverpool shirts to give away or exhibit. It is the everyday work of a big football club, coupled with the memories of one of its past heroes. The kids who now pop their heads in at the window of the club community offices probably have no idea who Brian Hall really is. He looks like just any other slightly overweight, middle-aged bureaucrat, an office worker. Wrong. Remember 27 March 1971 at Old Trafford: Liverpool v. Everton FA Cup semi-final replay, Liverpool 2, Everton 1. Winning goal: Hall; 73 minutes. Enough?

★

Like Big Ron, Little Bamber was born in Scotland, but in Glasgow, to a Scottish mother and an English father. His parents were still serving in the RAF just after the Second World War. There was a family joke that as soon as he could toddle, young Brian would stand at the front door waiting for his uncle to return from work to play football in the hall. There was no professional football background in the Hall family, though the Scottish side of it were Rangers followers, and his father watched Partick Thistle. When his parents were demobbed, the Halls moved onto a council estate in Preston and his father into an administrator's job in the National Health Service. They were one of the few white-collar families on the estate. Young Brian was a bright lad from caring parents and he passed the 11-plus to go to Preston Grammar School, where he played both rugby and soccer for the school teams, going on to represent Lancashire Grammar Schools at football.

A busy and committed midfielder, Hall went to a series of evening trials at Preston in 1962 and also watched as Liverpool schoolboys beat his Preston pals 9–1. It was a merciless slaughter. He was 15 years of age and, like Bill Shankly, a devotee of local hero Tom Finney, who had only just retired from the game. But young Brian had no intentions of becoming a footballer. For him, unlike for Ron Yeats who had signed for Liverpool just a year earlier, football was no escape from working-class hardship or from poverty and grind. Football was an enjoyable alternative to work, sure, but it was never going to be a substitute for it. When questions were raised about his choice of sport or education, it was a very obvious choice to make: he stopped attending at Preston, and prepared for university. *Where* he should go to study was also very obvious.

SERVANTS AND STARS: BIG RON AND LITTLE BAMBER

YEAH, YEAH, YEAH

Things other than football were already stirring, loudly, in Liverpool at this time. This was a heady period, especially for male youth in the city. The so-called 'Mersey Sound', led by the international pop-music success of The Beatles in the early 1960s, would soon thrust Liverpool into the world spotlight. The city's football clubs were also enjoying success together, with Shankly's Liverpool burning up the First Division, following Everton's 'School of Science' side that had won the League title in 1963. Even the new 'modern' Labour government of 1964 was led by a prime minister, Harold Wilson, who represented the Huyton constituency in Liverpool. Wilson also cleverly used his local connections to emphasise the youthful energy of his new administration – he liked his ministers to be photographed with the ubiquitous Beatles. This was also a period in which British drama, theatre and popular culture, more generally, celebrated specifically northern working-class traditions, probably for the first time. The Liverpool-based successful police series, *Z Cars*, for example, began to be broadcast on national TV. Liverpool, in the 1960s, was young and buzzing.

The regular televising of football highlights on the BBC began in Britain in August 1964, at Anfield. The choice of venue was highly appropriate. Liverpool were League Champions, and the club was guaranteed a large and vociferous following, especially as the British pop industry, a growing cultural and economic force in the early 1960s, was then dominated by Brian Epstein, The Beatles, and other Liverpool artistes. One emerging local band, Gerry and the Pacemakers, musicians and also fans of the club, reached the top of the singles' chart late in 1963 with a reworking of a grandiose old musicals' standard, 'You'll Never Walk Alone'. The themes of the song – struggle, pride, community, 'hope in your heart' – seemed ideal for the trials and emotions of football fans, and its 'walk on' chorus, slowly, began to be sung on parts of the Kop.

The Liverpool club, with Bill Shankly's enthusiastic support, eventually responded to growing informal pressure by agreeing to play the Pacemakers' version of the song on the PA before matches as a means of getting the home fans involved and of intimidating visiting teams. It was enthusiastically embraced by the players and the Anfield crowd, right from the start. There was now a central role for *youth* in the new symbolism at football on Merseyside. For writer Arthur Hopcraft, for example, his most vivid 1960s Anfield memory was not of the working men who followed the club in their droves, but of: 'The sight of a small, ragged boy appearing on the skyline of the Kop's acutely slanting roof, stepping gracefully down to the middle of it and sitting down, arms folded, a tiny symbolic representative of the bravura of his people.' It was a great time to be young, working class and a football fan from Liverpool in the early 1960s. And it was better still to be a student in Liverpool who loved playing football.

This was the dizzy world that both Ron Yeats and Brian Hall effectively joined in the early 1960s. The hard man Yeats, the football professional, became a bit of a celebrity in the city, especially after the Liverpool promotion in 1962, and he soon knew the local music and club scene in Liverpool:

> It was a great time then. I wasn't that interested in the music, but you knew most of the singers then, you met them at different functions. You didn't get pestered, I don't remember getting pestered then. But at six feet two and 14 and a half stone maybe you don't get pestered! We also knew all the Everton lads, we met the Everton boys socially – Roy Vernon, Alec Young – every week. We all used to go to a club in town and if we came back from an away game, the Everton boys would all be in there. Everyone knew The Beatles. And when you went to Europe to play, the first thing you would get is: 'Do you know The Beatles – yeah?' Their eyes would light up at this.

For the BSc maths student Brian Hall, going to Liverpool did not mean football at all, at least not initially. It meant music:

> When it came to choosing a university to go to in October 1965 there was only one choice. Liverpool was top of the list, nothing to do with football. It was The Beatles, Gerry and the Pacemakers, the whole Mersey beat scene. The Liverpool bands used to come to Preston and I saw them in church halls and local colleges. They were the best around. There was an energy about them that just appealed to me. And so I became a student in Liverpool in the 1960s, with all the music – and then ended up playing for Liverpool! Could it get any better?

Hall still had no plans to hitch up with a professional club, but a school friend wrote to Liverpool asking for a trial for him with the FA Cup winners and, on 5 October 1965, a university mate insisted he catch the 81 bus to Melwood to see what he could do. The bus driver, excited and honoured that he had a Liverpool trialist on his bus, actually got off and showed him into the ground. Hall's first sight at Melwood was of a junior goalkeeper who could barely walk after copping a boot in his, by now, black-and-blue genitals. Whilst the keeper staggered off to a cold bath, a shaken Brian Hall paraded his stuff and signed that night for Liverpool as an amateur. He was 18.

'I THINK WE'VE JUST SIGNED JIMMY CLITHEROE!'

Hall played his first game the following week for the Liverpool A team v. Everton A; and half the Liverpool schoolboys' team he had watched trounce Preston boys back in 1962 turned out for Liverpool, the other half for Everton. It was a major step-up, and a brutal contest. But within a month, this youngster, who still had no firm plans to play the game seriously, was actually in the Liverpool reserves team, making his debut at Old Trafford. He received expenses only, was strictly amateur, and he even continued to turn out for the university Maths Society team on Wednesday afternoons. Liverpool frowned. His attitude? 'All I was doing was playing football.' Youth coach Tom Bush and Joe Fagin at Liverpool even wondered if there were any other students like this one at college, and they sent a Reds junior team to play the Liverpool University first XI. It ended an embarrassing 9–0, the Liverpool side even easing up towards the end. They never looked again.

Hall was very different, of course, from most of the other players at Melwood in the late 1960s. Football was not the be all and end all of his life, as it was for the committed professionals and the tough young streetwise kids he now mixed with on training nights and match days. He was a hard-working and talented little midfielder, who was not averse to kicking back at opponents, so he got respect on the field. But he took plenty of dressing-room stick over his background and education (obviously), his height (5 ft 6 in. and going no higher) and his university maths. Players used to ask him to work out the odds on their 'Yankee' horse-racing bets, a complex series of cross-doubles and trebles. He knew nothing about betting, or about Yankees, which, naturally, creased up the older pros.

Some established players at Liverpool clearly also resented his freewheeling lack of dependency on the game and, at first, some senior pros in the reserves even refused to pass the ball to 'this fucking university boy'. He just gave them a mouthful back – and the ball eventually came. But it wasn't always easy, balancing the student life with that of also being an 'insider' at a top professional club. Embarrassment was only a short step around the corner at any moment. For example, in order to make summer training at Liverpool, as well as two shifts on his student holiday job as a bus conductor in Preston, Hall had to travel to Anfield in his bus conductor's uniform. It was a mistake. He looked like a northern comic:

> So here is this little 19-year-old kid, who looks about 16, rolling up at Anfield in a bus conductor's outfit. And I'm walking down the corridor, and big Yeatsy sticks his head out the door and says to St John: 'Saint, I think we've just signed Jimmy Clitheroe, come and have a look at this!' That's when the stick started. I get escorted into what was then the away dressing-room, the one used by the apprentices. I got directed to a hanger – I didn't understand any of this, of course. I just did what I was told. Then the big man himself walked in, Mr Shankly. I'd met him before, but only in the dressing-room, pre-match and post-match. He starts getting changed next to me: that's why I'd been given that hook. I could see a few smiles round the dressing-room now. Shanks says: 'Hello, son, how are you?' And then he clicks: 'You're the student, from Preston?' And then he's off: 'Tom Finney, what a player. Did you see him play, son?' He then went into this long eulogy about Finney and how wonderful he was. He loved him. All the young lads are listening now, in awe. And right in the middle of it all he suddenly stops and looks me up and down again and says: 'Son, do you need a degree now to be a bus conductor in Preston?'

After two mainly enjoyable years of dressing-room banter and reserve-team play at Liverpool, Hall was beginning to think, for the first time, that he might actually like to make it as a professional player, and he confided to trainer Reuben Bennett that he was thinking of giving up his studies to concentrate on playing. But he had picked the wrong man: Bennett had sons at teaching college himself, and he had seen plenty of promising young players chewed up and spat out by football. He laid into Hall: 'Don't you dare give up on your education!' This blast confused the university man: after all, Liverpool seemed keen on him, and yet here was Bennett cooling him out, preparing him for a career elsewhere in which his maths, rather than midfield calculations, were likely to be more useful. Hall resigned himself to quietly playing out his time under Joe Fagin in the reserves, and at 21 he contemplated a new career – in computers.

Before finally deciding whether to turn his back completely on professional football, Hall talked to Billy Liddell, who now worked as a bursar for the university. He asked Liddell if he had any contacts at a smaller football club – perhaps Chester or Tranmere Rovers – where he might play the occasional game after graduation? This inquiry got back to Liverpool, of course, and the following week Joe Fagin asked Hall if he had contemplated turning professional and that if he had, Bill Shankly was now ready to see him. Hall thanked him, but told him that he preferred to wait until after his final exams. Fagin just shrugged his shoulders, uncomprehending: what sort of lunatic was this?

When he eventually saw Shankly, in June 1968, Hall was also by now engaged to be married and had checked out graduate pay: new graduates at this time were earning around £1,100 per year. Shankly offered him £20 per week, plus bonuses, and a signing-on fee of £250: around £1,500 per year. Hall, astonished, heard himself asking for travelling expenses from Preston, and the manager, a face like thunder, silently rose and left the 21-year-old alone in his tiny office in the old stand, staring at the unsigned contract left on his desk. Hall thought he had blown the deal – maybe computers were not such a bad idea, after all. After what seemed like a lifetime, Shankly returned with another contract that he had typed out himself: for £22 per week. Hall, by now visibly shaking, signed. He was a professional footballer after all – at Liverpool.

Hall appeared 220 times for Liverpool between 1969 and 1975, scoring 21 goals. He won championship, UEFA Cup and FA Cup-winners' medals in the process. So, his was just another successful Liverpool career, out of different roots. Comparing university maths with studying at the Melwood Football Academy under Shankly, Fagin and Paisley in the 1970s, Hall observes today that every year in education the maths was getting more and more difficult, while at Liverpool the football got simpler. Every day on the Liverpool training ground the basic messages of 'pass and movement' were relentlessly hammered home. This was the genius of the Liverpool system – and the reason why Shankly reasoned that Lilleshall could keep all of its fancy FA qualifications.

Like Ron Yeats, Hall thinks that Shankly's greatest ability was to look a player in the eye and see a winner. The manager also had the gift of language, of inspiration, whereas Paisley, essentially a non-communicator, better understood systems of play. Hall played under Paisley as manager, of course, but he argues that the values of the club – the Liverpool Way – stayed exactly the same after Shankly's shock departure in 1974. The Liverpool dressing-room remained ultra-competitive, and Hall had few real friends there 30 years ago, but it also had a unity and a commonality of purpose. Like Hunter Davies in *The Glory Game*, Hall uses the language and symbolism of the family to describe the Liverpool club in the 1970s: a togetherness that linked the players, management, fans, and even the ground staff and ancillary workers at Anfield and Melwood. But he also regards this intense intimacy as very much a 'Liverpool thing'.

Rows and divisions would occur in the family, of course, but they would always be overcome for the wider good. It was a simpler game.

THE NEW LIVERPOOL

At 29 Hall got injured playing against Slask Wroclaw in the UEFA Cup in November 1975, but he insisted in playing on the matches coming up – Jimmy Case was, by now, stalking his first-team place. Eventually, he had to step down and Case stepped up. Too often on the bench, Hall – stupidly, he says now – got it into his head to leave Liverpool, despite Bob Paisley asking him to stay. He joined an old school friend Tony Waiters at Plymouth Argyle, to play and coach, but it was a disaster on the football side. Hall had public disagreements with the manager and was played as a striker. However, he learned a lot about working in the media, PR and commercial sides of the club, experiences that he put to good use when he returned to Liverpool to work on the community front.

Why did Liverpool fail later? During the club's 20-year cycle of success, the football industry was already changing. The old, successful formula – the transfer of management from one Liverpool insider to the next – *seemed* to be working, but the football world was really passing Liverpool by. It was Liverpool that would now have to change to catch up with the rest of the game. It was too easy to blame individuals – Graeme Souness or Roy Evans, even Peter Robinson – for what was a more general problem at Anfield: a failure, according to Hall, to connect effectively with the new global game:

> Liverpool was always a parochial club, with a family feel and atmosphere: it was inward looking. This used to be a strength. But the game had changed. When I was a player, the club was in control of your destiny; your wages were subject to appearances, crowd bonuses, all that stuff. Now you are dealing with players who are very much in control of their own destiny. How you motivate them to go out and give everything they've got, week in, week out, how you manage to keep hold of them, apart from anything else, and make them understand that you're the boss and it's your job to pick the team. How you manage to do all that today, I don't know. Roy [Evans] was old school, not very strong with the board, so it was always going to be difficult for him. But because the worldwide market place for players was changing, they were used to the new methods. Gérard Houllier wasn't introducing anything new to the foreign players he brought here. He was introducing it to the English players. That's all. They

[foreign players] came here and expected it. The first thing I saw
Patrik Berger do when he arrived at Melwood [in 1996] was to
go straight in the dining room and say, through his interpreter, to
the two women who served the food, what he eats. I couldn't
believe it. No one had ever seen it here.

Unlike the 1960s and 1970s, today's players also live in a media goldfish
bowl; they can be successfully traded on the basis of video coverage of a
few goals scored abroad and make enough money for the rest of their
lives in just two or three moves. Titi Camara, a liked but inconsistent
player at Liverpool, and a disaster at West Ham, has probably earned
around £2 and £3 million from his stay in England. Why leave a
comfortable living now – as Hall did for Argyle in 1976 – when this sort
of money is available? Building a believable, a convincing, team ethic is a
more complex problem today, and much more short term. And the
Liverpool fans today are harsher, more demanding and much less tolerant
of failure.

In the 1960s and 1970s there was no great Liverpool European legacy
to live up to: it was all still to do. Nevertheless, Bill Shankly and Gérard
Houllier actually do seem very similar in their approaches to reviving
Liverpool football club: find players in places you know best; recruit them
young and ambitious; 'sell' them a new football adventure; offer strong
leadership; inspire loyalty and trust. But in the 1960s global game did not
yet exist. And getting back to the top is always more difficult than getting
there, or even staying there. So being willing to 'go through brick walls'
or even simply being winners, like Ron Yeats and Brian Hall, is probably
no longer enough to secure real success in the new football business of
2003. Gérard Houllier knows all this, of course. But can he make it work
today as Shankly and Paisley did so gloriously with Big Ron and Little
Bamber 40 years ago? It is still a new football world to win.

CHAPTER 6

In Search of the Golden Sky

1 JANUARY 2003: NEWCASTLE UNITED 1, LIVERPOOL 0

'We celebrate together and we suffer together.'

Gérard Houllier

New Year's day at Newcastle United brings no respite in the League. A limp Liverpool midfield that, masochistically, includes both Biscan and Cheyrou (Murphy is suspended), relies too much on a recovering – and, let's remember, a still very young – Steven Gerrard. A poor match played out in atrocious conditions on a bog of a pitch is settled by an early, deflected Robert free kick. Baros, flinches, showing no guts – or sense – in the Liverpool wall and so contributes to our downfall. Thereafter, Liverpool show little creative intent or ambition – though coltish striker Neil Mellor does offer some welcome heart and application in his first League appearance as substitute. Salif Diao's idiotic sending off with half an hour left allows our hosts to glide to a 1–0 victory with the minimum of fuss or effort. Another spineless loss.

Later, journalists report a surprisingly genial and relaxed Houllier talking in an animated way in the press conference about the very 'exciting' challenges that (apparently) lie ahead for this Liverpool. His upbeat demeanour smacks of David Brent's reliance on the words of Dolly Parton in TV's *The Office*: 'If you want the rainbow, you've got to put up with the rain.' Perhaps part of Houllier is actually *enjoying* this slump, already anticipating recovery and the opportunity to say 'I told you so' to the fans and the press. He says later: 'You must not forget that the average age of our team tonight was 23 and a half. Even if our run without a win goes to 12 games, so what? We've got the foundations, so there's no problem.' No problem? Twelve winless games? Even after the brief promise shown at Highbury, we see no obvious rainbow, only storm clouds, but then nothing really surprises us now.

5 JANUARY 2003, FA CUP (THIRD ROUND): MANCHESTER CITY 0, LIVERPOOL 1

Pasty young Neil Mellor gets a surprise Liverpool start at Maine Road in this FA Cup tie, with internationals Heskey and Baros both on the bench. Traore replaces Riise on the left once again (no one understands this Traore fixation anymore, another Houllier stubbornness). Given our recent form, this is set up for a home win, but City perform as if this tie is just a training-ground run-out with absolutely nothing at stake. Perhaps the 10 foreigners in their starting line-up give not a toss for the world's oldest and most respected knock-out competition. It looks like it. Certainly the crowd can't be arsed – there are huge empty spaces in the ground today, as this TV lunchtime bore meanders, gently in the freezing winter sun, towards a deserved Liverpool win. Let us not look too deeply: just accept the fact of it.

Murphy and Gerrard dominate the midfield and Diao also looks commanding, for once, swamping his fellow African, the man from Cameroon, Foe. Even the chaotic Diouf occasionally looks threatening, madly chasing every lost cause amidst City's nervous, makeshift defence. City's Anelka, on the other hand, is lazy and anonymous. Lost. The winning goal is another Liverpool penalty – how else are we to score? This one was stolen by Smicer early in the second half. Murphy now looks utterly reliable from the spot and scores easily. But can we also do this in the League, and against a team that really wants to win?

'FOREIGN QUICK FIXES'

In the FA Cup, by the way, we now want to draw Third Division Shrewsbury Town. The Shrews have already disposed of Premier League opposition and we think they deserve another match up with a real giant. Their previous victims: only newly puff-candy Everton, that's all. A tragedy. PFA chief, Gordon Taylor, warns top English clubs not to use the transfer window to stock up on 'unreliable foreign quick fixes'. One (un-named) club chairman points, in the quality press, to Liverpool as an example of a failing club with 'too many non-British nationals in their team'. Meanwhile, as the gruesome Lee Bowyer is finally making his transferred way to West Ham, we have other pressing cup business to face, in Sheffield. Another test of the 'foreigners' thesis.

8 JANUARY 2003, WORTHINGTON CUP SEMI-FINAL (FIRST LEG): SHEFFIELD UNITED 2, LIVERPOOL 1

A fourth consecutive Liverpool away game, and so it is another ugly capitulation, just like it was before. Sheffield United are on their own little roll, a 12-game unbeaten League run and, with recent cup wins here against Leeds and Sunderland, they are also pressing hard for a play-off place. Neil Warnock is the home manager, so they will niggle, scrap and fight, on and off the pitch, and they have a strong and experienced core, as well as good young prospects, including left-sided Michael Tonge, currently linked with Liverpool. So this is not a match to be taken lightly.

South Yorkshire police could not be accused of taking this match lightly, either. Visiting Liverpool fans must negotiate lines of Sheffield's finest riot officers: helmets, vests, batons, the lot. Unsmiling, waiting, as if pulled in from another film set – or from another football era. We *know* in which era they truly belong. This seems to us like an unnecessary and ugly provocation. To our cost, we have unwillingly placed our livelihood in their nervous hands once before. But once inside, we can begin to see at least some of the reason for the extra police hardware. A large group of puffa-jacket-wearing baseball-hatted locals to our right audition as if extras in one of those *What Happened to 1982?* TV nostalgia specials. It's 'The Blades' crew, of course. They even, periodically, bawl (at us): 'You're gonna get your fuckin' 'eads kicked in!' Time-warp time.

Star Wars music greets the teams and a stadium announcer insists on calling United: 'Warnock's Red and White Wizards' and on adding stupid little descriptions for the local favourites ('The best goalkeeper in the Nationwide', 'The most valuable player on the pitch tonight', etc.). A whole 11-strong team of United mascots – Dumpy right through to Dopey and even Titchy – accompany the home team on to the field. United have had no cup-final appearance of any kind since 1936, so you have to know that waiting 67 years for this sort of night is likely to get local expectations up to fever pitch. Even so, this still ought to be a controlled win for Liverpool. But nothing is ever easy now. Nothing.

Having told the press today that Heskey needs to start repaying the faith shown in him at Anfield by scoring goals, and while also having another sly poke at the 'phone-in idiots' who have been criticising the manager and the team, Houllier plays his poker face by actually fielding the *same* players who started against Manchester City. This means Heskey and Owen on the bench, once more, and a convoluted 4–2–3–1 formation: Kirkland in goal; a back four of Carragher, Henchoz, Hyypiä and Traore; a deep-lying middle two of Gerrard and Diao; a more advanced three of Smicer, Murphy and Diouf; and a lone front man, young Mellor. Baros and Riise are the main men still out in the cold. Biscan has disappeared again, possibly for good. This system can play either very defensively – with the forward player becoming detached – or it can be aggressive and exciting, with midfield players offering support in numbers high up the field. I'll let you guess.

To be fair, we start well, Smicer and Diouf involved, and the passing is good. Mellor misses, close in, when he really should score from a pass from Diouf, and Sami is winning the aerial battle at Liverpool's attacking corners. Traore is under pressure from Ndlovu on the left, sure, but Gerrard is looking the class act we all know he is: that Tonge kid can't be playing. Ten minutes before the break we even score to back up all this promise and control, Hyypiä flicking on a Murphy free kick from the right for Mellor to nail with a header at the far post – and right in front of us. Heskey might take note. The Sheffield lads to our right now stand with creased red faces, arms spread wide, cajoling us forward – as if brawling will now solve their team's problems. Plain sailing.

But at half-time, we all know the danger that still lies ahead. Warnock will be positively blasting his players at this moment: 'What's the bleedin' matter? Get fucking into them! Stick your fucking foot in. Mess 'em up!' Houllier will be telling ours, more calmly, that things are going well, that we need to stand firm and try to sneak another, clinching goal. But give nothing away; keep your shape. This is the dilemma of our entire season: stick or twist. Lately, we have usually gone bust from here. Warnock wins the half-time, because the second period is a sprawling mess, United pumping it forward, scrapping, Liverpool grasping for control.

And now Diouf is suddenly 'supporting' Carragher at right-back, mainly by getting in his way. Worse, he is not doing his real job anymore; he is not frightening Sheffield defenders now, not even a little. And certainly not the way Ndlovu is still freaking out Jimmy T. on our left. United's Brown, desperate now, scythes into Kirkland high and late – and incredibly stays on. The entire Liverpool bench is up at this assault. Perhaps this is Sheffield's last desperate throw? Tonge is now clearly playing: advanced, wide left this half, fiercely ugly and bouncing on his choppy little stride, with the little Bluenose veteran McCall inside him. It is these two who have forced Diouf back and who finally undo us with 14 minutes left. We have had warnings. After a goalmouth mêlée, Carragher and the Liverpool centre-backs attack the same ball on the edge of the box and the wily McCall, expertly and instantly, feeds the afters to Tonge who, unopposed by Jamie, slides it through Chris Kirkland's legs.

This is trouble; we know it all too well, we can smell it by now. A corner from Quinn, six minutes later, is not properly cleared and Tonge, again, keeps cool on the edge of the box, makes space on his right side – and finishes by dragging the ball back low, inside Kirkland's right-hand post. Tonge now dances, with a tacky musical accompaniment, over to the Blades' ugly brigade who – need I tell you? – are positively stupefied with joy. Suddenly, a post-match kick-off seems an unnecessary distraction to them – one best left, no doubt, until after the decisive return leg. It ends 2–1, the second leg no longer the formality we had hoped for.

MY DAD'S BIGGER THAN YOUR DAD

In the following days this defeat feels worse, because both Houllier and even Thommo complain – moan – to the press: about the Sheffield pitch; about the touchline wind-up from Warnock, and about the 'physical' side of the United approach. (Did we expect them to lie down, like Keegan's City?) We even talk about relishing getting these clowns back to Anfield, presumably for a going-over. Houllier really loses it here, pointing to the terrible 'leg-breaking' tackle by Brown on Kirkland: 'I am looking forward to meeting them at Anfield, believe me,' he mutters. Is this a threat? Can we back it up? This match has not even been that heavy, bar Brown's stupid lunge. Our management team should grow up. And get focused.

At the Liverpool AGM this week – and there was no real rough stuff aimed at him from the floor – Houllier was off again, criticising the moaning radio phone-in fans and saluting the 5,000 'loyal' Reds who went to Villa for the 4–3 League Cup tie. It's funny that he thinks there is no overlap at all between these two groups, that the phone-in boys are all carping dickheads, while the Reds' away fans are resolutely behind him (and that he chooses Villa as his example, one of our only decent away performances in this drought). He doesn't know the half of it. 'Every game is a fight for life,' he said recently. 'This is the time for players to show they are men. We have to push to the edge.' But all this quirky, vainglorious media stuff just adds to the pressure and the hardship. Why doesn't he just keep quiet sometimes?

Houllier also says that he is still 'searching for the golden sky' at the end of the current, torrid phase. It's a phrase taken from 'You'll Never Walk Alone': 'At the end of a storm/ There's a golden sky.' It's carefully chosen. He's smart, *Le Boss*, he knows that, emotionally, we are right behind him. We have to be. He turned the club around, brought trophies back in 2001 and then almost died at the helm. We owe Houllier, and he still deserves our support. But our allegiance is not unconditional. How can it be? Intellectually, rationally, we are actually completely opposed to aspects of what is happening now. Houllier is ruthless enough to know that in the hard business of football, 2001 is already history.

11 JANUARY 2003: LIVERPOOL 1, ASTON VILLA 1

From today, we need to win 15 and draw the other one of our remaining 16 games in the League, even to reach last year's total of 80 points – which was only good enough, anyway, for second place. We still have to play all the top clubs away – save Arsenal and Newcastle – so our best aim even now must be to qualify for the Champions League, a top-four finish. As things stand, this may be beyond us. With a new ground still in the offing, missing out on a Champions League place is unthinkable for Liverpool. It means cash lost, but, worse, a place at the back of the queue for new signings.

Today, Mellor partners Owen and Riise replaces Traore in a match we *must* win. Diouf plays on the left of a midfield four, which, even from this vantage point, looks a tad optimistic. The somnambulant Heskey ought to be angry and ashamed, of course, that this rookie kid Mellor is now preferred to the England man. I wonder if the message has even got through to Emile? Hamann remains injured in Germany – how we need him back. There is still no Milan Baros in the squad, not even on the bench. A pariah, is he, since collapsing the Reds' wall at Newcastle? If so, it is the management of the madhouse.

Villa threaten from the start, Barry making an early chance for Dublin, but the match is scrappy, incoherent, and Diouf is already beginning to wander, offering some danger but also threatening our shape. Both sides look uncertain, as you might expect. It is a bumbling Diouf run on the right that makes Michael Owen's goal. As usual, our new man fails to pick out a Red shirt from a good goal-line position, but the ball falls to Michael anyway and he spears it past Enckleman. The relief in the ground bubbles over: a goal, at last, from the Boy Wonder. We even see a slip of an Owen smile! This must be a turning point. But 1–0 up is actually one of our worst places to be at the moment: we badly need to extend the lead and to head, for once, into the winning comfort zone.

Forget it. We get no chance to relax, because Graham Taylor has the Villa lads warming up early on the field at half-time, and they begin again much more tuned-in than Liverpool. Dublin has already missed another real chance before Hyypiä dives in on Barry within minutes of the restart and referee Durkin has no option. Kirkland sees the penalty kick all the way – low and left (he knows Dublin's style from their Coventry days) – but still can't save it. Now we can all feel the uncertainty, the panic, rise. I bet the Villa boys can sense it, too. We look, not for the first time this season, quite witless.

As home frustration rises, the Liverpool substitutes duly arrive: Smicer, Heskey and Cheyrou, in swift succession. But these are not the men to change a game. OK, Smicer offers width and some threat on the right, but the other two entrants are timid, hopeless replacements at the moment. So now we look a mess, a real shambles. Cheyrou is embarrassing, his body language telling you (and his marker) that he's hating all of this. Dublin heads over once more before the end when scoring would be easier. The crowd is strangling its own boos. Champions League? This is our worst League run for 49 years. We are (ha, ha) looking for the five draws we still need to get us to 40 points, and safety.

Back in the Flattie, venom predictably overtakes despair at last. It has been coming. A group of St Helens lads, regulars away and in Europe, have finally turned on Houllier, big time. They want him out and they won't be told otherwise. They also want the foreign invasion to stop. Voices are raised, men standing, their true feelings, the pent-up anger and the deep-seated prejudices that lie below, all are now just starting to come out. It's not pretty. 'What fucking African has ever been successful here, in England?' they ask. 'Lauren and Patrick Vieira,' I suggest. But these current Arsenal stars, these authentic successes, are not 'real' Africans, at least not for these angry Reds: after all, Vieira chose France over his native Senegal. The bitter complaints continue to tumble out, and these hardened, knowledgeable Reds fans do have a point about Houllier's signings. The dogs in the street would nod in agreement with them at the moment. So they deserve to have their concerns addressed.

TRANSFER BLUES

Houllier's questionable buys: draw up a list and look at it coldly. It makes troubling reading in the current situation. For example, and in the face of the Anfield boo boys, *we* have supported and defended Vladdy Smicer, right from the start, and he has put in some decent performances for Liverpool, especially in Europe. But he usually manages only 70 minutes in the Premiership (unless already subbed) and also looks no closer now to offering the sort of consistency and commitment we really need, home and away, than when he dipped out of his first Liverpool tackle. He is still a peripheral figure.

Jimmy Traore is different: he too readily dives in and goes to ground, and is crude and awkward, uneasy on the ball at full-back. He panics away from home. Bruno Cheyrou is simply bemused, frightened. Diouf lacks footballing brains (as well as brawn) and, thus far, offers no obvious, regular goal threat, a real problem for a striker. Can he play wide? His mate, Salif Diao, has his muscular moments but deals, largely, in destructive energy. But let's not be too hard here – the men from Senegal do need time to settle. Milan Baros may also do better given time: he has talent, but he is still a head-down, raw loner. And even the previously reliable Jerzy Dudek has started to creak, alarmingly, this season. Abel Xavier has not impressed at right-back and there are transfer rumours, and no one here – except perhaps Houllier himself – now believes in Igor Biscan.

Finally, Emile Heskey simply seems to have completely lost his game from the rampaging 20 goals start he made back in 2000–01: no Liverpool coach or adviser, seemingly, can help him find it. This makes *ten* big and expensive (nearly £50 million worth) Houllier transfer question marks; nine of them foreigners. And I'm not even counting Vignal, Diomède and others who have already passed through. All of these guys are decent athletes, but their technique, or their heart – or both – lets them down. Our imported players are either too young, inconsistent or too inexperienced in England – and many of them seem not good enough. This leaves Hyypiä, Henchoz, Hamann and Kirkland as GH's real gold-standard successes. Great buys, bargains even. Babbel and McAllister, too, and probably Riise. It's hit and miss on transfers so far. We also wonder how many of these question marks will ever become Liverpool fixtures, real players at Anfield. It's a fair question.

18 JANUARY 2003: SOUTHAMPTON 0, LIVERPOOL 1 (ONE!)

> 'There is a fine line between winning and losing. Imagine that we had just taken six more points – then we would be second. If we had got 15 points then we would be first.'
>
> Gérard Houllier

Gérard Houllier and his team may be driving us to distraction at the moment, but there is little wrong with Gérard's strange logic – or his maths. These mysterious 'missing six points', especially, have featured quite a bit in his interviews recently. Has he lost them down the back of the couch? Or, perhaps, an appeal to the Premier League to return them might be in order? After all, Charlton are trying to get a replay at Chelsea for having to play on a beach at Stamford Bridge. This kind of wistful day-dreaming comes directly from the 'If my aunt had bollocks she would be my uncle' school of football philosophising, but it seems to offer our beleaguered manager some comfort in difficult times. Our own dampened spirits demand more tangible signs of recovery. Admittedly, the south coast looks an unlikely place to start turning things around.

The King Alfred pub is barely five minutes over the main access bridge from the new St Mary's stadium and is a decent enough watering point before facing the home storm. This new ground, like Sunderland's, is within walking distance from the city centre, another plus. 'The pubs on the other side of the bridge are fucking rough,' the security guy deadpans to us. And this is no palace. Some of the St Helens lads are also here, upstairs with giant jugs of ale already on the go. A 5.35 p.m. Sky TV kick-off (are we *ever* off the telly?) means we can all watch the afternoon results feeding in. Everton and Newcastle win, and United beat Chelsea. Even Spurs are now above us after sneaking home at Villa. And what about: Brechin City 5, Cowdenbeath 7, crowd 693. We all wonder how the second set will finish.

The Liverpool talk here is all about the grinding out of a result today and possible UEFA Cup final preparations for Spain: 'I've told the missus, *you* take the kids to Blackpool for a week, I'm off to fucking Seville for the final for my summer holidays.' Football households are seldom places of equality and harmony, and watching 'new' football is hardly cheap: £28 for a ticket today, plus travel and ale. It's an all-day event. These boys are serious and dedicated LFC travellers, family or no family. But let me say now there are no signs at all that any Liverpool follower will have to book time off for European final duty in May. Auxerre will test us enough.

Diao is suspended and Houllier surprises everyone by actually selecting his best available combination this evening: Gerrard and Murphy in the middle with Riise in left midfield, Diouf playing wide right and Heskey, for once, up front with Owen. The key to stifling Southampton is to make Bridge play as a real left full-back (Diouf's job) and also keep Fernandes out of the game on the right (Traore and Riise, together). Then, you must boss young Beattie (Sami can manage here) and get at their slow centre-backs (Emile – the old Emile – to use his pace and weight). This is what we dream of.

Incredibly, in the first 30 minutes and in swirling rain in front of sell-out, raucous, standing Liverpool support, we manage to do all these things. Today, it is as if *we* are on an unbeaten run, rather than a club searching desperately for confidence and a foothold. Everyone does his job, but the key figure is Heskey. Having him restored up front, and looking powerful and determined once again (new coach Rushie is eyeing Emile coldly from the Liverpool bench), changes the whole chemistry of the team, and offers a reliable focal point high up the pitch. But Riise is also pressing hard against Telfer, a makeshift right-back, Diouf is operating as a real outlet for once and is also working back, while Steven Gerrard and Danny Murphy are scurrying like talented red slaves in the middle. We are pouring forward.

Fourteen minutes: hold the front page, Emile scores! No League goals since 14 September, we are impressed Heskey even remembers how. Our hero (again) he bustles in front of Svensson and meets Riise's looped near-post free kick perfectly with a cute downward header. It all looks so simple. It *is* simple for God's sake. Gerrard soon plays Emile in again, but this time the big man hits Niemi. The home keeper also saves from Riise and Murphy, and Michael is even buzzing away now, taking shots and looking for openings. We look good; no question. So, when the locals chant, originally: 'If Heskey plays for England, so can I,' we are able to jeer back with a knowing, light heart. All irony is suddenly suspended.

In the second half we do sit deeper but Southampton produce little. Even Strachen looks defeated. And when, on the hour, Gerrard slithers a perfect pass into the galloping Riise down the Liverpool left, and Owen breaks free in the centre, we just *know* the drought is over, that this will be at least a 2–0 away win. And so there will be no terrible torture for the final minutes as we hang on grimly again against the threat of a possible deflection, a defensive error or a lucky shot. Michael calmly collects the cross, moves clear of the home defence, sets himself and, as we rise to salute him, screws his shot wide.

So when the end finally arrives, with Kirkland's yellow jersey still mud-free, and St Mary's by now barely half-full, even Henchoz, our dour brick-maker at the back, clenches his fists in utter relief, while Kirky jigs in front of us, his first Premiership win secured, and Emile smiles that brilliant grin he has been sheepishly hiding for four, long months. '*Gér-ard, Gér-ard Houllier, Gér-ard, Gér-ard Houllier*' booms shamelessly from the Liverpool end. This chorus has GH and Thommo beaming and waving to us from the tunnel. Despite all the crap we have played, the mistakes and the cruel selection mysteries, these fans suddenly seem to have faith in him. Crisis, what crisis? And the rain still leaks from the black Hampshire sky as we burst out of the ground through gaggles of Saints fans to cross the dripping metal footbridge back into town – to celebrate!

TOP FOOTBALLER HAS BET SHOCK

The red-tops this weekend have Michael Owen blowing his many endorsements on slow horses, cards and football bets. Get used to it: old blue eyes likes a punt. One rag mentions losses of £2.2 million. Get real. Owen's people stay calm: yes, Michael does like a bet, but he has lost more like £30,000–40,000 over the past couple of years – about half a week's wages, which probably puts him level with most working men in Liverpool. Rubbishing all this hype, Alan Hansen recalls how bad Liverpool card players in the 1980s used to lose a couple of hundred quid on away trips – out of £600 a week wages – and that Bob Paisley used to announce the big race winners during the half-time team talk at Anfield. So Michael has some history to follow here.

21 JANUARY 2003, WORTHINGTON CUP SEMI-FINAL (SECOND LEG): LIVERPOOL 2, SHEFFIELD UNITED 0

He needs a gag sometimes, he really does. At the pre-match press conference, Gérard just cannot stop himself going on about the 'disrespect' supposedly shown by the United staff at the first leg. Warnock, for example, audibly compared the entire club wage bill at Bramall Lane to Michael's take-home pay. Big deal. He also claimed that Liverpool staff had told our players not to swap their shirts after the first leg. Sounds like the sort of petty gesture a fuming Thommo might well have made. But everyone in the game knows Warnock is a bad loser and a worse winner, so why get upset now, upping the ante, and so risk losing focus? We don't need to get dragged into a battle here.

The clog-dancers from Sheffield have also travelled across the Pennines with real hope. Not since a losing Wembley FA Cup semi-final against their Owlerton neighbours have United been this close to a big football weekend away. And so they flood the Flattie tonight, the Blades boys, with their songs about 'greasy chip butties' and news of their past glories, of 'running' rivals Wednesday. They even include in their ranks at least one dickhead in a Harry Enfield scouser wig and 'tache. *Très amusant.* Someone else buys his ale, obviously. We should forgive them for some of this – but not for the trouble later outside Anfield Road. These South Yorkshiremen have, after all, been a long time out of the limelight.

We are sited in the Main Stand, Kop end, so we get a good view of the minor celebs but also of the Kop winding itself up for another big Anfield night. Ron Yeats passes just in front of us, still fit, a giant of a man. Only his nose is gently flattened by too many clashes with foolishly ambitious centre-forwards from the 1960s. He's seen loads of nights like this – and much bigger ones. The Kop is in fractious mood tonight, a more souped-up local audience than normal this evening because tickets are just £14, and many of the non-Merseyside season-ticket holders who usually make up the great goal end will be snuggling up instead, in Swansea and Dublin, Milton Keynes and Essex, with Sky Sports.

From our vantage point you can also really *hear* the effect of seats on the Kop's swirling vocal support. Songs begin these days from all parts of the Kop and are seldom taken up by everyone together as they used to be in the 1970s and 1980s, when the core behind the goal orchestrated matters. The left and right sides today operate almost as rival choirs, occasionally colliding, less frequently hitting on the same good idea at the same time. In the Main Stand, the familiar minor scouse elites and entrenched season-ticket experts are rubbing shoulders with obscure football scouts, members of the new Liverpool fan base – young Asians, complete with Red scarves and also turbans – and the one-off visitors who have come for the low prices and, mainly, to worship in the Kingdom of Michael. Right next to me are two young girls, local kids of 10 or 11 years of age, being watched over by a wary female parent. They start tonight deep within their shells, intimidated by the alcohol breath and oathing, but by the end these little urchins are hollering and singing like the rest, only octaves and decibels higher. 'Would you still love the Reds if Michael left?' They giggle at such an idea, uncomprehending at what it might mean. They'll learn.

The narrow concourses of this ancient old building can no longer cope with the pre-match or half-time demand here. When men stood on the Liverpool paddock, and when I first started watching games, the ten-minute half-time period was not 'for' anything, except for the players to grab a cuppa and to listen to Shanks' pearls of wisdom. Today's 15-minute break is to encourage the crowd down below to buy ale and food or else to piss it all away. These are the reasons why the new ground is still on the agenda. The proposed 15,000 new seats cannot be squeezed in here, nor the new consumption and corporate spaces demanded by the club – and its modern supporters – for pre-match and half-time refreshments. Change will surely come.

The teams. We have agreed, all the way to the ground, that even Houllier knows he has only one decision to make from the team which dumped Southampton: Smicer or Diao to replace the suspended Traore. He opts for Smicer, a more attacking selection. Riise reverts to full-back. United are unchanged from that which finished in charge in the first leg. Liverpool need to score early to stop the crowd getting restless and to pin back that familiar anxiety, and we begin at a high tempo with a result to match. Diouf scores the goal, but it has its roots in United's fear of

The new great, roofed Spion Kop at Anfield in the late 1920s, a place of popular worship of the Liverpool goalkeeping legend Elisha Scott.(© Steve Hale)

The signing of 'seven foot' Aberdeen slaughterman, Ron Yeats, was crucial to Liverpool winning the Second Division title in 1962. Shankly and Paisley were already in command. (© Steve Hale)

Little Bamber, Preston's own Brian Hall: university graduate, bus conductor and terrier-like Liverpool midfielder in the 1970s.
(© Steve Hale)

Gary McAllister and pal tell Barcelona's Puyol that penalties win matches, UEFA Cup 2001. Liverpool struggled badly to replace the talented Scot. (© *Liverpool Echo*)

The mercurial Vladimir Smicer retrieves his own shot from the Basle net in the 3–3 Champions League drama in Switzerland. It was not enough – Liverpool were eliminated by the unconsidered Swiss. (© Dave Rawcliffe)

Liverpool player of the season Danny Murphy scores the winner in the late-night 4–3 League Cup victory at Aston Villa. Emile Heskey seems pleased. (© Dave Rawcliffe)

Michael Owen (who else?) seals United's League Cup fate in
Cardiff. But would it save Liverpool's season? (© Dave Rawcliffe)

Flying the flag for Africa. £10 million El Hadji Diouf
impressed at Cardiff, but less so in the tough grind of the
English Premier League. (© Dave Rawcliffe)

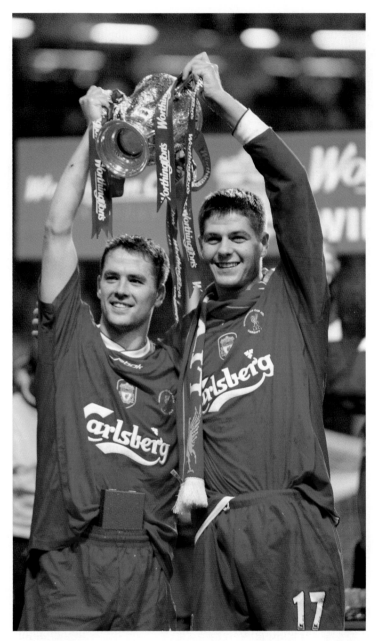

Boys from the Hood. Despite the foreign influx at Anfield,
Liverpool's future still rested with locals Owen and Gerrard.
Would they stay with an underachieving Liverpool?
(© Dave Rawcliffe)

Liverpool's Traore and Diao tame the new Blue Boy Wonder at
Goodison Park in 2003. It will not always be this simple.
(© *Liverpool Echo*)

Robbie Fowler struggles for a ticket on his Anfield return with
Man.City in 2003. Phil Thompson is unlikely to oblige.
(© *Liverpool Echo*)

Steven Gerrard avoids the post-match rush at Stamford Bridge.
Liverpool avoid the 2003–04 Champions League. (© *Liverpool Echo*)

Another new beginning. Parry and Houllier, the brains behind
Anfield, present a stylish Harry Kewell to the Liverpool press pack,
July 2003. (© *Liverpool Echo*)

Michael, because the Sheffield centre-back Murphy just doesn't deal with a regulation high ball and Michael latches on to the mistake, opening up for a shot, which the Sunday League lookalike keeper Kenny does well to turn away. Heskey, actually on his toes, lays this loose ball back to Diouf, who slides a low shot around defenders and in, off Kenny's left-hand post. The goalkeeper is motionless, like the Sheffield fans standing behind him.

Sami Hyypiä remarks later that 'Dioufy' has been showing his stuff in training and is getting more of the language, settling in. 'He'll be a big star in the Premier League next season.' These are the first real signs. Liverpool continue to attack, with United's best chances coming from set pieces, headers from Allison and Jagielka. Kirkland could *talk* more at the back, but he has been excellent since replacing Dudek. United have a go at the start of the second half, easily their best period, but they make no real chances. So when Steven Gerrard takes over soon it is one-way traffic down to the Kop end. But Michael, Smicer, Diouf and then Steven, himself, all miss presentable chances before, in the final minutes, Kirky has his one 'moment' of the match.

He gets tangled up with the giant Allison, stretching for a paceless punt into the Liverpool box, and as he drops the ball, the big keeper grabs for it once more − but *outside* the box. There may well have been a foul by Allison here, but the official gives United a free kick. Kirkland, fearing the worst now, even pushes directly into referee Wiley, protesting wildly about the challenge. 'He's off,' I tell everyone around me. Not only is this handling offence *outside* the box, but the big keeper's lost his head. He'll have to go. A visiting player would definitely be walking now, the crowd would see to that. Wiley, instead, brings out only a yellow card, and the free kick is deflected harmlessly away.

Extra time actually seems to pump up Stevie G. as others are fading, because now he is rampaging away, bursting past defenders, setting his own strikers away. His cushioned half-volleyed pass in the channel for Michael in the second period sublimely cuts out three Sheffield defenders and finally leaves the children's favourite in the clear. The kids next door are now beside themselves, pulling each other's hair in excitement. Owen looks up, leans back, and flips the ball over Kenny into the right side, before drifting off left towards the Kop–Kemlyn corner. Owen has *no* celebration now. Absolutely none. For a few moments he surveys the exultant chaos around him − and sees it as a mystery. It is almost as if he is saying to himself, and to us: 'How can a man who is so famous, who has scored at World Cups and is already so rich, still get excited about merely scoring a goal here?' Eventually, he raises his arms half-heartedly. Scoring goals should be his focus, his ecstatic moment. Instead it seems to mean nothing.

At the end, a fellah stops with his young lad to talk, as they leave the Main Stand seats. 'We're still not a good team, are we?' he rhetorically reflects, on this bitter struggle to the finish line. You don't easily fool these fans, even with another glory, glory day out in prospect. In the Flattie, later, the Liverpool performance divides the regulars: we played some decent stuff, sure, but we still struggle to score more than one goal in open play in 90 minutes. And this is against an immature side, not yet in the top two outside the Premiership. But a win at least means the season remains alive, and another March weekend in Wales is booked in. And in a season like this one, nothing else can be guaranteed.

WHERE THERE'S LIFE . . .

Manchester United breeze past Blackburn Rovers in the other Worthington semi-final, thus confirming the 'revival' of the League Cup, with a full-powered United v. Reds final lined up. It's handy for the sponsors that both Houllier and Ferguson seriously fear a season with no silverware, and also that the FA is making its by now usual bollocks over the FA Cup, allowing little Farnborough to transfer its home tie to Highbury, for example, for a highly paid beating. Meanwhile, the troubled insurance company Equitable Life reveals it owns a three per cent stake in LFC, worth about £3 million. The shares were bought four years ago and have been nose-diving in value ever since. 'A stake in one of Europe's leading football clubs is not unattractive,' says an Equitable spokesman, fooling nobody. 'We are very comfortable with our holding.' Our supporting investors should be made to watch home games. Let's see how 'comfortable' that makes them.

Apart from not getting knocked out, **Crystal Palace** 0, **Liverpool** 0 in the FA Cup fourth round, is almost all bad news. Cheyrou and Diouf offer little in this alien setting and in the Liverpool defence Traore is unconvincing for the suspended Henchoz (we really do need another centre-back). It is Jimmy's poor covering and Carragher's typical dithering which allows Adebola to reach Kirkland in the first half for a crunching head-on collision. After Sami performs a near-comic goal-line clearance from this explosion, our man is stretchered off in real pain, a big knee problem. He is soon in the back of an ambulance, no doubt careering around Croydon and wondering if the whole Liverpool thing might actually be over for him before it really gets going. We hang on for the final, embarrassing ten minutes, which includes Emile, nonchalantly, flicking a goal-bound header from Popovic over his own bar. It is depressing survival, no more – and we have one crucial man down.

ANOTHER LIVERPOOL CISSE?

On Monday, 27 January 2003 the Manchester *Daily Mirror* has a real go at Liverpool, big headlines:

- They have a squad full of international stars.
- They have a wise, world-renowned manager.
- They are part of the Premiership Big Four.
- They have some of football's best fans, so . . .

WHY ARE LIVERPOOL SO BORING?

Houllier, no doubt, will use this crap to try to draw the staff and the 'real' Liverpool fans together. Any clever manager would do the same, and the *Mirror* is trying to puff this up into a major issue once more. We won't get drawn into this media squirt, of course, but you don't have to be a genius to see we are still struggling. We have an active first team squad of 18 or 19 players, but only 7 or 8 of them are truly worth this famous red shirt, and Houllier's philosophy of playing is plainly not working. His new signings also have to front up – fast. He may be adding another soon.

Djibril Cisse, peroxide Auxerre forward and recent transfer target of Liverpool, talks to the French sports press about a possible move to England. 'I dream about playing for Arsenal,' he says. And where, as a young continental forward, would you rather play at the moment – honestly? The 21-year-old then reveals, impressively: 'I would like to be a woman, but I don't know why,' before admitting to already owning a Jean-Paul Gaultier dress. No prospects of any dressing-room stick here, then. The possibility of fielding, say, Smicer, Diouf, Cheyrou *and* Cisse together in the same Liverpool team in the FA Cup in some future dark and muddy corner of the Football League may be too much even for the strongest Red stomach. Meanwhile, Liverpool (or Palace) draw Leeds (or Gillingham) at Anfield in the FA Cup fifth round. Kirky won't be there: he has serious cruciate damage, probably a year's absence. A shattering blow. Cisse's Arsenal? They've drawn away to Manchester United: definitely best-frock time.

29 JANUARY 2003: LIVERPOOL 2, ARSENAL 2

We are counted into the city of Liverpool tonight by roadside actuaries. The club is doing research on traffic into Merseyside for Reds' home games, pending planning discussions for the proposed new ground and its growing capacity. The latest plan is for a 60,000 venue, possibly to open in 2005–06. But don't plan on a brick being laid if we finish out of the Champions League places this season.

Yesterday our esteemed manager was complaining in the press about

Arsenal's 'luck' (their many 'deflected' goals and the Jeffers 'penalty' against us), and also the Gooners' 'level of maturity' and 'continuity' compared to our own comparative youth and rawness. These are familiar themes and, to an extent, they are also ones that are self-inflicted. In the pub tonight I take a straw poll among the Liverpool heads and fanatics about the manager. No one now stands full square in the Houllier corner. Even those who think this recent poor run is a blip are strongly opposed to the current playing philosophy. Those who defended Gérard early on, those who assumed the excessive caution and direct play were a preface to a more sophisticated Liverpool approach later, are now disillusioned. Like Blair's stock with the Labour faithful, *Le Boss* just hasn't delivered in his second term and faith in him is diving. You can dislike Wenger and some of his players for their professional cynicism – and believe me we *do* dislike them – but you also have to hold your hands up and respect their pace, imagination and style. It is all of these things that make us the malcontents we are – and so fearful this evening.

> 'Christ, Cheyrou! Get a foot in. You don't even want to be out there. Keep the fucking ball!'
>
> 'Why don't you fuck off to Goodison? Why don't you stop fucking moaning? He's not the worst. Look at Carragher.'

This is myself and one of the Fellahs in Front, arguing wildly, after about ten minutes of this coruscating game. I am doing the hounding, but Houllier has insisted on starting this nailed on 90-mile-an-hour trial with one of his new recruits, the reluctant and faint-hearted Cheyrou on the Liverpool left. Well-known Liverpudlian John Mackin says that Bruno plays in 'gay' boots (white ones), the kind of semiotics which demands double the usual bravery, effort and skill to carry it off in front of the Liverpool sceptics: the many thousands of Kopite boot police. Instead, our new man looks intimidated and lost, as usual, the theme of my critique, although the point about Carragher is also a fair one. As the quality of opposition increases, so Jamie's glaring, basic deficiencies glow ever stronger. And this Arsenal, let me tell you, are top-quality opposition.

Liverpool actually start strongly tonight, Heskey powering away against Campbell and the suspect Cygan in the Arsenal defence, but the visitors need only one early break to flash up their ability and intentions. Hyypiä loses the ball high up the field and Bergkamp picks it up in the Liverpool half before spotting Thierry Henry busting a Gallic gut to get between Henchoz and Carragher. Henry makes his run, not like Michael might for Liverpool, half-expecting the ball to be delivered behind him, over his head or ballooned right up into the stand from a drunken full-back, but with complete assurance that the brilliant, sour Dutchman can deliver a curving 40-yard pass right into his preferred flight-path. When it arrives, bent on to Henry's right foot, Dudek blocks the shot, but only into acres of green filled by Pires, who scores. His 'marker' Diouf has given up on this little chore about 50 yards and seven seconds earlier when the two had been side-by-side on the edge of the Arsenal area. All of this has taken just moments to conceive. Our fellahs are already blowing.

And for the next 20 minutes it is like that scene in *Raging Bull* in which De Niro's Jake LaMotta is being savaged in a boxing whirlwind by Sugar Ray Robinson. Because Arsenal come at Liverpool from all directions now, throwing punches with unbelievable speed and pain. Pires and Henry double up on Carragher and are gone in a flurry of flicks and scything lay-offs. Bergkamp defies geometry with his passes, Vieira powers through tackles. I swear, there are times during this giddy spell when Henchoz literally *cannot find* the supercharged Henry, who seems to disappear into the sort of fourth dimension physicists speculate about, before re-emerging in a blur in the gut of the home defence, either to drive the ball against a visibly nervous Dudek or else crash it into the side netting. Point-blank headers by Vieira and Cygan are scraped away. We are on the ropes, sure, hanging on for the bell.

But even while this howling blizzard is threatening to engulf the Kop goal – and Liverpool with it – Michael Owen has two clear chances to equalise, two opportunities which must be made to count at this level, in this sort of storm. For the second of these, the entire Kop leans with Owen's body to the left, every Liverpool fan anticipating Michael's feeble low shot to Seaman's left-hand post. Even this goalkeeping pensioner easily sees the future, and saves. At half-time it's 0–1; punched near senseless at times, we are battling on and could even have landed some important blows of our own.

And at the start of the second half – after the Kop welcomes Seaman with the sort of ovation that must mean he has earlier blown up Goodison Park en route to Anfield – we actually hurt Arsenal. Riise is the source, a man suddenly back to form, pressing Lauren on the Arsenal right, before a ball over-the-top from Murphy ends up at Emile's feet with his back to goal at the corner of the Arsenal penalty area. Heskey, all power and determination again, holds off Campbell, delays for a beat, and then lays the ball back into the arriving Riise's path. And here is the important thing, the one big reason Riise now scores, and a lesson to some of the faint hearts in our team. He has an absolute focus, an almost reckless and scorching determination to reach this ball first. He probably doesn't even see Gilberto's body hurtling towards him from his right, which is the very first thing a Cheyrou, or a Smicer, or Diouf would have sighted. The cement-footed Seaman has no chance with the raking low shot delivered through a crowded area by the Liverpool left-back. And as a whooping, bare-chested Riise whirls his shirt like a helicopter blade in front of a boiling Kop, outclassed, pummelled Liverpool are suddenly right back in this contest.

Now, Houllier's pre-match comments actually begin to strike home. Having paraded all of their pace and slickness for a crazy 1–1 scoreline, Arsenal do, indeed, get lucky. Except it is not *all* luck. After Liverpool fail to clear from another mazy visiting attack, an affronted Dennis Bergkamp battles and pushes his way into a hopeful shooting position on the right of the home defence, including by physically handing off Carragher. And this is what makes Bergkamp a great player in England: he has that essential nastiness you need to play here, he refuses to be bullied. His scuffed shot glances off Henchoz and bypasses the already committed Dudek. Lucky Arsenal, indeed. Now Dr Houllier offers one last prescription, a kill-or-cure remedy.

Smicer replaces Cheyrou (at last) and is joined now by Diao and Baros from the home bench, for one last, late assault. Wenger responds by taking off the tiring Bergkamp but, crucially, replaces his forward with a defender, the creaking Luzney, to pick up Baros. This last substitution, a visitors' error, invites Liverpool on for one last assault. The TV post-mortem later concentrates on a dodgy corner won by Liverpool as we reach added-on time, but it really should focus on Diao's precise cross from the right or, better still, on Emile Heskey's controlled header, which powers the ball back from whence it came – and low into Seaman's net.

Despite the battering we have taken, we deserve this return for making chances and never letting our heads drop – for never falling all the way to the canvas under the Arsenal barrage. Later, Steven Gerrard describes Thierry Henry as being 'in a league of his own', and Arsenal as 'the best team I have ever played against in the Premier League'. Fair enough. Meanwhile, back in the Flattie, and after 'the corner that never was' is endlessly replayed by Sky to satisfy Wenger's griping, the entire pub of bubbling scousers quietens to a hush to hear Houllier gently chide his TV interviewer for even *suggesting* this contest was ever beyond Liverpool's grasp. His many doubters look into their beer and smile. He, at least, still believes.

EAST END KNEES UP

The exhausted cheers on the Kop at the end of the Arsenal game for the announcement of West Ham's 2–1 home win against Blackburn – the Hammers' first at home all season – are no idle signal of Anfield respect for a decent team down too long with the dead men. No one here really cares if they go down. It is, instead, a note of sheer relief that this uncertain Liverpool will not now be travelling to this East End theme park – hotel included – with the not-so-happy Hammers still looking for their first seasonal victory at home and with Di Canio, Bowyer, Les Ferdinand and Kanoute all available and desperate for some late relegation-busting success against ailing northern giants. We need not have worried, as it turns out. Not for a second.

2 FEBRUARY 2003: WEST HAM 0, LIVERPOOL 3

Baros for Owen ('rested' says *Le Boss*) is our only change, with Hamann back on the bench. Note how Houllier has suddenly ditched the rotation model, opting for a more-or-less settled formation to get out of this trough. Someone has been talking. West Ham start, inexplicably, with both Kanoute and Defoe merely looking on, manager Roeder opting for the toiling Ferdinand up top. But before the home subs have a chance even for a gentle touchline stretch, this match is already gone. David James, England keeper. How? His blunders multiply. After seven minutes of near-total Liverpool possession, Riise pings a corner into the home six-yard box. Now, either James has to come and flatten Baros, or the ridiculous Repka must challenge his Czech mate. Neither of these things happens. The score is 1–0. Two minutes later, in an act of blatant overcompensation, James *does* come for a corner he has no chance of getting, and his weak punch is positively bazookered past him and through a packed area by Steven Gerrard. Nine minutes, 2–0, game over.

Kanoute finally gets on in the second half, and even makes Jerzy produce a save, but the 'quality' West Ham forward players – Carrick, Cole, Sinclair, Bowyer and even Di Canio today – are flyweights, passionless pretenders. And the real tragedy here is that the home defence is even worse, filled with alarming chaos. When Sami reaches another Riise corner unchallenged beyond the far post, and heads back for Heskey to get his suddenly customary goal (get me!), Liverpool are home and dry. Owen and Hamann are able to enjoy a late stroll, for once, in our first comfortable win since – actually, since a home 2–0 against West Ham back in early November. Since, in fact, Michael was regularly scoring goals. Baros has worked hard here and he looks keen. There is a case now for giving him a run alongside Emile.

RISKY AND RISIBLE, MR RISDALE

Leeds United have been having a fire sale. After allowing O'Leary to spend, spend, spend two years ago, the gutless and faceless men from the PLC now demand their cash back. After Dacourt, Bowyer and even Robbie Fowler have been allowed to leave, so, too, is defensive man-for-the-future Woodgate – to Newcastle United. It is the final straw. Chairman Risdale, a hero and high-profile Leeds fan just two seasons ago, is suddenly a devil as he explains about the necessary belt-tightening. El Tel looks bemused, an unexpected fans' favourite. The Leeds supporters are livid, incandescent at the 'lies' they claim have been told about the size of the club's debts and at the willingness, now, of the money-men to asset-strip on this scale. 'We thought this was a football club.' Think again, boys. And remember, you had no money worries, apparently, while you were boozing it up in Milan and Rome.

5 FEBRUARY 2003: FA CUP (FOURTH-ROUND REPLAY): LIVERPOOL 0, CRYSTAL PALACE 2

The press image this week of Houllier and Steven Gerrard battling through the winter blizzards to Stevie's personal hearing at the FA might well stand as one of the signifiers for this troubled Liverpool season. Actually, *Le Boss* – or Shackleton, as we wittily now like to call him – seems increasingly bizarre in his accusations and interpretations; frostbite seems to have set in. He is genuinely bemused, for example, that Steven's assault on Naysmith in the derby game should be dealt with by the men-from-the-ministry with a three-match ban. What else could he have expected, given the TV evidence of this horrible two-footed lunge, intentional or otherwise? Perhaps, without Gerrard, GH even fears Palace in this FA Cup replay? It's crazy, I know.

At least Hamann is back tonight, but also Cheyrou gets another start. You explain it. Baros is rewarded for his good work at West Ham by a predictable return to the bench. Trevor Francis, a student at Houllier's feet, actually leaves out his own best player, Tommy Black, and comes to defend. This means that for 45 solid minutes this is a game of Liverpool Shots In – or rather Shots *Out* – towards, and into, the Kop. Even old white-boots Bruno has a couple of reasonable goal tries, but mainly it is Michael who is the culprit, once more, as Liverpool swarm all over Crystal Palace. Referee stops the fight, for sure. Owen wants every chance on his right foot, if possible, a sure sign of his recent nose-dive in confidence. He misses them all.

Seventeen goal attempts, and no goals. Is this all bad luck? There is more to it than that. At this level, if your main striker is wayward, distraught, you need intelligent, reliable replacements to fill in: men who, above all else, are confident and sure in front of goal. Houllier says every team needs at least four good strikers. At the moment we have none. Instead, apart from Michael, we have gathered a whole collection of forward players with no real record for regular goal-scoring in the English game. Tonight, no Liverpool player steps up to show Owen how to do it. The truth is, no one is capable.

At half-time Crystal Palace are just happy to still be in the game – but two minutes into the second half they should be out of it. Palace, strangely, pack everyone up in the Liverpool half for a rare attacking corner, but when the ball breaks to Emile Heskey, suddenly he is away over halfway like an overdeveloped child in a seven-a-side contest, clear of all pursuers – except for a sprinting Michael Owen on his right. What is going on in Emile's head now? He has 70 confusing, long yards to run before Berthelin comes out to face him. His mind must be racing. Heskey has seen Owen available to his right, no doubt about it. Most of the fans will say that a good, confident striker would score this goal himself, and, by doing so, show the necessary responsibility, and greed. And, for sure, this is what Emile thinks: 'I *have* to take this on.'

This decision is wrong, of course. A good, confident, intelligent and mature striker would make the simple pass to Owen, who would then walk the ball into an empty net. This is, after all, an example of just the sort of team play GH is always extolling. Heskey – a really nice lad but, like so many of this current squad, lacking a native football intelligence – fails on all possible counts and, muddled, he gently chips the ball into Berthelin's astonished hands. Deathly. Houllier says later that this miss deflated the entire Liverpool team – and much of the crowd. I hope it mortified the Melwood coaching staff, and all the psychologists and the various hangers-on who are undoubtedly now on the club payroll, precisely to prepare players for this kind of crucial, pressured decision making. Palace are visibly lifted by this collapse. Incredibly, they know they have a real chance. We all know it.

On 55 minutes, a Palace break down the Liverpool left finds Adebola flicking a simple crossed ball beyond the Liverpool far post. Now, you can bet your life that if there is just one thing that dipstick manager Trevor Francis has drummed into his talented young left midfielder Julian Gray, it is that even if Diouf tracks him back into the Liverpool box, the Senegalese does not know how to play defence. He will not pick up. And, sure enough, when this deflected cross reaches Gray he is splendidly alone, with the entire Liverpool right side ball-watching. He volleys cleanly past Dudek from a sharp angle: no other thought even enters his mind. In fact, it is the sort of directness and uncomplicated technique that

Diouf, our expensive cul-de-sac of a wing-man, might try to study and reproduce. So after all the fancy forward footwork, after all our huff and puff, this is goal-scoring made simple. One clear shot: one priceless goal.

Soon after this catastrophe the experienced Dougie Freedman – a total head loss this – smacks Hyypiä with an elbow, and it is 11 against 10. Hope, perhaps, out of this stupidity? But – and this is how bad it really gets – nobody in the Liverpool crowd sees any prospect in this unexpected bonus. Palace simply sit deeper and let Jamie Carragher have as much of the ball as he wants on the Liverpool right. 'He can be your *extra* man.' Well, thanks. Thanks a lot. You might imagine now that our advanced coaching genius Houllier will pick up on this and that Carragher, who is by now being roundly abused by the eggheads in the Kemlyn lower, is the obvious man to replace with Baros for the final, frantic 20 minutes. Indeed, 30,000 people can see the sense in this. All the safety stewards have nodded their assent.

Only one man sees, instead, that it is Danny Murphy, Liverpool's best player, the team's only intelligent, inventive spring, who actually demands replacement. (Does the entire Liverpool bench see it this way?) And so it is done, another deathly illustration of modern, interventionist football management. It is our final white flag. Before the end, Gray still has time for one more dance down the Liverpool right and to cross for Stephane Henchoz to bundle the ball into his own net. We turn to the officials for help: blow up, for Christ's sake, so this gut-wrenching torture can finally be over. The Main Stand boos the end – then cheers the Palace players. Was it ever more clear? We have too few real leaders, men who really hurt with defeat, who simply will not accept it. Players, in short, who really understand the Liverpool Way.

HOME COMFORTS?

Coming back from FA Cup disgrace against Palace, and needing a decent performance and a solid home win to pacify rising disquiet among the Anfield faithful, Liverpool, instead, offer more tired League rubbish in **Liverpool 1, Middlesbrough 1**. Riise at least provides a smart second-half equaliser to Geremi's free-kick opener, following a flash of Michael brilliance. Our one comfort is that Owen might be reaching for some real form at last. But another stumbling 1–1 home League draw against our can't-win-away opponents means a stunning and quite unprecedented *seven* consecutive home Liverpool Premiership matches without a win. Moreover, in none of these matches have we really deserved to win, not one. Liverpool are currently offering relegation home form and few signs that Houllier's famous, and much talked about, form 'corner' has been turned – or even sighted in the distance. We have, as one wag put it recently, apparently made enough turns this season to have completed 50 laps at the Monaco Grand Prix.

We could easily identify the spine of the Liverpool team back in Houllier's successful side of 2001. The Liverpool squad of 2003 looks callow and weak by comparison. No doubt, Houllier will describe this latest setback as merely 'character-building' for his inexperienced new men, as he has, contrarily, seen every recent Liverpool reverse. But not *every* defeat, not every desperate home League failure makes us stronger. Some just highlight the key absences, the key structural deficits. They erode our belief. Houllier says he is at Anfield for the long haul, so perhaps, for him, this is merely another season, simply part of the longer-term building process. But we see FA Cup ejection in 2003 by lowly Palace and this latest drab league draw with a limited and unambitious Boro as more vital chances lost – as more costly signs of our season sliding down the drain. And worse, we are even starting to fear that the new Liverpool – perhaps the entire Houllier project – is in danger of becoming a castle built on sand.

FA PREMIER LEAGUE TABLE AT 15 FEBRUARY 2003

	P	W	D	L	F	A	GD	Pts
ARSENAL	27	17	6	4	57	29	28	57
MAN. UNITED	27	16	6	5	44	25	19	54
NEWCASTLE U.	26	15	4	7	42	32	10	49
CHELSEA	27	13	9	5	48	27	21	48
EVERTON	27	13	6	8	35	32	3	45
LIVERPOOL	27	11	10	6	38	26	12	43
TOTTENHAM	27	12	6	9	40	37	3	42
CHARLTON	27	12	6	9	36	34	2	42
SOUTHAMPTON	27	10	9	8	28	26	2	39
MAN. CITY	27	11	5	11	38	38	0	38
BLACKBURN R.	27	9	10	8	28	31	1	37
ASTON VILLA	27	10	5	12	38	29	2	35
LEEDS U.	27	10	4	13	32	34	0	34
FULHAM	27	9	6	12	31	34	-3	33
MIDDLESBRO.	26	8	7	11	30	30	0	31
BIRMINGHAM C.	27	6	8	13	23	40	-17	26
BOLTON W.	27	5	10	12	30	44	-14	25
WEST BROM.	27	5	6	16	20	41	-21	21
WEST HAM	27	4	8	15	28	52	-24	20
SUNDERLAND	27	4	7	16	18	42	-24	19

CHAPTER 7

Rick Parry: The Man Who Sold the World

SWEET FA

'English football is in crisis, up to 30 English clubs are facing bankruptcy and hundreds of players are heading towards the dole queue.' Thus begins Simon Banks' book, *Going Down: Football in Crisis* (2002). And he had a point, but only up to a point. Because let's also be honest, even the dogs in the street knew that 30 English professional football clubs would not soon disappear, because we had heard too much of this sort of apocalyptic sooth-saying in the past. When pushed to the very edge, bankrupt football clubs tend to steal someone else's money, or else draw on their supporters' energies and resources – and then carry on.

Also, the whole concept of what actually constitutes 'the game' in England has rather changed since the fateful summer of 1991, when David Dein, from Arsenal and, yes, Noel White, representing Liverpool, approached the Football Association about plans hatched by a group of elite clubs to break away from the Football League. Liverpool FC, note, always seem to be in the vanguard of major change in the English game, going right back to John McKenna's election to the League Management Committee in 1902. The moment of the hooliganism crisis in English football, the Hillsborough disaster, and Lord Justice Taylor's public concerns about lack of effective leadership in English football had precipitated what had been a growing unease among the larger English clubs, in an era of free-market theocracy, about income-sharing and centralised policy-making in the historic football family. Something had to give.

At this precise moment in the early 1990s, the Football Association, itself threatened by power-sharing ambitions from both the Football League and the PFA, decided that its own future lay not in an extension of its historic role as an independent regulator of the sport, an imperfect restraint on overcommercialism and inequality, but rather as a sidekick to what would become the new commercial engine of English football. From this point on, any sense that the notion of 'the game' might be taken to express clear links between the English professional elite and the fate of the smaller professional clubs, and those that struggled on outside the ranks of the professionals, was pretty much lost. As Sky kept on telling us, it was, indeed, a 'whole new ball game'. Instead, the FA's *Blueprint for Football*, published in 1991, sought to rationalise its unholy marriage with the top English clubs by claiming that a new slimmed-down 18-club FA Premier League would actually aid the ambitions of the England national team. Let me surprise you: the reduction in the number of clubs never came. Instead, club managers whined more and more about their players being used for international matches. Throw in a fiscal crisis in the embryonic satellite TV industry, which meant the two new businesses effectively falling into each other's arms, and, hey presto, welcome to a new world. We suddenly had the first sports league in Europe developed by and for television. Nothing would ever be quite the same again.

It is not that some of the problems facing English football in the early 1990s were not real enough. The English game *was* dogged by the following issues: problems of hooliganism; poor spectator facilities; a crude, unprofessional approach to marketing and promotion; a TV cartel that kept broadcasting fees unrealistically low; and a threadbare and fractious leadership. No change was not an option, but where was the vision and strength of purpose in English football? In an era of globalisation and with new international TV sports markets to serve, it seemed clear that the ambitions of larger English clubs, like those in other European countries would, indeed, become more strongly tied to those of similar clubs abroad. A radical new direction was needed in England, one which could free up the existing structure to allow the developments that were necessary at the top end of the sport, while also ensuring the well-being and long-term survival of the smaller clubs. Producing a new regulatory framework to manage these changes was the challenge facing the FA in 1991. Like a fighter on the take, they ducked it, and threw in their lot with the Premier League chairmen. It was a crucial abrogation of responsibility.

All of this meant that while the FA Premier League grew greedier, richer and stronger – and increasingly sceptical, contemptuous even, of any sort of effective regulatory framework – the Football League also grew richer, but much more slowly, and became considerably weaker. To be fair, the problems in the Football League were, partly, the old traditional ones: a large number of fully professional clubs, too many of which were poorly run, which recruited too few spectators, and which paid their players far too much. The level of long-term and innovative thinking here was painfully low, at least until supporter trusts began to organise the rescue of local basket cases and introduce an element of fiscal common sense and real community involvement in the smaller clubs. By opting for the Premier League route, the FA had effectively opted out of even the possibility of useful intervention here. It certainly did too little to encourage the larger clubs to help tend to their weaker neighbours, or even to see the financial crisis at the bottom of the professional game as part of the FA's wider responsibility to English football. Indeed, new FA chief executive Adam Crozier, who was brought in partly as a credible opponent to the commercial excesses of the Premier League clubs, ended up out of a job because he threatened to replicate their business practices and steal into their markets. And mimic their debts! FA expenditure on staff, offices and jollies doubled under Crozier, a glossy advertising man recruited from the Saatchis.

Crozier then chose to pursue a quite grotesque and corporate-driven new £750 million Wembley stadium project, while the lower end of the professional game seemed to be imploding during his watch. The FA's input on regulating football 'for the good of the game' turned out to be an impressive new website, a vague and under-resourced commitment to equity issues and £40,000 per year spent on ex-policeman Graham Bean, who chased down asset-strippers and illegal payments made by shifty Football League managers. Crozier's attempts to limit Premier League influence on the new Professional Game Board were too little, too late. His number was already up and football governance in England, it seemed, was slowly going mad.

But there was something else here. A 'new' crisis in the Football League also grew directly out of the distant, burgeoning coffers of the Premier League. The new Premiership TV deals – in excess of £1 billion by 2000 – coupled with the later collapse of the ITV digital deal with the Football League, opened up financial chasms within and between the new leagues. Within the FA Premier League, the original, proud emphasis on an even distribution of the TV cash was becoming more and more difficult to sustain. Yes, unlike in Italy and Spain, the top clubs were still bound by collective deals for TV rights, and 50 per cent of TV income was distributed evenly between all clubs. But the other 50 per cent, distributed on the basis of merit (where you finished in the table) or coverage (how often you were featured in live coverage), was helping to open up very large gaps between the club at the top (reportedly around £30 million from all TV in 2003) and that at the bottom (around £17 million). Add to this deficit, returns at the top from regular involvement in the Champions League – say between £10 and £25 million – and the elite now seemed pretty much uncatchable. Top clubs paid much of this new income to players in the shape of higher wages and, according to accountants Deloitte and Touche, wages are easily the best predictor of League performance. In the satellite age of collective bargaining, some clubs were becoming a lot more equal than others.

But between the Leagues, things were actually much worse. As the cost of *not* being in the Premier League began to escalate – some estimates suggested that relegation/promotion could now be worth up to £25 million – some clubs began to do crazy things to try to reach the top level, or to try to stay there. Dodgy agents vigorously greased their palms on all of this overt desperation, often acting unscrupulously for both club and player – and scoring a huge commission both ways. The FA looked away, while the clubs shrugged their shoulders and carried on dealing. In recent years, a number of the aspirant middle-range clubs – Leicester City, Nottingham Forest, Bradford City, Ipswich Town, Sheffield Wednesday, Derby County, Sunderland – have either faced savage cutbacks or even extinction because of overspending and then relegation from the Premier League. It was like the bends in reverse. Some promoted clubs – Watford and West Bromwich Albion, for example – bravely chose financial rectitude over reckless speculation, and thus opted for certain relegation. It was very hard to swallow.

The Premier League fobbed off half-hearted attempts at regulation by New Labour in the late 1990s by suffocating government attempts at football reform from within Blair's own abject Football Task Force. The Task Force outcomes, instead, were supporter trusts to help rescue the basket-case clubs and a vapid cul-de-sac that is the new terrrain of customer charters and the Independent Football Commission, to cover fan complaints at the elite level. This was not headline stuff. Radical new proposals followed at an urgent rate from the sinking Football League. These included salary caps and more flexible, performance-related, contracts for players. At Blackpool, they tried to cut players' summer pay, and one club, Wimbledon, was even allowed by the FA and the League to relocate elsewhere in search of a crowd. It seemed inescapable, even as the elite was still negotiating salaries in excess of £60,000 per week for some top stars in the summer of 2003, that the wages of some very ordinary middle-ranking players would have to nosedive. There were soon reports of First Division players halving their salaries and yet moving up into the Premier League. However, being paid up to £1 million per year while still being *outside* the top 700 professional footballers in England might also seem a tad excessive, even to the most committed fan. They were the football years of boom and bust, indeed.

PROTECT ME FROM WHAT I WANT

Despite these problems, the Premier League had its defenders for sure, and a lot of good things came out of 1992 and after, some of which is too easily forgotten now. For some commentators inside and outside the sport, for example, the new League marked nothing less than the beginning of the social and cultural rejuvenation of football in England and the emergence, once again, of the popular Victorian tradition of the modern English football stadium as an important source of local civic (and commercial) pride. New football grounds in the 1990s and after became a central community and commercial focus once more for local business and cultural aspirations. Look at the success of the new football venues at Middlesbrough, Sunderland and Bolton, as a marker.

Today, a stadium development for a Premier League club can help revive local interest and set commercial pulses racing, and a top football club can help to achieve invaluable marketing globally for a supportive city. This was especially so as TV money was used to recruit a roster of world-famous football stars. By 2003, English club qualification for European football competition would no longer mean simply cancelling all police leave. Instead it would send City Fathers scurrying round for discussions about product synergies, business fairs and corporate hospitality. It was a new and enticing world out there.

At the core of this recent shift in football's fortunes, of course, has been the arrival in the sport of a new administrative and entrepreneurial elite that now aggressively and effectively sold the sport and its products, especially via TV, to new audiences. This new elite – Bates, Dein, Parry and later Kenyon among them – has a more expansive view of new football's marketability and, unlike those who used to run top clubs, the new order had good business sense and saw profit as integral to the practice of sports governance and sports administration. Whereas in the past local, small businessmen may have bought into the local football club in order to bolster their own civic and business status and to do a little business on match days, today's top football–club owners are much more diverse in their commercial links and aspirations – and more geared to achieve commercial stability and success as a result. Public flotations had arrived, too, as a welcome means of increasing investment in the clubs and ensuring better regulation of their affairs – even if it was also more difficult to tell *who* actually owned the top football clubs in England these days.

At the same time as this commercial revolution had occurred, recent measured falls in incidents of hooliganism at club football in England, for example, indicated the popular rediscovery of the much-cherished and at least partly mythical image of the English sports crowd as one noted for its mutual tolerance and sociability. In the recent decline of overt racism in English football, the small overtures made by some clubs towards black and Asian fans, and the apparent growth in active female support at English football matches, the game now better reflected, so its supporters claimed, the integration and diversity of modern British culture. Look at the Kop at Liverpool these days – black and Asian fans from outside the city are a routine feature in the non-season-ticket-holder seats. All-seated stadia have been an important part of this move to a generally much more inclusive and civilised climate at top English football matches.

So this was the 'up' side of the modern football revolution, some big pluses. But there were many claimed 'downs' too. For opponents of the new game, the recent period should be read as no less than the effective end of the local and organic football crowd. It signalled the loss of the self-administering and creative football end full of the 'vim and vinegar' of Arthur Hopcraft's famous characterisation in *The Football Man* of the Spion Kop at Liverpool and of other great, largely working-class, standing terraces of the 1980s and before. In its wake came the overly regulated, individuated, surveilled and high-spending, seated, middle-class football audience. From here, English football stadia at the top level were now increasingly dull and boring places to be. They were places where crowds, like those at 'prawn sandwich' Old Trafford and 'Highbury the library' Arsenal, had to be urged by officials to offer more vocal support, and where safety, rather than excitement or involvement, had become the stifling order of the day.

The sounds of the English football stadium today are, in fact, increasingly the jarring Americanised public address promotions of corporate sponsors, and the inane pre-match slaverings of neck-tie guys with an on-pitch microphone. Racism and hooliganism also still exist, despite what the commercial interests contend. It is just that the media servants of top football are now less willing to report it. It is no coincidence, as the non-believers point out, that Rupert Murdoch, owns BSkyB, the Premier League's biggest advertiser, but also *The Times* and *The Sun* newspapers. Hooliganism in the Premier League is bad news to the Murdoch stable, which means it just doesn't happen anymore, or, at least, it doesn't appear on News Corporation screens and news pages. The racism focus on correcting the behaviour of fans is just an easy way of avoiding difficult questions inside clubs about why their own staff are so uniformly white – and why so few black players ever graduate to the Big Office in football management.

The sorts of people who now, increasingly, make up Premier League football crowds, according to these sceptics, are no more than an ersatz following of promiscuous *consumers*, with no real footballing tradition or local ties, save that which is concocted and sold to them by the sport's new marketing gurus. These new followers at top clubs have no real attachments to their clubs born out of the traditional ties of region or place: they are pointedly customers (not supporters), who choose their clubs rather than the other way around. Look at the way the people in Milton Keynes have suddenly been delivered a First Division club, one that actually belongs in south-west London, in Wimbledon. There is little earning here of the right to supporter status via the long-term material and psychological deprivation suffered – and welcomed – by the true devotee. These new fans, in short, have it far too easy. Their passion for the sport, if it exists at all, is highly contingent, ultimately transferable and it is substantially shaped by the new ways in which the sport is mediated and packaged by the Sky Sports cronies. These fans will be lost when the sport eventually sheds – as it surely must – its current, hyper-real, 'this year's model' vogue.

Finally, the sport's new entrepreneurs are, themselves, in the business *only* for profit, not for love. Plenty of owners have profited directly from public flotations and football's new, sexy corporate image. Greed rules football, and underpins the new Premier League, where the elite no longer cares for the foundations of the sport or the smaller clubs. Globalisation and deregulation have helped riddle big-time football with corruption, implicating officials, agents, managers, players and crooked bookies. The game was sick, these critics cried. Worse, it was dying.

So whom do you blame for the current excesses or, indeed, praise for the game's economic and social rejuvenation? Who is the man who sold the English football world? What about settling on the guy who designed the Premier League, and who was also the Premier League's first chief executive? He is now the chief executive at Liverpool. What about starting with Rick Parry?

★

Eight Premiership clubs are currently publicly listed and a number of these are in potential danger of the same sort of 'economic rationalisation' that occurred at

THE LIVERPOOL WAY

Elland Road in 2003. Chelsea boasted debts that were even larger than the reported £77 million festering at Leeds, before being 'rescued' by a mysterious Russian oil billionaire, Roman Abramovich. Rick Parry, for Liverpool, said the Anfield club will remain in private hands because: 'We think it's right for us, philosophically as much as anything, because we are still a football club at heart, focused on silverware and winning trophies.' This is the theory at least. Liverpool also revealed news of a £100 million sponsorship deal with Reebok over the next six years, an announcement which was designed, no doubt, to take the heat off the manager and allay fears that we could be 'another Leeds', especially if Liverpool struggle even to get into the Champions League slots this season. The message here is that we will not go bust or have to flog Michael Owen or Steven Gerrard if Liverpool finish outside the top four. On balance, this is good news.

I interview Rick Parry at Anfield. He has rushed over from Melwood to meet up and he looks a little dishevelled, one button missing or undone from his shirt and his greying curls are doing a kind of Harpo Marx number. He has very little of the off-putting gloss or even the world-weary conceit of a chief executive at a major football club. He is an impressive and willing communicator. Many people have argued that he was successful at the Premier League because he was very good at what he did, but also because he could manage the deranged egos of the 20 club chairmen, without worrying too much about his own. He is also obviously a real fan, as well as an inveterate enthusiastic moderniser, not a common combination. You sense he would much rather talk about the possible make up of next season's Anfield midfield than anything else, but not far behind in his conversational preferences are the ways that Liverpool FC will have to change to keep up with the elite clubs in Europe and the world. He believes in football in permanent revolution.

★

'I THOUGHT IT WOULD BE TWO MONTHS OF GOOD FUN'

Rick Parry says that his first connection with the game was in the cradle. But fast forward just a little and he is working as a management consultant at Arthur Young's in Manchester and involved, in the late 1980s, in Olympic bidding. This high-profile brief led to some consultancy work for the Football League in 1988 – at exactly the time the League was already tearing itself apart over the distribution of TV money. Indeed, when Parry and his colleagues first presented to the League, at the Holiday Inn in Plymouth, his clients were already split and at each other's throats. In this surreal atmosphere the presentation was actually an irrelevance; history had already moved on. It was an early insight for Parry into the bizarre world of professional football administration. It both intrigued and appalled him.

Parry's work on Olympic bidding had meant some contact with Graham Kelly, by now at the FA. The men liked each other and within two weeks of Manchester's bid crashing in late 1990, and with Parry wondering exactly what he was going to do with the rest of his life, Kelly phoned, out of the blue, with another brief. David Dein from Arsenal and Noel White from Liverpool had been calling. They wanted someone to produce the outline of a new Premier League, but, crucially, this time it would be sanctioned by the FA. Parry, by now unsurprised by anything the game could throw at him, was still sceptical: 'I thought it would be two months of good fun and nothing would never see the light of day.' He could not have been more wrong. Plans for the new League also fitted very well with the FA's ongoing power struggle with the Football League:

> The reason the FA was interested in the Premier League was not that it was a good idea. It was because they were at daggers drawn with the Football League. Because the Football League produced their *One Game, One Team, One Voice* document on power-sharing, Graham [Kelly] was sort of outraged and said it was ridiculous. Charles Hughes [FA Technical Director], a bright guy, said, 'Hold on, at least these fellahs have got a plan. We're supposed to be the governing body of the game. Where's our plan? Maybe we should produce one.' This became the FA's *Blueprint for Football*. But the Premier League didn't come out of the *Blueprint*. The Premier League was shoehorned into the *Blueprint* as part of the total. It was seen as a power struggle between the Football League and the FA. The League wanted power-sharing, the FA didn't and the FA said, 'Right, we're now going to take control, we'll do the commercial bit.' They never envisaged the idea of a new League structure at that time. It was a great coincidence.

The FA and the big clubs liked Parry's programme for change – they liked it so much they asked him to lead it. He was genuinely thrilled by the challenge of his new job as chief executive of this extraordinary new development in the game. 'Fantastic!' he says today. He twinkles now with the memory – and the sheer madness – of it all. Shaping the club chairman into line was like walking on hot coals: personalities were always full on; there was the residual bitterness of the 1988 split to contend with; there was little common sense or strategic thinking; policy was based on short planning cycles; everything was high emotion and done in the glare of the spotlight and in a cut-throat atmosphere. It was, blissfully, a roller-coaster ride for the new chief executive, who never seemed to lose his cool or his direction. Forget *Footballers' Wives*, this was the real stuff.

Parry argues that the old structure of the Football League was run through with vested interests and Byzantine voting arrangements. It was an impossible vehicle to run a modern sport. He's right, of course. But what exactly was wrong with the old way, and of what was he most proud in his new creation?

> Firstly, the clubs would vote on what suited them and their Division, and then maybe what suited the game as a whole. A management committee, which was, again, divisionally based, was exactly the same. So you had no independent view to say: 'Hold on, let's genuinely think what is right for the League as a whole.' The most satisfying day I can look back to was the day the founder members' agreement was signed, which was the very first meeting of the clubs. In one meeting we got the basis of the constitution and the TV-sharing formula agreed. That's probably more than had been agreed in the previous hundred years and definitely more than has been agreed since! But we did that in half an hour, and everything flowed from that. The one-club one-vote agreement gave a degree of equality. We agreed to no committees, which made life difficult, but it also got rid of all the 1988 suspicions. But the establishment of the independent board and empowering the smaller clubs through one-club, one-vote are the basics which made it all work. We said to the press, 'Watch us over the next decade because what we now have is a body which is relatively streamlined, is not bogged down by politics and bureaucracy and is actually going to be capable of making decisions.'

The key thing here, which rather gets lost in all this talk about streamlining and escaping the terrible policy straightjacket of the Football League, was that the new Premier League would no longer have to even *think* about the 'good of the game' at all. These times were effectively gone for good. What really mattered now were the interests of the clubs involved at the top, and those that might one day be promoted into the Premiership. This made the world a much simpler place for the chairman and the new chief executive, especially since the FA had long since given up any notion that it might actually hold some sway over the League that now carried its name.

When Parry and the clubs cut the first deal with Sky for live TV coverage in 1992, he knew they would be attacked. But he was also convinced that it would work. Fans complained about the live game disappearing from terrestrial networks and there were howls of protest from UEFA and across Europe about the Premier League plan to have 60 live games on television. No one had gone for this kind of coverage before, certainly not in Europe. Either Parry knew what he was doing or he got lucky, because the new policy of more live games, but shown to a restricted TV audience, minimised the negative impact on crowds and actually seemed to market football more effectively. Attendances at matches climbed, despite warnings that fans would either get saturated by TV coverage or would forget the game, which was now 'hidden away' on Sky. Rising ticket prices and the subsequent 'gentrification' of active supporters Parry blames squarely on the Taylor report, not the Premier League. Clubs needed to raise income, after all, to pay for all the stadium changes. He thinks that, in some places, yes, it might have gone a little too far, but he also defends the rights of clubs to set their own ticket prices. 'They manage to get away with it,' he chuckles now. The market, it seems, will out.

Parry is also proud of the Premier League's work on producing the football academies and new systems of youth development. So the new League, as he's keen to point out, was not all about setting up massive TV deals and dividing up sponsorship cash. However, the size of the former plainly astonished and impressed the larger clubs – and fixed Parry's reputation at an early stage – and the latter was also important because it challenged the voting bloc power of the elite clubs. When early disagreement over the Carling sponsorship had the seven largest League clubs voting together, in opposition, in their so-called Platinum Group, the rest of the clubs walked out of the meeting. It was a seminal moment; bloc voting soon disappeared, too. Also important was the resolution over the distribution of TV income. At one extreme the big clubs wanted most of the cash, at the other the smaller clubs wanted equal distribution. What was fashioned, instead, was a merit-award formula. It was not perfect, Parry accepts, but it was a signal that this was, to some extent at least, a 'league of equal opportunities'. Moreover, the formula held, even as elite clubs around Europe were soon striking their own, independent TV deals.

MR PARRY GOES TO ANFIELD

Rick Parry was king of the world, leader of the fastest-growing sports business in Europe in the mid-1990s. He had been in charge of the FA

Premier League for six and a half years. Now, he wanted out. After the accusations and bluster about the original 1992 Sky TV deal, the new 1996 deal was voted in by the clubs after just 20 minutes. For Parry, this was both immensely satisfying and also a signal for a new direction: 'I actually quite like change, and moving through uncertainty. There wasn't much that was now uncertain about the Premier League, I guess.' With the European Commission and others getting more involved in football's affairs, which meant the chief executive spending more and more time with competition lawyers, he thought that maybe he had already passed the high point with the new League. It was time to move on. And there was plenty of uncertainty – bucketfuls of it – at Anfield Road in the mid-1990s.

Parry had always fancied the idea of working with a club. Saturday, after all, was the culmination of the football working week, but for the League's chief executive it was an anti-climactic day off. He wanted to be *part* of the game on Saturday and not just *at* one. He had been approached by other clubs, but wanted to work for the club he supported, Liverpool. Secretary Peter Robinson, the vital overseer of Liverpool's dominance in the 1970s and 1980s but out of his time in the new era, had intimated he would soon be retiring and Parry rang him. Robinson was not yet ready to leave – he had planned to go in 2000. So Parry moved to Anfield, with some misgivings: this was Liverpool after all, so maybe three years in waiting could be endurable. The club he joined was actually buoyant, and with a realistic championship challenge already in progress under Roy Evans. But clearly Liverpool had also been left behind, on and off the pitch, by Manchester United. Parry sees the United era as a good opportunity well taken rather than any strategic planning for change at Old Trafford:

> I don't put that [United's success] down to any great strategy. The game is cyclical, definitely. You are not going to stay top of the pile forever, and it was somebody else's turn. Where United were fortunate is that their 'turn' coincided with the formation of the Premier League and the new riches. United could have been owned by Michael Knighton, for goodness sake! So the idea that somehow their success on the pitch, the flotation, the formation of the Premier League are all part of the Grand Plan – well, life isn't like that. But did they make the most of their opportunities? Yes, of course they did, and you have to admire what they achieved over the decade. The game and the world was changing.

These changes included Bosman, the influx of foreign players, the more scientific approach to training, and the more enlightened approach to diet and preparation. For Parry, the sense he got on arrival at Liverpool was: 'If we keep doing it the way that we did in the '70s on and off the pitch, then it will come back.' Commercially, the club was not in a complete backwater: they had had good kit sponsorship deals for some time, for example. But what impressed Parry most was that the club had insisted on maintaining some positive standards in this area, standards which were not always adhered to elsewhere:

> I hate to use the word 'brand', but it's a word that fits. The great thing that Liverpool had never done was to prostitute its brand. And that is terrific. There is a paradox for Manchester United that they are, simultaneously, the most loved and the most hated brand of all, which is kind of tough from a commercial perspective. The 'brand values' that we have developed for Liverpool, well, the key word for us is 'respect'. In the '70s and '80s we were not loved by everybody, but there was always a respect for Liverpool, and that's a value that I think is extremely important.

HOULLIER ON BOARD

Gérard Houllier arrived at Liverpool soon after Rick Parry. Parry knew the Frenchman from listening at the Premier League to his presentations on youth football. The feeling inside the Liverpool club at this time was that for Roy Evans it was a case of close, but no cigar. New coaching ideas were needed, but without losing the input of the valued Evans. It was Robinson who recruited Houllier, initially as a coach. But Houllier also wanted to pick the Saturday team and the idea of joint managers developed out of the willingness of the two men to work with each other. Parry thought it could work, and it seems unlikely that this was a strategy designed, simply, to get rid of the loyal Roy Evans. The harsh truth, nevertheless, was that if it didn't work, Evans would be for the high jump. And so it turned out. For Parry, Houllier seemed like the ideal candidate for the new era, basically because he offered both change and continuity. He understood the Liverpool Way:

> There is a natural conservatism here, but also rightly so. You need to have that understanding of the Liverpool Way and what Liverpool is all about. That doesn't mean you can't bring fresh ideas. But if you don't understand that, you won't get very far

here. But Gérard had both of these things, so he was the ideal candidate. The new science is not mumbo jumbo, but clearly the French had been doing something right. From being in the doldrums, they now knew how to produce a player. Anyone who had been involved in producing the French players for the 1998 World Cup had been doing something right. We also needed more discipline here. Everybody harks back to the white-suit FA Cup final [of 1996, when Liverpool players paraded pre-match in some very dodgy suits and shades], a moment that said: 'We need to do this differently.' We couldn't have a repeat of that. Gérard's approach to discipline was not about throwing teacups or screaming. It was very simple: 'My door is always open, but if you don't like my methods, come and tell me. And you will be out of the door because we're doing it my way.' Planning, attention to detail, recruitment, a new training regime. It all changed here.

Houllier's arrival also increased the international knowledge at Liverpool. Houllier had, after all, been a FIFA technical expert at World Cup finals, so was likely to know something about players and trends in the world game. The profile of the top players was changing, he contended. Vieira and Petit, now the powerhouse young players in the French national team, were close to Houllier's profile of the new model footballer: athletic, physically imposing, hard running, adaptable. But where actually was the balance between this kind of physical resource and the finesse and the skills needed to break down determined international defences? It was a conundrum Houllier would often face in the years ahead at Anfield.

In 1999 the Liverpool and Manchester United squads passed en route to contrasting European destinations: United were bound to play a crucial and glamorous Champions League match in Turin with Juventus, while Liverpool were off to some obscure football backwater. For Parry it was a defining moment: the Liverpool staff vowed it would never happen again. The successes in 2001 maybe 'came too soon for the fans', in terms of raising high expectations, but not for the club. But Parry is also 'realistic' about where the new Liverpool lay in the international football pecking order. In the new global game, the Anfield club would have to recruit better and younger than many of their rivals:

> Given the structural changes in the game, we didn't envisage ourselves being a Real Madrid or a Barcelona, or even a Bayern, a club with limitless cash. It's a different world now, a world in which

Real Madrid can sustain a debt of £170 million and nobody cares. We couldn't just buy whoever we wanted. We always reckoned we would have to be smarter and maybe try a little bit harder and make sure that we were identifying the outstanding players younger. So, if we are not in the market to buy Zidane, then let's find the next one. But we also wanted to be very close to that top tier. I had an idea that, if the Champions League revenues were producing the polarisation which was leaning towards the European 'superclubs', clubs which were bigger and more powerful than the rest, then we had to be in there. The necessity was sustained participation in the Champions League. That wasn't an aspiration, a goal. That was a necessity. The goal was winning the Premier League, winning silverware. This club is about winning trophies. Three cups was good [in 2001] and I would not have traded them for Champions League qualification. But to also qualify for the Champions League was fantastic. We were a year ahead of Champions League qualification in terms of our targets.

In this sense, the 2002–03 season was in grave danger of turning out to be a 'failure' for Liverpool. But Parry also sees the current period, essentially, as one of transition. He is aware of Liverpool fans' concerns about how the team is performing and playing, and he admits that the famous 'slump' this season has hurt everybody at the club. But he thinks that the management team is actually not that far from building a very good team here, and that the Liverpool performance in 2002, in finishing second without a manager for most of the season, was incredibly heartening. However, it also set very high expectations among the Reds' fans, and winning the League this year, especially with inexperienced new players to bed in, was always going to be very difficult.

In Europe, meanwhile, it is no longer a level playing field. Liverpool's resources simply don't match those of the super elite, though the club's income in 2001–02 still placed it in the top ten in Europe, and, admirably, wages were under some reasonable control. Liverpool were ninth in income – including a boost from Granada TV – but twelfth in wages and thirteenth in net transfer spend for 2001–03. Bayern Munich has managed to suppress wages and maximise income and performance perhaps better than any other European club in recent years. In the 1970s, of course, the differentials in turnover and wages between Liverpool and Manchester United were actually very small because it was a pre-merchandise domestic football market. By 2002 United's turnover was 50 per cent larger than Liverpool's. Liverpool could also spot and recruit the outstanding players in these periods. But even United's transfer spending and wage bills in their dominant years of the 1990s were not that excessive: they raised plenty of their own talent, something Liverpool can also do – and must now do to remain competitive in Europe. So the necessity for the club is always to be in the Champions League. This is the bottom line in the new era, and according to club revenue and to wages paid by Liverpool, an annual appearance in the quarter-finals of the big European club competition should also be a *minimum* aim. The aspiration, of course, is to win the Premiership. But you need to be in the Champions League to make a Premiership title challenge feasible. The two things go hand in hand.

EUROPEAN FOOTBALL RICH LIST
(Adapted from *World Soccer*, July 2003)

		Revenue 2001/02 (Euro millions)	Wage bill 2001/02 (Euro millions)	Net transfer Spend 2001–03 (Euro millions)
1.	Real Madrid	252	140	96
2.	Man. United	207	98	80
3.	Juventus	195	103	42
4.	Bayern Munich	176	38	38
5.	Milan	162	107	87
6.	Chelsea	161	77	40
7.	Barcelona	148	102	53
8.	Roma	144	90	(0.1)
9.	**Liverpool**	139	69	22
10.	Arsenal	127	85	34

A WORLD STILL TO MAKE

What of the future? The new stadium on Stanley Park is still part of Liverpool's new direction. A huge amount of detailed work still needs to be done, but a planning application will go in for the summer of 2003, with the aim being to open the new venue in 2006 at a cost of between £80 and £100 million. It sounds like a huge chunk out of the club's budgets, especially if Champions League football is not guaranteed over the next few years. Why must the club have it? Change again:

> Because you can't stand still. Absolutely doing nothing is not an
> option because the old Main Stand will need replacing sooner

rather than later. And bearing in mind if we had to rebuild the Main Stand now to Green Guide standards we would end up with a capacity of 42,000 – so we would actually be going backwards. We wanted to expand where we are, emotionally, but also from a business sense as well. But it was clear we were not going to get local-authority backing. There was the small matter of 250 houses to demolish, so it just wasn't going to happen.

The economic case seems compelling – but only if the club can raise the cash, and the costs stay reasonable. Parry is very clear that the proposed new stadium is not being built as a monument, or as part of a fixed or inescapable commitment, as happened at the FA or at Arsenal, for example. The venture does not go ahead, come what may. If the costs get too high, or Houllier cannot get Liverpool into the Champions League consistently, then things might well stall. It's a difficult balance to strike, but damaging the future development of the team is to be avoided, of course:

> The broader point is that we are up to £1 million per game worse off than Man. United. That's one hell of a handicap to overcome. If you are going to be up there with those 16 European super clubs, you have to progress. We will have a 60-something capacity ground. We looked at 70,000, but the economics of that did not make sense. I don't get the sense that there is a huge undercurrent of opposition [among fans] to the move. For us, a new stadium is a component of having a successful team. More income of up to £400,000 a match means it will be worth £10–12 million a season in revenue, but it also has to be paid for. At every stage we are saying we want a new stadium to raise money for the team. If at any stage things go wrong, or this escalates to the point where it makes no financial sense, we won't do it. A new stadium is a means to an end, not an end in itself.

Liverpool does not yet have enormous debts. For Parry, this year's example of Leeds United is a 'salutary lesson', a warning to all clubs. But Liverpool are not at risk. There will be belt-tightening, but the club will still be standing. Is the Leeds example – or those of the middle-range clubs – a sign of *structural* weaknesses in the game? Parry thinks hard about this. He says the English game is characterised by feelings of extremes: it is either all fantastic or all disastrous. There was too much optimism before the slump and too much gloom and doom now. This is true. He now becomes Mrs Thatcher: you cannot spend above your means. Spending tomorrow's money today – on the basis of expected gate receipts or TV income – is a big risk. Too many clubs here are too quick to borrow against future revenues for team-building. But the answer is not regulation, he contends. Clubs need to learn from their own, stupid mistakes. Domestic salary caps make no sense if you are competing in Europe and regulating salaries in Europe seems impossible too, even though the G14 Group have recently been talking about restricting wages to 60 per cent of turnover. Who is going to enforce it? 'I wouldn't hold my breath that too many clubs are going to stick to it,' says Parry. 'We'll run our business according to the formula we think works here. Sixty per cent of turnover as a limit on your wage bill is fine, but we will do it here because it suits our business, not because G14 tells us to.' That's clear, then.

And the size of the next TV deal, the future financial lifeblood of the game at this level? Parry plays deadpan. OK, there will be no more 400 per cent increases on the previous deal: those days have long gone. But if the next deal is the same as the last one, the top clubs will be happy. There may be no real competition to Sky in the TV football marketplace this time, but then why would Sky want to shaft the Premier League? The relationship is entirely symbiotic: football needs a successful Sky and Sky needs a successful Premier League. Cutting the TV money also damages the product Sky desperately needs to survive, because most of Sky's subscribers are subscribers for Premier League football. Sky and the Premier League rise and fall together. There will be no major fallout between satellite TV and football, though the European Commission's interest in increasing competition is a potential cloud on the horizon. In the summer of 2003 a new £1 billion TV deal over three years was struck with Sky. More of the same, except that 138 matches would now be shown live.

Parry thinks there will be 'more realism' regarding players' salaries in the future, with perhaps more flexibility on players' contracts. He talks throughout here, using examples from across the continent; he knows what is happening on TV issues, salaries, stadia and so on in Germany, Italy and Spain. He's impressive on all this, and has a sophisticated overview of the European football landscape. He really shows a convincing sense, too, of where Liverpool and the Premier League are placed on all these matters. He is more circumspect, however, about the current tensions between the FA and the Premier League. He clearly disapproves of the FA's new overt commercialism and financial speculation. The FA is important to the game precisely because of its traditional reliability and stability, while so much of the rest of the sport was in flux. It usefully provided some checks and balances for the English game, a necessary anchor. But when the FA starts to go over the edge, gets into huge debt, then perhaps it is time to worry. Perhaps the lunatics really have taken over the asylum.

Parry is appalled that the FA might not be able to deliver on grass-roots initiatives, because the FA's role should be exactly here and for fielding international teams; that's *why* the FA exists. Parry also does not approve of the idea that the Premier League might somehow 'run' the FA, precisely because those useful checks and balances in the game will disappear as a result. Maybe the streamlining of the FA, which gave much more power to the chief executive, was actually a bad thing. Here, of course, Parry conveniently contrasts the 'necessary' revolution inside the Football League back in the early 1990s with the very different functions performed by the FA, which now seemed to be challenged by the ambition and recklessness of the Crozier style of management. I don't go all the way with him here, because I am much more wary of the ambitions of the Premier League than he seems to be. But he has a point: chairmen might make a complete mess of their own club, but if the FA starts crumbling, then it is general alarm bells.

I guess I like Rick Parry. He has a kind of benevolence, and a sense of the importance of the club and its supporters, that is both engaging and reassuring. I'm sure he believes in the Premier League, for all of its ills, but then show me an architect who wants to take a sledgehammer to any of his own constructions. This means Parry, at heart, is a man of the market – clubs and ticket prices must find their own levels. He offers us nothing much here. He is a hard businessman, I'm sure about that, but I also think he is generally working for Liverpool supporters not, simply, despite them. He has ambitions *for* the club that most fans would share, but he also has to deal with the dirty economics to bring these ambitions about, and the difficult business of change. Unlike most football fans, though, he likes change, and positively welcomes it. This could be a real worry, of course, except that he also makes tacit commitments here not to prostitute the Liverpool 'brand'. (He, at least, is very happy not to talk about 'brands' at all.) We need to hold him to that promise, and remind him of the signs of hideous LFC branding that are already very apparent in L4. Rick Parry helped change the face of English football, all right. And he is not yet done.

CHAPTER 8

Salvaging Respect

I SECOND THAT EMOTION

A 'relationships' expert (it says here) has compiled a survey that shows that football matches are rated higher than bars, the theatre, walks and the cinema as the perfect location to meet your dream partner. Researchers claim that football provides would-be couples with an external event at which they can get rid of date-related stress, and which offers a good topic of conversation. Football provides, say our boffins, 'an arena in which you can share a roller-coaster of emotional and physical reactions'. Anfield, this season, is more likely to be a convenient site for the negotiation of divorce.

20 FEBRUARY 2003, UEFA CUP: AUXERRE 0, LIVERPOOL 1

European dreams. Such is the sheer unreliability of Liverpool's League performances in 2002–3 that it is fast becoming clear that victory in the UEFA Cup, or even in the maligned Worthington Cup, might be our best – perhaps our only – chance of honours and even making Europe next season. So this mid-week meeting with talented, little Auxerre matters to us, even if United and Arsenal – and ambitious Newcastle – are also back playing with the European Champions League big boys as we squirm among the Euro also-rans (in fact, among teams like us). The big press story of this UEFA Cup tie is the meeting of old French coaching chums Houllier and the remarkable Guy Roux, a man who has been involved at Auxerre since 1961, thus making Ferguson's lengthy stay at United look just a little like a bit of part-time casual labour.

Roux, like GH, has also had his health problems, enduring a recent double heart by-pass. The two friends last met in a French hotel in 2001 when they were both recuperating from life-threatening surgery. Each of these men know that there is more to life than football – and also that there is also no living without it. 'We're both workaholics and passionate for the game we're in,' says Gérard. 'Guy is a cunning, clever person who is enjoyable to spend time with.' 'Gérard is like a half-brother to me,' confides Roux to a surprisingly gooey press pack. 'That's why it hurts me to see him criticised. I know they have had a dip in form since November, but people need to remember that when Gérard took over Liverpool were a mid-table team going nowhere.' This raises two questions for me: what, exactly, is the French translation for 'dip'? And has the great French coach Roux looked at the Premiership table recently, because *this* Liverpool, Houllier's new team, is also rapidly heading towards mid-table obscurity.

Traore starts tonight, with Riise and Steven Gerrard restored in midfield and Diouf now a fixture on the Liverpool right. Questions need to be asked. Hamann is left on the bench. Merseyside cab drivers have begun to talk recently about Hamann's supposed run-ins with Houllier over the continuing omission of his mate Markus Babbel, a man barely seen since his early substitution humiliation in the League Cup at Villa. The word on the street is that Hamann may return to Germany in the summer. If true – what, you doubt scouse cabbies? – it is another sign that experienced players who are willing to speak their mind may get short shrift from *Le Boss*. The less outspoken pairing of Owen and Emile Heskey lead from the Liverpool front tonight. Michael – 19 goals in 40 European games – needs just one more to overtake Ian Rush's European record for Liverpool. But these two hardly ooze goals at the moment. We'll settle for 0–0.

Liverpool's bright start soon gives way, predictably, to stirring home pressure, with Carragher and Traore in their usual European frantic-cum-panic mode. But after Emile fluffs a rare breakaway chance in the second half, and just as Auxerre actually start to believe they might even win this ordinary tie, Sami Hyypiä, of all people, pops up with a calm finish from Danny Murphy's poked pass to deflate home hopes. (Hyypiä's recent biography – a book so uninspiring it might alienate even his biggest fans – reveals that Sami's worst moment as a young player was to be substituted by his coach father – for a *girl*. This *is* Finland, remember.) The final quarter hardly passes without incident around the Liverpool goal, but this is a good away win in a tricky venue. Not a good Liverpool *performance* mind – but when did we last see one of these?

THE O'NEILL MAN COMETH . . .

A draw at home in this tie will now see Liverpool through, and to a possible UEFA quarter-final meeting with Martin O'Neill's Celtic, who take a 3–1 lead to Stuttgart. O'Neill, by the way, has always been a Reds fan, has reliably bought a house on the Wirral, is in daily contact with Rick Parry, and has already made a couple of major signings for his new club – Liverpool. You mean you hadn't heard? You must be reading the wrong newspapers.

Meanwhile, at Old Trafford towers, Sir Alex and his favoured son Becks seem to be having their own relationship traumas. The grim Scot scuffed a stray football boot in his star's direction following an FA Cup home loss to Wenger, and Beckham copped it above the eye. Cue public outrage and financial downturn. United's share price fell by 2 per cent as rumours spread that the sainted – and powerfully branded – one might leave the global club. Posh is already in Milan visiting estate agents, while mysterious investors and bidders stalk United shares. 'Forget *24* or the *West Wing*,' puff up the broadsheet business pages, 'because the home of Manchester United rarely disappoints lovers of intrigue, power battles and personality clashes.' Right.

23 FEBRUARY 2003: BIRMINGHAM CITY 2, LIVERPOOL 1

'Failure is part of success.' Gérard Houllier

Birmingham City are on the very cusp of being the sick men of the Premiership, fighting for their lives to stay out of the relegation shite and backed by a crowd capable of howling down the moon. So you don't want to come to St Andrews carrying doubts and passengers. You need absolute belief and quality to ride the early storm here and to buy the right to play, because this ugly home team will find every point of weakness, every minor shaft of uncertainty and flood them with corrosive poison until you fall apart. Manager Steve Bruce says: 'As a player my philosophy was that I was not blessed with any great ability [no argument there] but I always had a go and that is what I like to see in my team.' So this is no Rinus Michels, this new Birmingham boss. Robbie Savage is the 'I can-give-it-out-but-can't-take-it' midfield menace who sums up the crude Bruce dictum: barely any real football talent but relentless and game, a non-stop piercing toothache that will erode your will unless you deal with him, take him out of the contest. We need to stand up here. Instead, all our pretenders play today. We are suckered to another humbling defeat.

The Birmingham fanzine *The Zulu* describes our pub-of-choice this afternoon, the Hen and Chickens, a mere ten-minute gambol from St Andrews, as hosting customers who are 'the ugliest in Brum'. Local Bluenoses have not been close to sobering up since a 3–0 drubbing of Villa. There is eager talk here of the forthcoming return at Villa Park – and not all of it is about football. In short, this is decidedly an 'old' football venue, one sited in the post-industrial wastelands of the second city, and one designed to shake violently awake any marketing man who thinks the game here has been taken over by the Midlands literati and droves of season-ticket holders drawn in from the so-called 'creative' industries. They still admire a bit of rough and tumble here. You'd better be ready.

Nor is *The Zulu* overly respectful of its illustrious visitors today. Instead, it devotes page after near-intelligible page to the recent 'fuck-ups' made by Houllier on Merseyside and to mauling a visiting team that 'has no leadership on or off the field'. Bloody cheek! On the way to the ground – a tin-pot Homebase nightmare, by the way – Paul Hyland spots a dilapidated Mini wrecked in a front garden and one remembered, he claims, from a Liverpool visit here back in the 1980s. Even today it still feels decidedly edgy around this venue and you can see how the visit of a Chelsea or a Leeds – or even a Villa – might still pump up the local volume in these parts.

The Liverpool fans' entrance is guarded by a couple of hundred police, all of whom seem to want to check your ticket. Would anyone *forge* a ticket to come here? Liverpool fans complained that last time they were in Brum, in the same lower tier at the Railway End, piss came through the ceiling from above. Then the coins started coming. We don't get any of that today, which is a bonus, naturally. In fact, a nice 'supporter charter' in the club programme asks the home fans to 'arrive sober' and 'show respect for visiting fans' and also to 'applaud good play and goals by both teams'. What planet do these people come from? But for £30 there is little to shout about in the away sections in terms of space, design or comfort. At half-time the riot police even 'guard' the squalid away toilets, who knows why. Don't ask me about it.

We have been talking hard about our visit here, about how it is a trial for fans and especially for the players. You need guts and character to win here, perhaps even more than skill. Gerrard is out, suspended, which means the increasingly unconvincing Diao has to play. Traore replaces the injured Henchoz at centre-back, while Cheyrou is selected on the left and Baros replaces Michael. All of this is bad news: all of it. Steve Bruce has already told the press he fears Michael, that he always promises goals and that the home team might suffer the backlash from his recent failing form. In the Birmingham dressing-room now Bruce will be ridiculing this bunch of visiting faint-hearts, telling his own try-hard losers that Liverpool will not want to know today. Even Didi Hamann, on from the start for a change, has no appetite for the battle and he plays like he really *is* waiting for a flight back to Bayern.

But the worst offenders, predictably, are the new recruits, Diao and Cheyrou – and also Baros. The Senegalese man Diao is now playing as if he is, possibly, competing for the sobriquet of one of the most expensive and limited footballers ever to wear the Liverpool red. He offers little class or creative intent and is comfortably outfought and outplayed by the Birmingham midfield, by Savage and his buddies – by real British journeymen. Bruno Cheyrou is just lost, no stomach for this conflict, horrified at the brutality of it all: the old Shanks description of a player 'with a heart like a caraway seed' seems to fit him perfectly. The bench even call him over for a rallying chat during the trench battles. And Milan Baros – much worse than Diouf today – is all head-down stupidity, fooling some of the travelling Liverpool supporters with his mazy, going nowhere, running with the ball. Emile, meanwhile, slinks into that familiar marginalisation we have all grown to know so well recently. With Carragher over-run by Dugarry and Lazaridis on the Birmingham left, and Traore floundering against Clinton Morrison, we are a mess – and heading for another defeat.

As all of this is playing out in front of me, I suddenly realise how few of the Liverpool team on show today I actually *like*, have some real respect for. Hyypiä and Murphy, OK, they are wholehearted and talented, hate to be beaten. They are the Right Stuff. Hamann is usually reliable, though not today. Riise *can* do it and Carragher is a loyal tryer – if a blindingly limited one. But after that? With no Michael, Steven Gerrard or Henchoz in the side? And playing like this? Our squad players are weak and ordinary. And not suited to this sort of battle. Diao pointlessly gives away a free kick on the right just after the half-hour mark – an obvious danger: Birmingham have already missed chances right in front of us. Savage floats the ball in – Dudek, of course, *never* comes for these catchable crosses – and Carragher lets the puny Stephen Clemence out-jump him to score. It's 1–0 at half-time, and once behind we know this Liverpool team is already done for.

Gérard now directs the team as if he wants to make absolutely certain of defeat. Because just after the hour Michael finally comes on. ('*Who?*'

bellow the Brummies loudly when Owen's name is announced over the PA, sniggering at their own joke. Nice touch.) Fair enough, you might think, this is a sensible move. Cheyrou is already making his way to the bench, positively pleading to be replaced. Heskey could easily go and not be missed, Diao too. But it is Carragher who gives way – and the hapless Diao is moved to the right side of a reformulated back three. Disbelieving, he poetically double-checks with the bench. '*Quoi? Trois? Avec moi?*'

This move is a bit like offering raw meat to a slavering dog you are deeply afraid of: you simply stir its feral juices, get it coming at you for blood. Dugarry and Lazaridis are soon pouring through on the Liverpool right, and immediately into a space from which Diao is entirely absent. Morrison jubilantly slides in the simple, low cross. A sucker punch, and one positively *invited* by the Liverpool bench. Only Michael's gentle late conversion of Murphy's cute pass offers any hope, the young striker then banging the ball about in the home net as if exorcising demons produced, no doubt, by the sheer lack of chance-making talent assembled around him. It's 2–1. It's awful, awful.

CRISIS? WHAT CRISIS?

Later, Houllier will talk about how the officials were 'not brave enough sometimes' to give Liverpool penalties, a familiar and wilful missing of the point. This is another terrible, gutless Liverpool away defeat. 'Don't fucking clap that!' I shout at the dismayed – but hardly heartbroken – Liverpool supporters who gather around the exits at the end for a better sight of their fallen heroes. Christ, what do they want from us, this team? Unconditional love? Houllier even scoffs at the Birmingham match-day programme for suggesting that this Liverpool is now a club in crisis. What, a club with early title pretensions that has now conceded miserable away defeats at Sunderland, Fulham, Birmingham and Charlton? A club with a huge wage bill struggling even to make the top six, with just one confirmed goal-scorer who, himself, has often lost the finishing art and who, perpetually, looks in the gloomy depths? A club where £20 million spent on players in the closed season seems to have bought nothing of real value. In crisis? I don't think so.

On the morning of **Liverpool 2, Auxerre 0** Danny Murphy – fast emerging as the sensible mouthpiece for the current Liverpool team – sounds out a warning: 'As footballers you have to be realistic' (a novel idea this one). 'If you're not performing and the team's not succeeding, certain things are going to change and it could be you. I don't want to leave here because there's only one way you're going to go from Liverpool and that's downwards. We are all fighting for our futures.' (Some are fighting rather harder than others.) In the Flattie, the Liverpool fans refuse to accept the manager's definition of the problem. Here, it is all 'new manager' talk again. The Reds' collapse at Birmingham was both shocking, but also shockingly predictable. There is profound anger, but also real unease and uncertainty here. This is not a sacking club and knee-jerk responses to managerial mistakes and inadequacies are rightly regarded by true Reds fans as both crude and entirely alien forms of control. But Liverpool stalwarts in this debate also point out that this emphasis on the need for change is no hasty overreaction: that the 'problem' has been clear for quite some time.

Only after a witless Diouf leaves the party on the hour, replaced by Hamann, do Liverpool finally take control of this tie and score the goals that kill off Auxerre. First, Murphy cleverly flicks Michael through the centre of the visiting defence and the Golden One finishes neatly, beating Ian Rush's club-scoring record in Europe in the process: 20 goals in 41 European matches, and 129 in 247 Liverpool games. Murphy then nicks the second himself, a keeper's blooper. For a man whose career has seemed in almost perpetual question for the past two years Owen's is an amazing strike rate. In a season where his play has sometimes been wretched – and the service to him has been even worse – he will still end up with 20 League goals. Michael's running and pace have been absent too often this season, but he has at least done his job while others around him have often been floundering.

BACK TO THE FUTURE?

The city of Liverpool has started a public consultation for the endorsement the council seeks for re-introducing trams nearly 50 years after the last tram ran in Liverpool streets. The new tram network is about putting the city of Liverpool back on the international map – and about 'catching up' with Manchester. When, a decade ago, our north-west rivals proposed trams as an environmentally sound response to the new pressures of modern transport systems, we scoffed. Now the 10-year-old Manchester Metrolink will soon be doubled in size, with a new £820 million project involving three new lines and including a direct link to Manchester airport. With the arrival of the modernisation of Manchester transport, in the shape of the trams in 1993, also came the new Manchester United. Was it all coincidence? In that year Ferguson won the first championship for United since 1967. Six more titles have followed for United as Liverpool – the city and the football club – struggled.

THE LIVERPOOL WAY

In 1977 Liverpool, already League Champions, lost to United in the FA Cup final at Wembley. Six years later it was revenge in the League Cup final, the Reds recovering from a 1–0 deficit with a sweet extra-time clip from Ronnie Whelan. The 1983 final team contained Rush, Dalglish, Souness and Hansen, all candidates for a best ever Liverpool XI. But only once since the fateful year of 1985 – the awful 1996 FA Cup final surrender – have the then defending European champions Liverpool played Manchester United near the business end of a major football competition. In 1985 it was an FA Cup semi-final, an ugly and poisonous affair at Goodison Park, when rival fans spat violent hatred at each other and Liverpool escaped for a replay with an undeserved extra-time last-minute equaliser from Paul Walsh. United took the rerun in a spiteful match at Maine Road – and won the final against Everton.

So the history of meetings of these clubs in the latter stages of Cup competitions has tended to show United desperate for something to rescue their season, with Liverpool more determined to reassert their national football authority. Not this time: this latest meeting in the unconsidered Worthington Cup final is taking place in quite different circumstances. For one thing, United suddenly seem uncertain, cowed by Arsenal at home and worried by the quality of opposition in Europe. For the first time, Ferguson seems determined to put some early silverware in the OT locker just in case the wheels come off his challenges for the major prizes once more. He looks shaken in his convictions, drained by a recent home FA Cup defeat by Wenger.

Meanwhile, Houllier's Liverpool are adrift in the championship, out of the FA Cup and unconvincing in Europe. The Frenchman also badly needs this trophy. Supporter bragging rights are another crucial issue here, of course. Houllier could sell ice in winter but he is also under pressure from the media and from Liverpool fans: victory today, against bitter rivals, will make everything glow just a little bit differently. So this is much more than what detractors call a 'Mickey Mouse' cup final, and not just because £25 million out of the £40 million generated by the Worthington Cup stays in the cash-strung Football League. Ferguson has even rested players from a mid-week United Champions League clash with Juventus to have them fresh for this final. It seems that these two English football dynasties – and their managers and frantic worshippers – suddenly need this three-handled piece of silvered tin very badly indeed.

2 MARCH 2003, WORTHINGTON CUP FINAL: LIVERPOOL 2, MANCHESTER UNITED 0

Nire aitaren etxea / defendituko dut. / Otsoen kontra
(I will defend / the house of my father / Against the wolves)

Gabriel Aresti

'Fans come together for crunch match' is the sports pages headline in the weekend papers. It is a surprise – a disgrace, actually – to learn that the reference is not to Cardiff doings but to the India v. Pakistan World Cup cricket clash in South Africa this spring weekend. What? You really think that this tetchy minor sub-continent sporting spat fought over with stumps and sticks is more combustible, more disputed, and more important than this tribal conflagration between the English north-west's football best in deepest South Wales? Get a life – and a sense of sporting proportion.

We bed down in Swansea – the Mumbles – in the Saturday preamble for a Sunday meeting, and end up in a friendly local bar that tells you all you need to know about the troubled state of sport in South Wales. The history of Welsh sport is marvellously recalled here – the pub walls are crammed with proud black-and-white images of great boxers, footballers and rugby players from the valleys; the odd golfer, too. But the locals have now lost their way – in this pub they are divided in their football allegiances between two of the English powerhouses, Arsenal and Manchester United – and they spend the afternoon glued to Newcastle v. Chelsea on Sky Sports while both Swansea City and Swansea RFC struggle for ascendance – and support – in vital home games just a couple of miles down the road. Swansea City – a club that changed hands recently for £1 – could easily end up in the Conference at the end of this season, while their union mates are likely to be swallowed up soon by Welsh rugby restructuring. These developments would mean no top professional club sport based in Swansea. It is a sad, if predictable, tale.

In Cardiff, on a breezy, sunny Sunday, United and Liverpool supporters mix only uneasily. We see celebrity Reds fan, Tory MP Michael Howard, in the pub we are in, so there is also some pretty 'uneasy' mixing here. Police lines have even been set up in the streets around the stadium, like Beirut checkpoints, to keep apart the main bulk of supporters from the two clubs. On the field, Danny Murphy has gone too far for some Reds this week by admitting that Liverpool players do not, in fact, hate their United counterparts at all: after all, many of them are close buddies at 'Team England' gatherings. Even United's Phil Neville has said that his graceless brother Gary is 'misunderstood' in his supposed scathing public views on scousers. We'll accept none of this vain attempt to defuse the M62 enmity. It is, after all, what we all live for.

This feisty and mutual disregard among the affiliated will all work for Houllier – but only if Liverpool can overcome United this afternoon. Plenty of Reds followers are saying it already in Cardiff: '*If* we can just win today', as if the desperate moments of the season will dissolve from view as a result. Even Danny Murphy has said that winning in a final against United is more important to him than winning the UEFA Cup again. Despite himself, Houllier may actually agree with this, at least for one day. So rather too much is already at stake here, which also means that too much will also be forgotten in victory.

And there *is* more than a little malice in the South Wales air. You don't have to look too far this lunchtime to find small regiments of Liverpool outriders, shirts dragging outside designer jeans, and on the edge of enemy lines searching side streets and bars before kick-off for suitable targets to pick off. 'Fuckin' turn right, down 'ere!', an urgent half-whispered command from the rear and the hesitancy which follows at the front reflecting the constant tension in these circles between the fear that a wrong move may be a fateful step too far, and the desperate holding off of approaching big-match ennui. The skirmishes that follow, as always, are satisfying but inconclusive. Everyone lives to fight another day.

Michael Owen says he is actually spurred on, inspired, by a match with United – he was once sent off at Old Trafford, remember – and by the expectations of the crowd and his teammates that he will score: 'There is nothing more exciting than stepping on a plane knowing that I'm flying down to Cardiff to face Manchester United in a cup final,' he says. 'That gives me an extra 5 per cent over a usual game.'

Houllier also mentions, again, the training-ground work done on Owen's volleying, heading and his weak left foot: 'If you see the way he heads a ball now, or holds it up, it's different.' But this season almost all of Michael's previous progress on his left side seems to have vanished as he has struggled for form – and fitness. He puts his own lack of sharpness down to tiring weights work to build up muscle strength and fight off injury. Michael, at 20 years of age, was left out of the 2001 Liverpool Worthington Cup final team, his first big club occasion. His omission was also a sign of GH's policy of protection towards young players, his rotation fixation and the relative strength of the 2001 Liverpool squad compared to that of 2003. Owen, already a World Cup veteran, still didn't like being left out. It still hurts:

> It wasn't a pleasant experience, sitting on the bench. At the start of the day, when you find out at 11 o'clock that you're not playing, that's a low point. It wasn't easy. I'm a professional and I don't enjoy not playing. After the game a couple of the lads said I took it quite well and that they didn't know if they could have handled it like that. It got a bit better as the day went on, and I joined in the celebrations. But I'm not trying to kid anyone. It was a nightmare. Anything that happens to you, you have to turn it into a positive. A couple of months later I played in the FA Cup final and scored twice. It's hard to deal with at the time, but if you deal with it the right way it can help you in the long run.

This is a bit of Houllier in Owen: the need to turn disappointment into a weapon. But it is also a reminder of how close Liverpool came to losing that first final to an inferior Birmingham side in 2001 – a decent Brum penalty shout away from disaster in extra time, and Liverpool substitute Owen still rooted to the bench. It also reflects the young professional's concern to play in the really big games. Michael may be flush with fame and cash, but it is *playing* that still matters to him and, in his own mind you can tell, that after missing the semi-final second leg and the final in 2001, he feels he never really won that first medal at all. I bet he still hides it away. You don't win things in football sitting on the bench. Period.

Danny Murphy has also had interesting things to say this week about 'the Liverpool Way', in the process making Melwood life seem like a therapeutic alternative to *One Flew Over the Cuckoo's Nest*, while also surprisingly raising serious questions about some of his own teammates:

> If someone has an opinion, or a point of view, the manager encourages them to express it. We have lots of meetings and try to express views rather than bottle it up. If you want to scream and shout, you can. It's healthier, no pent-up aggression. That said, we are not falling out with each other. We are a good, tight bunch of players. When you're used to having a decent amount of success and it suddenly goes the opposite way it's difficult to deal with. One thing we've got going at our club is experienced staff who are very good at noticing any negativity or pessimism. Our problems have not come from lack of effort on the pitch – more a lack of quality at certain times. All you can do about that is get

your own house in order. You can't play other people's games for them.

Who does the screaming? Igor? Milan Baros? We wonder if everyone always feels *that* easy about getting things off their chest at Liverpool training. Are the decisions and tactics of the back-room staff routinely dissected and criticised, for example? Somehow, I doubt it. And what about those closing comments, from old Danny boy? A 'lack of quality' in the squad and an obvious frustration about this in his: 'You can't play other people's games.' You don't hear this kind of thing very often, this sort of blunt honesty about the inadequacy of fellow professionals. Even the fiery Keano, over at Old Trafford towers, only tends to mutter this sort of stuff in the lonely darkness of the home dressing-room. Murphy, basically, says here that we have a few fellahs who are just not up to the job. No names, of course, but we all know who he means. Does anyone scream *that* out at Melwood?

None of them start against United: none of the out-and-out Liverpool failures or any of our many deeply troubling question marks. This is important, because in order to win this final our best side has to play – and at the very top of its game. Our big-game players have to perform. The 'big-game player' is, of course, a coach's hazy (and lazy) concept and a good subject for journalists' late-night liquored-up debate. But it has some meaning and relevance here. Currently, everyone in England loves Chelsea's Franco Zola. The press lap him up and he has great skill and a good attitude. But is he a real big-game player; does he have the necessary steel to deliver when it really counts? I wonder. Eric Cantona was the same: great, brilliant, in the humdrum of the English Premier League but exposed in my opinion as a flat-track bully in the real big time, especially the top games in the Champions League. Perhaps even the horse-faced Van Nistelrooy has his own doubts. Mentally, they are all a little wobbly.

United also have fellahs they can rely upon, of course, but we have a few who can, and usually do, rise to the big occasion. They must do so today. Michael Owen, obviously; Didi Hamann always brings everything he has to the big stage; Hyypiä tends to get better the better the opposition; and Steven Gerrard has started to live more comfortably inside the top matches. We need a couple of other things to happen today. Seba Veron must play for United to slow up their midfield and reduce their tackle potential; and all the things we have been hearing about Keane's drive disappearing with his recent hip injury must be confirmed. Riise and Carragher must stifle Beckham and the increasingly inconsistent Giggs. And we *must* score first. This last thing, above any other, is crucial, and it reveals our essential weakness under Houllier. We are no comeback kings; we have no second option to drawing our opponents on and striking as they advance. Nor, currently, do we have the confidence to come back from behind. We must get ahead – and try to stay there.

On this beautiful, breezy day the authorities have closed the Millennium Stadium roof, an instruction from Sky Sports, apparently the game's new governing body. In this unnatural space it is Liverpool fans who make the early running, 'You'll Never Walk Alone' belted out and multiple flags to the ready: '*Don't Bomb Iraq: Nuke Manchester*' reads one. All right, it's only a joke – and a bad one. But it is at least a connection made to the event, a piece of real theatre and imagination from the cheaper seats. United's response? Pathetic kids' cup final flags, bought from vendors outside, and a children's playground song : 'Build a bonfire, build a bonfire/ Put the scousers on the top/ Stick City in the middle/ And burn the fucking lot' they sing, these doyens of the terrace creatives. Twenty-five years' travelling around Europe, and numerous Radio 4 explorations of Old Trafford fan culture later, and it suddenly dawns on us that the OT cognoscenti, the ultimate aficionados of the global game, have absolutely no songs they can really call their own. They have come only to gawp, to spectate, that's all. This now feels good. We can win this match.

LIVERPOOL (4–4–2)

	Dudek		
Carragher	Hyypiä	Henchoz	Riise
Diouf	Gerrard	Hamann	Murphy
	Heskey	Owen	

	Van Nistelrooy		
	Scholes		
Giggs	Veron	Keane	Beckham
Silvestre	Brown	Ferdinand	G. Neville
	Barthez		

MANCHESTER UNITED (4–4–1–1)

Look for yourself, bar Kirkland, our top 11 all start; even Houllier has got the rotation message by now. These are our *only* real 11 Liverpool players at present, though Diouf is still unreliable. Which means that Dudek has a chance to atone for his dreadful Anfield gaff, Riise is at left-back, and a restored, and 'when they attack' Henchoz is in again at the rear. We look solid, purposeful on paper. Veron starts for United, who play with Scholes, primed to support Van Nistelrooy up front, a piece of sophistry on 4–4–2. United look strong, but not unbeatable, with Keane struggling and Ferdinand and Brown hardly brimming with experience or powers of concentration at the back.

You can forget most of the first nervy 38 minutes. United have much of it territorially, but with the exception of a clever Van Nistelrooy flick from a Giggs feed that eventually spins wide, nothing of note really happens. Liverpool look comfortable but uninspired, and United lack real tackling might in midfield, where Keane is deep-lying and peripheral and Veron is getting caught on the ball, his usual, expensive, luxury self. Dudek looks secure in the Liverpool goal, untroubled. Steven Gerrard has been growing into the game from a slow start and the Liverpool four in midfield are slowly beginning to get on top, as we had hoped. Beckham looks distracted. Diouf is also keeping the dangerous Silvestre fully occupied on the United left, even if his promptings produce only the, by now expected, diet of miss-hit crosses and almost passes: 'As maladroit as a Rochdale reserve,' one newspaper unfairly sums up his erratic show today. He's actually doing OK.

David Beckham is not built to defend. None of his sponsors pay big money for injury-risking tackles and DB07 shows of gut-busting defensive cover. Here he is just lazy, lacking both bravery and concentration. He stands off Steven Gerrard on the edge of the United box, and half-turns to the Liverpool man's shot, offering only a stretched leg as a kid messing about in a playground might hope his gesture shows willing, while praying no exposed limb takes the full impact. In fact, Gerrard's speculative punt spins crazily off Beckham's wavering calf and loops over Barthez into the Frenchman's top left-hand corner. Defensive coaches now have a new video cut for those brutal Monday morning diagnoses on how *not* to defend strikes from distance. Steven, meanwhile, shirt whirling above his vested chest, seeks out the Liverpool dug-out for wide-eyed congratulation. Roy Keane, on the other hand, mutters more expletives at the fancy 'English bollox', the United faint-hearts, who have lately been ruining his life. So Liverpool have secured their 'must have' lead and, better still, it is only six or seven minutes from the sit-down session during which our players will collectively convince themselves they can now win this contest.

This still leaves time for Dudek to save from Veron and for Henchoz to wrong foot the rebound from Scholes over his own crossbar, praising his good fortune with clenched fists, before the players head for the echoing silence of the tunnel. They, at least, can now seek counsel and support from the manager and his back-ups. Right now Houllier will be gently urging organisation and workrate, pumping up Emile, and working on how best to release Michael when we can. Phil Thompson will be thumping his chest, calling loudly for more of the same, heart and belief, a second-half performance from real men. Sammy Lee will be checking for injuries and praising and cajoling in turn, noting every United weakness and each balancing Liverpool strength. In the stands we, the fans, can only listen to our own hearts thumping, both fearing and anticipating the next 45 minutes and every potential calamity that now bars our path to this trophy. Despite all this season's trials how could anyone, possibly, want to be anywhere else now?

Liverpool start well in the second period, with Michael being blocked by Ferdinand, and Emile coming close to earning an unlikely penalty. This is not what we had expected. More like it, soon after these assaults, Van Nistelrooy twists in the Liverpool box and around Riise – but shoots wide. Heskey departs injured on the hour – another big-match surrender – and his replacement Baros is soon breaking from distance, at pace, spreading the United defence in panic. Steven Gerrard (who else?) bursts irresistibly outside him, demanding the pass, and Baros actually delivers, takes the right option for once. Barthez batters the shot away, pointing to where the new danger now lies. But with Gary Neville finding room on the Liverpool left, Dudek suddenly has a busy period himself: his saves are solid and routine rather than spectacular. Scholes forces him once, that's all. We are reaching the critical, gut-wrenching moments of this match, with Liverpool mainly pinned back, but also threatening to break for the conclusive second goal. Our big-name stars have mostly delivered: Gerrard and Hamann, especially, are starting to splinter the centre of United's midfield, forcing Keane to retreat, while Veron is just disappearing – as we knew he would. We are winning this game physically, and mentally taking charge.

And it is Didi who secures this victory, and Michael, of course. Silvestre has had a miserable time against Diouf, who has made the Frenchman uncertain and tentative all afternoon. All this tension now explodes, as a weak Silvestre header to Ferdinand on halfway is critically short and is gobbled up by the battling Hamann, who straightens up to release Michael with a free run on Barthez from the centre-right. Ferdinand actually gives this up, stops trying to close Michael down, but even after 86 draining minutes Roy Keane still has the strength and the will-to-win to career back and hack at Owen in the box. But the England man doesn't even notice. Michael's shot flies past the hunched United goalkeeper Barthez. It is over.

Real football fans now simply write off the next few minutes. Show me any *real* fan who can tell you how the players celebrate a defining score like this one, or even what happens in the next couple of minutes of play. 'What? *They* had a penalty? Sorry, missed it, mate.' 'What? Vladdy's on – and he missed a sitter? Who went off?' Even in the 'mixed' area on the halfway line, where we are sitting among stiff suits and some glum United day-trippers, there are scousers in front of me, big, grizzly fellahs, who now insist on a full-on winners' snog: 'Do you mind if I kiss your husband, love?' These fellow foaming ranters and I can't watch this game now. We don't want to – *won't* sit down. Sod the suits, and the critics, and the hopeless Houllier tactics, and our terrible summer buys. This is not the time. You have to suck all the pleasure out of divine minutes like these. So luxuriate in the sight of the United end rapidly clearing, and Liverpudlians everywhere smiling and bouncing. You have to dance now because we have all been on the other end, of course: remember Cantona's sickening late Wembley winner in 1996? I spent the whole of the next day – my birthday – in bed. It is frightening, actually, how it can make you feel, losing or winning an important football match. How else, one is sometimes tempted to ask, are you supposed to know whether you are truly alive at all? And that, in its own way, is also a little frightening.

Later, in a local bar, with Liverpool flags stretched in every alcove, we even break out the bottles of post-match champagne and drift off into pleasurable drunken exhaustion. And our garbled, stewed, victory mantra for this memorable day in a thus-far forgettable season? 'I love my team, but more than this I love my club.' Also: 'We are better than them. We always have been. We always will be. And we were today.' So this is how we differ even from Houllier: stupidly, pig-headedly, wrongly, we still believe we are the best. This is our creed: we have to believe, because we have no other option. On a nearby table, one of a gang of beaten young United supporters spectacularly throws up at this final insult – a fan's instinctive response to defeat. And who, in these simultaneously wonderful and terrible football moments, can really blame him?

HOULLIER – FOR EVER?

This Worthington Cup win sets Rick Parry and his colleagues off into another predictable 'Houllier must stay' session with the press. The great man will sign a new contract before the end of the year, we are told. 'Our belief in him never wavered,' says the Liverpool chief executive, convincing no one. 'We don't panic at Liverpool.' Well, at least not *off* the field. Houllier has recently been fielding overtures, apparently, from Paris

St Germain, who are struggling in the French championship. It is a useful time for the manager to be publicly seen to be batting off potential suitors. 'People are trying to make me go on a tour of all the French clubs,' he says with a sly grin. 'But more than ever I am happy at Liverpool, even if we are not where we expected to be in the League. I love Liverpool and all the players who repay me for that. I'm working in an extraordinary atmosphere, which I could never find anywhere else.' Parry sums up, by denying that the cup win offers an opportune moment for the club to shore up Houllier's recent shaky position: 'We have always been happy with the direction we are taking with Gérard. Sunday hasn't changed that.' Nor, apparently, has a record of just two Liverpool League wins in the past 16 matches. This taste of victory is sweet all right – but it will not last for ever.

8 MARCH 2003: LIVERPOOL 2, BOLTON WANDERERS 0

Back to League work, and you have to admire Sam Allardyce, the Bolton boss. He took over at the Reebok back in 1999 and then got the Trotters into the play-offs in his first season. But when he actually brought Bolton up in 2001, securing a 10-year managerial deal into the bargain, we all waited for the up-and-at-'em relegation struggle which would surely follow. The Wanderers survived in 2002, but not by kicking lumps out of their betters or by spending cash they did not have on expensive English maybes. Instead, meat-and-two-veg Sam scoured the continent and managed to sell the north-west club to World Cup-winner Youri Djorkaeff, among others, bringing in new talent on clever short-term loan deals. And it was this extra bit of quality that helped them stay up.

And in this 'after the Lord Mayor's Show' post-Cardiff match-up, Bolton look well capable of springing an upset – by outplaying Liverpool and *losing* at Anfield. We play with Michael alone up front, 'supported' by an especially hapless Smicer and by Diouf. Henchoz is missing – for six weeks – so Traore starts. Bolton begin with Campo in midfield, well clear of the destruction he can sometimes wreak in his own defence. For much of the first half Campo, Okocha and Mendy control the match for Bolton, but though the Argentine Salva looks impressively tall, he also plays like a punch-less drunk up front. Sami misses a nailed-on chance from a corner at the Kop end, before Michael Owen eventually evades Simon Charlton on the Bolton right as the half-time toilet-stop approaches, and chips over Jaaskelainen for Diouf to head in on the very goal-line, his first League goal since two on his debut in August. He has not much looked like scoring since. It's 1–0 at the interval: not deserved.

The second half proceeds much like the first, though Vladdy gets much worse, even than his dilatory first-half show, and is soon substituted, to cruel Main Stand cheers. Vladdy even raises modest home applause for the arrival on the paddock of one Bruno Cheyrou. Within seconds our new man is leaping extravagantly over a stray Bolton leg, so I suggest he might better try hurdling rather than football. 'Or hairdressing?' suggests Rogan Taylor next to me, not sure what I had said. He may be right.

The Bolton left-back Charlton now has strong claims for the *home* team man-of-the-match, because he soon prostrates himself in front of Diouf – no tricks required – who then delivers to Owen at the near post for a simple finish. Even Diao gets a Liverpool run-out at the end; that's how easy this finishes. Not.

CELTIC FC: A DIZZY FOOTBALL DEMOCRACY?

Celtic, our forthcoming UEFA Cup opponents, have much in common with the modern Liverpool – and plenty that is impressively different. Celtic, like Liverpool, had been tortured in the 1990s, dominated and humiliated on the pitch by a hated local rival and left behind in vital commercial developments. The Scottish club's revival began when a headmaster's son and businessman from Croy in central Scotland, Fergus McCann, and other investors, stepped in to head off bankruptcy in 1993 and raised £21 million in a club share issue in 1994 – including, for the first time, shares bought by Celtic fans, to the extraordinary value of over £13 million. The cash was needed to buy new players but also to redevelop Celtic stadium. Today, the new Celtic Park is rivalled only by Old Trafford as a club venue in Britain. With 53,000 season-ticket holders, it makes Anfield look dated and small, which it is.

The reclusive and blunt McCann soon got rid of manager Lou Macari, bringing in ex-Celtic player Tommy Burns as his replacement, but the loyal Burns could do little to disrupt Rangers' dominance of the Scottish game and, facing a record tenth consecutive Rangers title in 1997, he too was sacked by the now increasingly unpopular McCann. Up stepped the Dutchman Wim Jansen to pilot Celtic to a titanic UEFA Cup meeting with Liverpool in the 1997–98 season. In the spring of 1998 Jansen duly delivered the Scottish League title to the East End of Glasgow for the first time in a decade, but 48 delirious hours later he resigned, unable to resolve disputes with the club chairman and the general manager, Jock Brown. Celtic fans were in uproar. Imagine Houllier resigning 48 hours after Dortmund in 2001 because of 'differences' with Rick Parry!

The embattled McCann then famously sounded out Houllier himself for the Celtic job – 'I had a nice choice,' quipped Houllier – before recruiting instead the quiet 62-year-old Slovakian coach Jo Venglos on a low-spend managerial ticket. He also resisted overtures by Kenny Dalglish and pop singer Jim Kerr to buy the Celtic club in December 1998, including a proposed £8 million investment in a new Celtic academy. In 1999 McCann sold up his original £9 million stake in the club, for a hefty £40 million instead, a move which left 45 per cent of shares in the hands of fans and small investors. A major football club substantially owned by its supporters? There is no English equivalent. McCann's departure also heralded the arrival of Kenny Dalglish as technical director at Celtic and the (disastrous) appointment of former Reds hero John Barnes as Celtic coach.

This new 'Liverpool' connection with Celtic did not last. Poor League form and elimination in the Scottish Cup by unconsidered Inverness Caledonian Thistle was the final straw and the Dalglish–Barnes axis soon fell. But under new chairman Brian Quinn and ex-Leicester City manager Martin O'Neill – and as Liverpool were also reviving under Gérard Houllier – Celtic swept the board in 2000–01, winning the Scottish Treble and finally deposing Rangers as the modern driving force in Scottish football. Recent Old Firm ambitions to gain entry into the FA Premier League, however, seemed no closer to bearing fruit in 2003 than they had ever been. Perhaps only drastically declining TV income in England could sway the English authorities, but UEFA would also lodge vigorous objections to any 'creaming off' of clubs by the most powerful leagues in Europe. There looks to be nowhere but Scotland for the Old Firm clubs to go. And so beating English clubs in Europe is everything to the Scots. Watch out.

20 MARCH 2003, UEFA CUP QUARTER-FINAL (FIRST LEG): CELTIC 1, LIVERPOOL 1

A Glasgow–Merseyside love-in is more in prospect here than the 'Battle of Britain' suggested by the headlines we usually get for a high-powered Euro meeting between Scotland's finest and top English opponents. But with a real war currently brewing in the Middle East, even hardened red-top sub-editors are minding their sporting language now. In any case, the Liverpool–Celtic affinity has grown ever stronger since the canny Bob Paisley signed Dalglish to replace Germany-bound Kevin Keegan in 1977. 'He was the only man I'd have sold you to,' Jock Stein told the young Kenny, before sending him on his way with a jaunty: 'All the best, ya wee bastard.' Celtic fans used to travel down to Anfield to watch the great man play. He did not disappoint.

With whom do Celtic's fans have other major supporter tie-ups in

THE LIVERPOOL WAY

England? Well, with Everton supporters, traditionally, though I also wonder how strong this link might now be, especially given the fawning new Celtic–Liverpool relationship? And Celtic also has this strong and thriving Irish-Catholic thing going with Manchester United. This means that later tonight we will be in a big Celtic pub, the Crown, on Duke Street in Glasgow, enjoying ourselves with our Celtic mates, while being invited to admire a framed and signed red football shirt that once belonged to – one Ryan Giggs. It is all part of the new – and confusing – social order in British football fan allegiances.

This Glasgow trip starts badly for us: Chris and Paul Hyland don't even make it on to the East Midlands morning *bmibaby* flight to Glasgow on which we are all booked: they have no photo ID, apparently compulsory in these dog-days, even for internal flights. I only get on board by flashing my out-of-date Liverpool FC European Travel Card. The war against terrorism has its first football victims. Undaunted, they drive up to Scotland, which means I can take in some of the local sights and also get a bet on – it's Cheltenham Gold Cup day. We eventually get some dinner – Arbroath smokies and haggis, no less – in the famous Charles Rennie Mackintosh Willow Tea Rooms on Sauchiehall Street, before heading down, via the Celtic shop, to the Horseshoe pub, which is already jam-packed with aled-up Reds. The Gary Mac 'Allouette' song is being hammered out here and John Mackin is happily steaming away, as always. Here we also manage to catch up on the final leg of my racing wager, erroneously cheering on a rival horse in the chaos of the bar before learning that the nag we had been furiously opposing – the race winner – was actually carrying my cash! Off to the bookies for the winnings, all of it later spent on warm Glasgow ale. Great night ahead, clearly.

We had been prepared, of course, for the pre-match Celtic Park performance of 'You'll Never Walk Alone', but nothing can really prepare you for this. This famous old song is much abused now. Feyenoord fans sing a mangled version of it. I have even heard it used in Australian rugby league – to accompany players sent to the sin-bin. But there is no abuse here. In fact, *everyone* here sings the proud old lady, with both reverence and commitment, led by Mr Marsden himself – a nice touch. This is both an awesome and a slightly disconcerting experience for any Liverpool supporter, because they really do believe it is *their* song, these Celtic sympathisers. It is almost as if the power and passion – and sheer scale – of performance somehow confers ownership, a lesson for everyone at L4. Perhaps it should.

Note this, too: unlike the 500 versions of the 'authentic' Liverpool scarf now churned out in all colours by Planet Reebok and the club, most

Celtic fans favour the unmarked simple green-and-white bar version for their mass YNWA display. This contains a message, too: that *this* is the official Celtic scarf, available for £3 or less from market stalls and cornershops everywhere. It looks brilliantly subversive and effective here, a 1960s throwback and a very simple statement about resisting the worst effects of the football–commerce synergy. Could we even start the same trend at Anfield, I wonder?

Both teams huddle before the start, another quirky club connection, and there is as much green as there is red in the Liverpool section as we kick off. Reds followers are crammed into a corner nearest the end Liverpool are defending in the first half, so we get a great – if unwanted – view of the early calamity that is a goal for Celtic, after just two chaotic minutes in the engine room of the Liverpool defence. Hartson has already gone close, fooling Traore and lobbing on to the Liverpool bar, but now Riise (at the front post) and Carragher (at the back) are both at fault in the next Celtic attack, before the ball is returned low into the Liverpool box for Larsson to nudge home. Weeks out with a double-jaw fracture, the Swede needs only seconds to damage us. The Celtic fans are now bursting for more, but it is Liverpool who take charge, forcing the home team back and quietening the crowd. Within 15 minutes Riise even makes a diagonal run right at the Celtic defence, before reverse-passing to Heskey, who surprises everyone – including himself – by showing quick feet and arrowing an unexpected low shot into Douglas's left-hand corner for the equaliser.

The celebrations around us are extreme, the Liverpool singing almost non-stop. For the rest of the half Liverpool control the play, carefully passing and keeping the ball. The pattern repeats after the break: Liverpool are in charge, with Gerrard supreme, but only two clear chances are created, missed by Owen and Heskey. But in a match run by the visitors – this vaunted home crowd is now perfectly silent – Liverpool manage only five shots in total, two on target. It is an opportunity missed. Drawing 1–1 after this ragged performance is no hardship for O'Neill's team. Like us, they often improve away from home, especially when someone else is pressed to make the running. Our home form should frighten nobody and O'Neill knows better than anyone how to win at Anfield. This tie is only halfway over: no one yet has a clear advantage.

MAN SPITS IN GLASGOW SHOCK

Before the end, there is an incident that keeps the press happy. Diouf falls into the home paddock to our left – but beyond our vision. Something obviously happens here, as he climbs out of the crowd, because the locals are soon bawling and booing at Dioufy – and a couple of them are even dragged out and away. Houllier soon substitutes our boy, to gales of hoots and Scottish curses. We see later, on TV, that a shaven-headed Celtic Bhoy has laddishly patted our man on the head as he has been sent on his way back on to the pitch, and the Senegalese has taken offence – or fright – responding almost instinctively, by spitting back towards this guy and his mates. In these parts, you get more respect – and understanding – for nutting an opponent than gobbing at him, so Celtic fans are apoplectic at this 'disgusting' gesture. There will be a price to pay for it, clearly, despite Houllier's mutterings about 'cultural difference'.

JC – BUT NO SUNSHINE BAND

Jamie Carragher knows well his own limitations: 'I'm not a player who's going to be getting eight or nine out of ten,' he says. 'I'm looking for it to be seven most weeks. Some of the others can reach the heights that I can't, but there are players in the side who maintain a consistent level of performance, a solid, steady seven. I'm talking about myself, Stephane Henchoz and Didi Hamann. I think I've done that this season.' (Actually, we wouldn't rate JC alongside these two proven internationals, he's a regular five, but you can see what he means. So I'll let it pass.) And Liverpool?

> For the last three seasons we've been improving, but we're not kidding ourselves. We haven't been that close in the League. It's not like we've been missing out narrowly. Arsenal and Manchester United are better than us. We need them to come down from their present level, as United did last season, and we need the manager to add to the squad in the summer to push us up a level. More than anything, it needs Arsenal to drop a notch. At the moment they're as good as any team in Europe.

Some of this is painfully true, and one area where the Liverpool manager will need to recruit – is right full-back. Arsenal? Well, Valencia comfortably dump the north Londoners out of the Champions League this week. Like the willing Carra, these soft London boys still have a lot to learn. This is also proved in **Tottenham 2**, **Liverpool 3** in the League, where Jamie boy actually does OK. But not Jerzy Dudek. Houllier thinks Taricco is messing with 'spitter' Diouf, and the Liverpool manager even bad-mouths the Spurs man in the tunnel at half-time. It gets worse. *Le Boss* then has his head in his hands when the Argentine swerves a little tester at Jerzy soon after the interval, who shovels it gently into the

Liverpool net. His mistake-free Millennium day out is suddenly history.

But the injustice of all of this seems only to rile Steven Gerrard, who now gives us half an hour of the devastating energy and skill we last saw from him at Villa Park in the League Cup. He makes a goal for Michael, and then one for Emile, and even scores an absolute belter himself, after a pulsating run from halfway. He stands head-and-shoulders above the rest here. Even a late Sheringham knee-trembler is not enough to rescue Tottenham. A 3–2 win at the Lane. We are still – just about – chasing that Champions League slot. But first, get the ale in, the Jocks are coming.

20 MARCH 2003, UEFA CUP QUARTER-FINAL (SECOND LEG): LIVERPOOL 0, CELTIC 2

'One Henrik Larsson, There's only one Henrik Larss-on.' It takes us fully ten seconds to meet up with our first, ticketless Celtic drunk in L4. There are a few more in the Flattie tonight, which is converted by the landlord and his Scottish visitors, for one night only, into a Gaelic ceilidh, and one filled with gormless Republican songs of sadness and defiance, pounding out over the PA. This is already a painful evening out. For all our buoyant talk now about flights to Madrid or Malaga *when* we get through to the final in Seville, it will only deteriorate from now on.

Michael Owen has been expanding before this game upon his problems and his new fitness regime, recalling his injury fears with England during the World Cup finals and also his new approach to conditioning. 'I do a lot of heavy weights every day, building up the strength in my muscles again,' he told the press. 'Some of the other lads go upstairs, maybe have a cup of tea or a game of pool before training, but I'll be in the gym for a 45-minute session with the weights. I'll do more afterwards. It's a sacrifice worth making. My pace is my chief asset and if this means I'm going to keep my speed in the long run, then it's worth it.' Good man.

The story of this match? Let me keep it brief: less pain involved. Celtic fans are in the Kop, and all over Anfield, in fact. No trouble, not a hint of it. Diouf is left out, because of his Glasgow spitting episode. Smicer plays: dreadfully. In the first few minutes Riise turns his ankle in a block tackle, but this multi-million-pound football business we call Liverpool has no one, apparently, who can replace him on the left. This means he hobbles on, and makes no attacking progress at all. One minute before the half, the Liverpool wall jumps over Thompson's skidding free kick. We are 0–1 down. Hartson scores again later, a pearler: 0–2. THE END. There, I feel better now. Spanish holidays are overrated.

THE LIVERPOOL WAY

TROUBLE IN MIND

Hugh McIlvanney – a bit of a Glasgow-nostalgic and certainly a Ferguson-lover, but a good football journalist nevertheless – said that the Scottish win at Liverpool depended on the morale, commitment and positive approach taken by Celtic. He has rather a different view on Liverpool, arguing that Celtic had 'thoroughly exposed the deficiencies in imagination, in tactical ambition, and in willingness to take creative risks that bedevil the current Liverpool'. This was powerful stuff. 'Lack of width on the pitch may be a vital symptom,' continued McIlvanney, but he made it clear that, in his view, this was not the deep source of Liverpool's problems. 'Limited breadth of vision at management level is a more fundamental concern, and all the affection felt for Gérard Houllier cannot blind us to it.'

He's right. No matter how you want to dress it up, no matter what excuses you want to offer – and injuries and loss of form can bedevil any side – this has been an awful, directionless, few months for Liverpool. All right, away at Celtic we had at least looked competent and assured, but at home we so patently lack ideas, real passion and belief, it was almost as if that trip to Glasgow had already been erased from the minds of the Liverpool team by the mere sight of a gleeful Martin O'Neill arriving in L4 to set yet another Anfield trap. He is a hard man to get past, no doubt about it, he's a real winner.

Now Houllier is talking about the 'eight cup finals' we now have left. This is another familiar Houllier tack, a last-gasp, just-in-time approach to football management: the idea that every single match can be built up on the basis of its own 'all or nothing' status, as a means of motivating the players to deliver their all. But no player can keep on playing cup finals. And our shabby form – eight home draws and plenty of gutless away losses – means that we must try to win every remaining contest. These must-win cup finals include away fixtures at United (who are bombing on again), Everton (who can't wait) and, as a forbidding last-gasp closer, at Reds' graveyard Stamford Bridge.

How are we doing? Well, currently, we are level on games won with the mighty Charlton Athletic, and just one above blubber-headed Manchester City. Impressed? Consider this: we will now definitely finish behind Newcastle United, a team with an unfeasibly popular and geriatric manager and no recognisable defenders. And we are still 14 points off leaders Arsenal – who have suddenly hit a wall. We have supplied dim-witted Sunderland, under the hapless Wilkinson, with more than one-fifth of their entire points haul. And, whisper it in these parts, we are still behind Everton in the League table. This means that the

Bluenoses could be lording it, playing next season with the big European fish, while the LFC grandees face getting out the route map for tempting UEFA Cup treks to outer Slovenia. It's eight cup finals all right.

FA PREMIER LEAGUE TABLE AT 22 MARCH 2003

	P	W	D	L	F	A	GD	Pts
ARSENAL	30	19	6	5	64	32	32	63
MAN. UNITED	30	18	7	5	48	27	21	61
NEWCASTLE U.	30	18	4	8	49	34	15	58
CHELSEA	30	14	9	7	52	31	21	51
EVERTON	30	14	8	8	38	34	4	50
LIVERPOOL	30	13	10	7	44	30	14	49
BLACKBURN R.	30	12	10	8	37	32	5	46
CHARLTON	30	13	6	11	39	38	1	45
SOUTHAMPTON	30	11	10	9	32	30	2	43
TOTTENHAM	30	12	7	11	43	43	0	43
MIDDLESBRO.	30	11	8	11	38	34	4	41
MAN. CITY	30	12	5	13	40	44	-4	41
FULHAM	30	10	8	12	35	37	-2	38
ASTON VILLA	30	10	5	15	31	35	-4	35
LEEDS U.	30	10	4	16	37	42	-5	34
BIRMINGHAM C.	30	8	8	14	27	42	-15	32
BOLTON W.	30	6	11	13	33	47	-14	29
WEST HAM	30	6	9	15	32	53	-21	27
WEST BROM.	30	5	6	19	21	46	-25	21
SUNDERLAND	30	4	7	19	19	48	-29	19

CHAPTER 9

A Scot and a Hard Place:
Gary Mac and Gérard Houllier

'HE WAS A GEM FOR US'

During one of the (many) low points during this 2002–03 Liverpool season, Gérard Houllier puffed out his cheeks, expelling air in that characteristic Houllier way, before contemplating a response to a key question from a sympathetic journalist: what exactly was still *missing* from this current Liverpool team? It had talented players, goal-scorers, decent defenders. The squad was full of internationals. What was going wrong, why didn't it seem to gel? The Frenchman looked wistfully into the middle distance, hesitated for just a second, before coming back with a name: 'Perhaps,' he said dolefully, 'we still miss Gary McAllister. He was such a gem for us.'

*

Houllier is right, of course. Few players have had such an extraordinary impact on a major football club, at such an advanced stage of their own careers, and in such a short space of time, as Gary McAllister did at Liverpool in the period between 2000 and 2002. McAllister was a very unexpected and a very atypical Houllier signing. In a period when the new Liverpool manager was busy recruiting younger players, mainly foreigners, who had their careers still well ahead of them, McAllister was 36 years of age when he arrived at Anfield – and a Scot. Liverpool, like most top English clubs, had, seemingly, stopped shopping in Scotland for players way back in the 1980s. Moreover, McAllister's playing career was apparently in steep decline at Coventry City after his earlier Championship success under Howard Wilkinson with Leeds United back in 1992. His international career with Scotland had nose-dived, gone completely sour, after the Jocks had actually started booing one of their own. Maybe it was McAlllister's dogged determination never to hide or to stop trying to pass the ball in a poor international side that finally got him the bird at Hampden? Or perhaps his critics north of the border simply could never really forget his Euro 96 penalty miss at Wembley – against the hated English.

Who knows? McAllister's retirement from the international game seemed only to confirm his likely slow drift into retirement and football management. He was a bright, likeable man, with firm ideas about how the game should be played. With his contacts and experience in football, and his level-headedness and determination, he had a reasonable chance of making it as a manager. Good luck to him. This is how we thought about this Scottish guy, McAllister, back then: a player that Roy Evans, say, could certainly have used well to help bring the title back to Anfield in the mid-1990s. But now it was way too late. That is until Gérard Houllier invited McAllister to join Liverpool in 2000. Nothing would ever be quite the same again.

So when I meet Gary Mac, among his own coaches now, at Ryton in Warwickshire, during a tough first season as player-manager at First Division Coventry City, he still has that strange whippet's shape, and alien's bald head; a lean running machine. He is genuinely touched – and chuffed – when I tell him that Liverpool supporters still sing the 'Gary Mac' song in pubs at Reds away games. I honestly still don't think he can really believe what happened to him – and to Houllier's Liverpool – in those few short months back in 2001. None of us can.

★

Gary McAllister, son of a Ravenscraig steel engineer, a Motherwell boy with GCSEs and something to say for himself, was always destined to be a professional footballer. From seven or eight years of age he was tracked by local clubs in the west of Scotland, and by 12 he was already getting calls to visit big clubs in England – Newcastle United, Leeds, Forest. But family links with Matt Busby, who also hails from the same area, coupled with his obvious ability, meant that while his mates were playing at the 'Well' during the summer months, between the ages of 11 and 16 McAllister was away down to Old Trafford. Here, he teamed up with other budding United hopefuls, the prickly Mark Hughes and a brutal Belfast man-child called Norman Whiteside. At 16 both Hughes and Whiteside signed with United, but a new manager, Ron Atkinson, fancied less the slim young boy from Motherwell. There was nothing down for him at United. 'Devastated' by this early setback, McAllister joined his local club after all – and waited. He had not given up on his ambitions to play football in England.

Working as a trainee at Motherwell McAllister describes as a '9 to 4 job': cleaning up and painting the stadium; tending the pros' kit; and two sessions of training a day. For £40 a week, it was hard, but enjoyable, graft. At 16 he was tossed into the reserves – 'You grew up playing against men very quickly' – and Motherwell was in its familiar turmoil at the time with the young McAllister greeting, and then losing, five managers during his four-year spell at the club. At 18 he was playing regular first-team football, wide on the right, and was already, in the vernacular, a 'good professional'; a man who enjoyed training and who, like both Shankly and Houllier, also saw the clear links between hard honest weekday preparation and playing to win at weekends. At Motherwell, the young McAllister actually saw an early sign of what was to be his future at Liverpool, in his relationship with the ageing ex-Scottish international Alfie Conn:

> I'm not a very good loser, so that gives you a good determination during the week, not to be losing at anything. If you win during the week, even in the little five-a-sides, it suggests you might not be too happy to lose at the weekend. I don't think it's something you can just turn on, on a Saturday, that desire not to lose. It's something you have to develop during the week in training. And I was very lucky, as a youngster, I played with Alfie Conn – Celtic, Rangers and Tottenham – who was from the very top end of the game. He was just coming to the end of his career, but the thing you pick up instantly is that he's right at the other end of the game to you, so you can learn from him. And later, of course, I'm the one who's at Alfie's age when I go to Liverpool and work with Steven Gerrard.

He now wanted a move, preferably to England. It was an ex-Liverpool man, Gordon Milne, then manager at Leicester City, who came to the rescue. The Motherwell target for English clubs was actually a tough little flame-haired midfielder, Ali Mauchlen, a man described by McAllister, with some affection, as, 'Horrible on the field, would do anything to win.' Milne paid and watched in among the Motherwell fans for the Lanarkshire Cup final to observe his target. He picked up from local supporters, and from the evidence of his own eyes, that Mauchlen was the club leader, the local sergeant major, but also that the wiry McAllister, the 20-year-old, was the local guy with the real football talent. Milne was convinced: he bought them both. McAllister was supposed to be a makeweight in the deal, but the true story is that he actually cost more than the Motherwell captain, at £150,000.

The Leicester City dressing-room was frosty, at first, to the new arrivals – established players were being replaced by these upstart young imports – but both became fixtures in a Leicester team that was struggling to find its level between the First and Second Divisions of the old Football League. McAllister liked Milne and thought that he had obvious 'Liverpool' attributes: 'He wanted players to be brave, and get themselves on the ball. Bravery in football is not just about clenched fists and being a "big man". Milne wanted people all over the pitch to stand up, take responsibility.' Sadly, Milne didn't last long. He had little money to strengthen the City squad, and so Leicester were soon relegated, leaving the Liverpool man out of a job. David Pleat took over at Filbert Street, an attack-minded, self-proclaimed 'thinker' about the sport, whom McAllister thought had good ideas and who was certainly 'clever' in his training techniques.

But at 24, the Scot was already eyeing another move, and he was canny about his future. He refused pay rises at Leicester as he approached the end of his contract, knowing that a tribunal would base any transfer fee on the level of his wages. He fancied Forest, under Brian Clough, still a major force in the early 1990s, and also a move that would mean no family upheaval. The two clubs agreed a fee only for McAllister to follow his gut instinct and pull out of the move. It was a mature decision reflecting single-mindedness and focus. And brave. Clough was furious.

Leeds United had just been promoted into the First Division in 1990, under Howard Wilkinson, and McAllister knew all about that manager's long-ball reputation. But he also saw a large, talented squad at Elland Road and liked the tone of Wilkinson's pitch – it was a very different style from Clough's – so he moved to West Yorkshire and never regretted it: it was the 'six best years', footballing wise, of his professional life. In 1992, briefly with Eric Cantona in the ranks, Leeds even overcame a 12-point deficit to Manchester United to win the last 92-club Football League title. McAllister was not just a winner but a champion.

There is no doubt that Wilkinson became a very big influence on McAllister's career. Despite Sgt. Wilko's many critics – check out Sunderland fans – the Scot still regards him as an important English moderniser. He was certainly a coach who pointed up crucial lessons that both stretched McAllister's playing career and would also be reinforced later, under Gérard Houllier's regime at Anfield. The main themes here were that quality training was the key to competitive performance, and that it was an athlete's physical and mental preparation and sheer hard work that produces the very best footballers:

> There are generational changes. When I first came into the game there were a lot of 'technicians' and people who never, maybe, got about the park, like they get about the park today. Fitness wasn't in the same planet as it is now. I'm lucky again because I've bridged the generations. Howard Wilkinson, at Leeds, pointed it out for me. He said: 'You're not a bad player, but you could be so much better if you did this and did that.' He opened my eyes to the fitness side and the diet. It gave us an edge; it definitely gave us an edge. He didn't just want players in training to be filling in the hours. People who couldn't meet his demands on the training side were just jettisoned, and he got someone else in. As much as has been said about foreign influences, coaches here, like Wilkinson, were important men. And that's when the penny dropped for me. It's not by chance or coincidence that you watch Zidane and it always looks as if he's got ten yards of space. He has the best touches in training as well. Now that's not by luck. It's because you're the hardest worker. He's continually looking to make space and there is a lot of cleverness in his movement. It's just what you learn through experience: the best players are the hardest workers.

Frustrated by the failure of Leeds to kick on from this title success and later by Scotland's defeat at Euro 96, McAllister then agreed to join the new management team of his old Leeds colleague Gordon Strachan and Ron Atkinson at Coventry City. It seemed an unlikely move, but McAllister was now over 30 and already had one eye on a coaching future. City were also 'throwing a few quid around, making some splashes'. They had big plans with these Scottish winners and 'Big Ron' was now in place. McAllister stayed for four years, which meant a welcome family move back to the Midlands, but Coventry never quite made the top-six assault the board had both wanted and expected for their outlay. It was now time to sell again, a transferred Robbie Keane soon flying off to join Inter Milan. But in his last year at Coventry in this first spell there, the evergreen McAllister still scored 13 goals. Was he really winding down as a top player? Gérard Houllier came calling.

THE LIVERPOOL WAY

'THERE WAS A VIBE COMING FROM LIVERPOOL'

Liverpool was also a club still in transition in 2000, and one trying desperately to qualify for the Champions League, for the first time, under Gérard Houllier. The whisper in the game was that the Anfield outfit would need a calming playing influence to help the new crop of players mature, both on the field and in the training camp – especially if this young Liverpool team qualified for the Champions League. But Gary McAllister still seemed an unlikely choice, especially when Liverpool cracked under pressure and finished the 1999–2000 season with five awful scoreless performances, thus throwing away their top European slot. McAllister certainly thought so too – but was then pleasantly surprised:

> My agent looks after two or three Liverpool players, Gerrard and Carragher among them. So Houllier says to my agent at the end of the season: 'Who have you got I might be interested in?' Now he had known of me because Houllier is very close to the Scottish FA and Craig Brown. And there was a vibe coming from Liverpool that they had got rid of quite a lot of experienced players up there. Familiar names, big names. Houllier didn't think these guys were good for the young players, all the 'Spice Boys' business. They might need experienced players in Europe. Now, they'd missed out on the Champions League by losing to Bradford in the final match. So I'm watching Liverpool losing these two or three final games, thinking my last chance to play for this big club with great support is going. But after that final game they came out and said they thought they were missing out on a bit of experience, not just on the pitch but also in training during the week. I thought there might still be a chance. The season ended and they got me in – and there was no negotiating. I signed right away. I was 36.

There were plenty of things that really excited McAllister about this gloriously unexpected last hurrah at Liverpool. For one thing, he was very aware of the tradition of great recent Scottish players at the club – Dalglish, Hansen, Souness – and he was extremely proud to now be a part of that group. He wanted to maintain and strengthen this Scottish flavour at Liverpool, even in an era when player recruitment had gone global. He was the sole Scot in the Liverpool squad, and he was generally troubled and, frankly, mystified by the decline in young Scottish football talent.

McAllister was also aware of the footballing knowledge of the Anfield crowd, recalling the 9–0 Crystal Palace thrashing, and noting that even as the goals piled up, Liverpool supporters in the stands were still calling and applauding little set plays at throw-ins and in defence – the sorts of things, in fact, that only professionals tended to recognise and respect. But he was also anxious, eager to please, and aware that, to some Liverpool players, his arrival might not have looked like a really great signing:

> As much as the Scots and scousers got on well, and I knew that wouldn't be a problem, but I sensed the negative little vibes when I got up there, y'know: 'What are we doing? We've just missed the Champions League and we sign him!' I know I wasn't the signing they [the players] were looking for, so I knew I had to quickly try to turn people around, because I'd only signed for one year and I didn't have much time. I thought I could show them, physically at least, that I could still run, and so the pre-season was important for me. I tried to show them in pre-season that I still had the legs for this level, because Liverpool was going up another niche from Leeds. Everyone knows that Liverpool are a massive club, but it's not until you go there that you realise the size of it: the European Cups, the fans. It just grabs you when you go up there, it's special.

McAllister began to study Houllier's coaching and preparation methods almost from the beginning. He noticed plenty of similarities between the Frenchman and Wilkinson: for example, their absolute insistence on good timekeeping and respect; the highly structured nature of their coaching sessions; the smart and formal turnout of players for matches or any other club occasions; the kit colour coordination even on different pre-season training days; the emphasis on discipline; and the general school-masterly attention to detail. The positive lesson he took from all of this, for his own later introduction to football management, was about the importance of the erosion of the identity of the individual in the training and playing context: in other words, that the team was everything – a familiar Houllier mantra.

But what really charged McAllister about his Liverpool period, what brought the very best out of him, is precisely what divides top footballers from the rest: he positively welcomed the attention, the pressure, and the intensity of the battle. He accepted, even embraced, the fact that, such is their media coverage, top footballers at top football clubs are simply never allowed to fail. This only adds, he concluded, to their resolve and status. He liked, especially, the togetherness and even the fear that came from the sort of striving to win titles and cups that binds and melds a group of footballers in the white-hot football crucible that was the Liverpool experience in 2001. Like all the great Liverpool players, in short, McAllister was not afraid of winning or of losing, but only of the professional's ultimate crime – of letting down the crowd, and especially his teammates:

> The intensity of it all was always something that I really liked. It was like playing in a major championship for your country, where you're eating and sleeping football. You love your family and your kids before anything, but when you get involved in something that means everything, that's when you don't want to balls it up for your mates. You need that wee bit of fear in there: that you don't want to let anybody down. It's that feeling that players at the top clubs cannot afford to have an off day. If they do, they just get mullered. It's that which drives the top players on. Just the fear of letting people down.
>
> I've been in changing-rooms where there are factions and little groups, especially where players have different languages, but there was none of that allowed at Liverpool. As soon as you got into Melwood, no one was allowed to have their own culture, their own special language.

He would certainly need this sort of intensity and strength. McAllister was sent off in his very first Liverpool start, away to Arsenal, the first sending-off of his entire professional career. Miserable and ashamed, he got a phone call after the game from his wife, which changed his whole mindset. She had been diagnosed that day with breast cancer. Just two matches in, and his dream Anfield move already seemed to count for nothing. Other priorities had now taken over. Houllier, typically, told McAllister to take off as long as he needed – to forget Liverpool. In fact, he missed six games, returning for a 4–0 away drubbing of Derby County. He then figured in another 13 straight League games, eight of which he started. Until the end of the season McAllister was left out of only two League matches, starting 21 League games in all, coming on in a further nine, and scoring five crucial goals, including four in four consecutive winning games in the successful run-in for a Champions League place. The first of these was an extraordinary, never-to-be-forgotten, 44-yard, injury-time free kick to win the derby game at Everton. McAllister feels this was one of his very best Liverpool games – and one of the club's best performances during his brief spell at Anfield. He was already an immortal to the wearers of the Anfield Red. Here was a man who had probably been brought in to improve training, start a few games, and pass on his experience: he was now one of the first names on the Liverpool team sheet. We wanted him in.

How did he manage to maintain this level of fitness, and his appetite for the game, at 37? What was McAllister's secret? It was, partially, the little tricks and tips he had learned at Leeds about looking after himself, of course. He looks about the same body weight today as when I first saw him at Leicester City, incredibly, almost 20 years ago. But coming to Liverpool also inspired him. Don't believe it is all one way, this idea of the old head coming in to organise and fire up the youngsters around him. McAllister was drawing, too, on plenty of the energising ability and excitement around him at Anfield. He was especially lifted by the promise of Steven Gerrard — at least as much as it was occurring the other way around:

> As much as I was brought in to do a specific job, I also get caught up with what's going on, y'know, so you get bouncing off other guys, the young players, who have got a drive which lands at my feet as well. As much as I'm trying to pass things on to them, I'm lifted by them, by the young players. A lot has already been said about Steven Gerrard, I know, but he is a very special player, believe me. When you play with him, he has such a drive, and a surging power. He's really explosive. You see it in training, in the tackle, in anything he does. He has everything as a player. You'll see him come out over the next few years. He is very special.

There were other McAllister Liverpool highlights, of course: a penalty clinically taken to defeat Barcelona in the UEFA Cup; cunning free kicks to down both Coventry and Bradford City (both were relegated); the free kick as a substitute that led to Michael Owen's first goal at Cardiff and so, ultimately, to Liverpool's 2001 FA Cup glory; a man-of-the match performance in a breathtaking night in the UEFA Cup final in Dortmund. (He still claims that Didi Hamann and other Liverpool players had no idea that the golden-goal rule was in operation that night.) Houllier told McAllister immediately after the FA Cup final that, at 37, he would start the UEFA Cup game, his first European final. 'I sometimes sit down,' says McAllister now, 'and I wonder if it ever really happened at all.' We all do, Gary, we all do.

Liverpool offered McAllister an extension on his original one-year deal for 2001–02 — what else could they do? However, his second season didn't quite work out. He still made 14 League starts and figured in 25

League games in total in 2001–02, but his legs had just about gone at this level, and so had his goals. He saw some early Champions League action, but as the season reached its (anti-)climax, McAllister figured less and less in the Liverpool first team. The absence of his unique combination of enthusiasm and running power, his control, intelligence and calming influence, as well as the quality of his passing, his goals and his linking up of defence and attack, were cruelly missed.

On reflection now, he seems the perfect Liverpool midfield player, and he was probably the single key player in the 2001 Liverpool Treble season, and so also a central figure in the making of Gérard Houllier's reputation at the club. This all begs the obvious question: exactly why had it taken us until his 37th year to realise what Gary McAllister could offer us? And what might we have achieved had he been signed earlier, by Roy Evans or even by Houllier himself, in his first season's campaign? Ifs – there are always too many ifs in football.

Towards the end of his second Liverpool season, when he could already see the end coming, McAllister started examining the Liverpool youth set-up and he also began having chats with Houllier about his future plans to move into football management. There was even talk of a coaching job at Anfield, but nothing was firmed up, and when Coventry City approached with a player-manager's post, McAllister took the plunge. He follows a strong recent tradition, of course, of ex-Liverpool players moving into the football hot seat. He has all the credentials, and more, to make a success of it. He also hopes to loan in a few more Liverpool youngsters. I could think of no one better to supervise and nurture them.

His final home match, as a Liverpool substitute against Ipswich Town, produced the sort of ovation, whenever he even stepped off the bench to warm up and when he finally got on the pitch, usually afforded players with ten years or more Liverpool service and a hatful of titles and medals behind them. 'Like a Liverpool legend,' he smiles now. 'I'll never forget the reception I got that day, till the day I die.' He means it. Whenever he goes back to Liverpool McAllister is still mobbed and grabbed for handshakes, not as a celebrity might be, but as a real footballer, a man who only came very late to the Liverpool Way. But also as a man who grasped hungrily at the Houllier challenge, with both feet.

GÉRARD HOULLIER – AND LIFE WITHOUT GARY

With his veteran talisman, McAllister, now away in the managerial toils at Coventry City, life back at Liverpool had become noticeably tougher for a recovered Gérard Houllier. It was Sir Bobby Robson who had first pointed out that reaching the top four was tough enough in the

Premiership, but every single improvement on your position in the top places becomes ever more difficult: almost like winning a mini-league in itself. So it was proving for Houllier, who had taken Liverpool to fourth, third and second position in consecutive seasons, but was now finding it a real challenge to aim for the top spot, faced, as he was, by the continued excellence of Arsenal and Manchester United. He is confronted daily by their presence as obstacles to a possible Liverpool title and by the media obsession with the intense Ferguson/Wenger rivalry, which rather sidelines Houllier.

Houllier resisted all suggestions that his illness had changed his fundamental approach to the job. To talk about more delegation, he suggested, was nonsense: Liverpool work as a team, always. 'I'm not detached,' he said in October 2002. 'It's not a job you can do at a distance.' But now he would need to show all his application and skill. Liverpool were even in a dog fight for one of the four guaranteed Champions League places in 2003, an absolute bare minimum necessity for maintaining continuity and competitiveness in the club's attempt to battle back to a position of ascendancy in the English game. He may not have wanted to admit it, but Houllier and his team were struggling.

Houllier, almost for the first time, was also starting to get a mixed response, at best, from some Liverpool fans and also from the national press in 2002–03. In 2001–02 his illness had quelled any possible public expression of concern or criticism about any perceived weaknesses or inadequacies in his tactics or players, but all bets were now off. There were a few opposing camps already setting up in trenches. One was of the extreme tabloid variety, which fetched up with hysterical accusations that Liverpool were now simply too one dimensional and, worse, just plain 'boring'. Some ex-Liverpool players – denounced by Houllier as disloyal – also chipped in. In these sorts of accounts, Houllier had simply lost the plot, perhaps influenced by his illness. He had done good things in repairing the Liverpool ship, but now he had taken the club as far as it could go under his stewardship. He should step aside, or upstairs, and let another, younger, manager take over. Some Liverpool fans also favoured this position – increasingly, reasonably sensible ones had even been here.

Opposing this critique were friendly journalists from the more pro-Houllier tabloid camp or, more usually, from the slightly more considered perspectives of the broadsheet press. These were people who, after all, knew Houllier and liked and respected him – certainly a lot more than they did some of their own tabloid buddies. They rightly thought the Frenchman to be a positive addition to the English game, a civilised and intelligent man and a man with all the right values, who was now brutally set upon by the ugly, British gutter press. For these guys, the manager had not only saved the Liverpool club from the storm it had been engulfed in since the early 1990s, but he had righted the ship, trimmed its sails and got it sailing in exactly the right direction once more. He stood for long-term stability and good sense, and was a sophisticated marker against the spivs and half-wits who often managed English football clubs. If Houllier's Liverpool occasionally slipped off course, well, that was to be expected, given the stormy passage it had faced. Houllier had not become a bad football manager overnight: he just needed more time to produce the consistent upward trajectory for Liverpool that the fans wanted, and indeed expected.

Somewhere in between these views came the more calculated and thought-through critiques of Liverpool by journalists who were not just looking for a blousy headline to sell a red-top, but who were also increasingly unwilling to offer Houllier the benefit of the doubt in what was becoming a taut and uncomfortable Liverpool season. Perhaps the most sophisticated and also the most searching of these critics was an old Houllier adversary, James Lawton of *The Independent*. He returned to the 'Houllier and Liverpool' issue a number of times during the season, perhaps most tellingly after the barely believable Liverpool defeat at Sunderland, on 15 December 2002. Too often, Lawton argued, a steady supply of the ball – which is a gift for a skilled and crafted football side – is experienced, instead, by the current Liverpool team as a burden. Liverpool, it seems, would prefer the opposition to have the ball and to respond, perhaps by reflex, only to their opponents' failings. So what exactly *is* the current Liverpool philosophy, James Lawton asked. He went on to describe it in *The Independent* in an article that appeared on 16 December 2002:

> It is one of relentless pressure. It is of the early ball, the long throw-in down the line, the willingness to concede possession in the belief that you can win it back in positions of danger. It is a policy which precludes the staple of Liverpool's success in their greatest years, the game-shaping cleverness at the back . . . Now the need for craft is ignored in a way unthinkable at Old Trafford and Highbury . . .
>
> There is also the sense of interchangeable players, who do not have the time and the underpinning to develop belief in their own powers. Jari Litmanen was a player of lovely touch and sophisticated instinct but he rarely got a game . . . Asking Houllier to do nowt, to let a group of players grow organically rather than

by constant, Dr Frankenstein surgery seems to be too tall a requirement of a passionate, hyperactive man . . .

It is not, the Sunderland result stressed over and over again, a matter of personnel. It is how you see the job, and what precisely you bring to it . . . It is not, clearly, a deficiency of talent. Houllier has surrounded himself with gifted players. The question concerns quite what he does with their gifts. His worst critics would say he flattens them out, he tinkers relentlessly. No one is quite so wedded to the value of rotation . . . What is Liverpool's natural terrain, what is their game? They had better have some answers if they ever manage to climb over the brick wall that grew considerably higher on Sunday. (Article copyright of James Lawton and *The Independent*.)

This was a very cold and cruel assessment of the Anfield situation – and Houllier's role in it – but it did seem to strike some important chords, especially with concerned but essentially supportive Liverpool fans. Houllier's 'fiddling' *was* drawing plenty of comment in the Liverpool crowd, and so too was his defensive caution. The rigidity of some of his systems had also featured strongly here, even when the new Liverpool had actually been winning trophies. But back then fans could at least be comforted by victory and by the reasonable expectation that this Liverpool team would eventually be encouraged to mature and grow and to play in what we thought was the true Liverpool Way. Houllier's admirable credo was still that his players needed to 'live for the job, not use the job to live well'. We all agreed with that. But there seemed a danger now that his team might be kept on the leash, perpetually adolescent and confused, that it may not be allowed to detach itself sufficiently from its 'father'. These, believe me, were deeply troubling thoughts. We needed some answers.

*

These are important and difficult issues to confront, especially for fans who feel, as we do, deep down, very emotionally committed to Houllier, for his decency and all his intelligence and heroics, and for his fans' devotion to the Liverpool cause since 1998. I had not interviewed him since November 1999, when he still seemed so enthusiastic and excited by what then lay ahead. He also talked then with such a refreshing intellect, freedom and range – almost with a sort of innocence – that one already feared he might not survive the daily assaults and routine double dealing by the British press. So here I was to talk with him again, back at the new Melwood, with its retractable steel-gated entrance, its sweeping new reception area and multi-million-pound treatment centres, offices, saunas and artificial surfaces and all the rest of what goes into preparing footballers, who earn in a few days what it takes most people in this city a whole year to compile. Patrik Berger comes into the reception area, as I wait, wearing a pair of those naff denims, patched with sand-coloured thread so that some grifter can add a couple of hundred quid to the price. Berger is leaving the club, so he hangs around now like a sixth former with no lessons. It's depressing.

The most striking thing of all about this new Melwood development is Houllier's new office. It is directly up the main stairs and it juts provocatively out, in a glass-and-steel protrusion, to overlook all the playing areas of the training ground. This viewing turret, itself, conveys a clear message, of course: it pretty much shouts that this is where the head honcho hangs out, and that he sees everything that goes on here: every unpressed press-up, every incomplete lap. In the 'soft' area of Houllier's office, where we are going to talk, there is: a tactics board; a wide-screen TV; a large card that reads: 'United we win, divided we lose'; a 'Welcome to Melwood' sign; a huge get-well card, signed by hundreds of people, presumably from when the manager was ill; and a series of shelves carrying multiple framed copies of photographs of recent Liverpool triumphs: Cardiff; Dortmund, with Gary McAllister to the fore; the cover of France Football, *commemorating Michael Owen's Ballon d'Or for 2001; a picture of the players' huddle; and one of the Houllier Kop fan mosaic on the night he returned for the Roma match. Alex Ferguson is very jealous, apparently, that Houllier seems so loved by Liverpool fans. Fergie has never had a crowd mosaic – or a single song sung for him at Old Trafford. I wonder why.*

You can 'read' the open display of these photos in a number of ways, I guess: a collection of uplifting memories; or a comforting reminder of past triumphs, a sort of security blanket. This seems strange. In the past, one day after winning the League title, Ronnie Moran used to cheerfully say: 'Right, that's over, forget it. We all start at zero points again now. Let's win another.' There were no photos of last year's triumphs in Bob Paisley's office or the Anfield boot room; it was all looking ahead to the next challenge. But the pictures here are obviously also carefully designed to reassert the collective – Liverpool players and staff after major finals interlocking arms and facing their supporters. The players' huddle. There are very few individual images here. But there is a copy of the photo voted the best picture of the first ten years of the Premier League. It also sums up much of Liverpool in the League in the 1990s and beyond: Michael Owen, Smicer, Rigobert Song and a few thousand Kopites, all with heads in hands, as Michael has just squeezed wide another chance against the Mancs in the Jamie Carragher 'two own goal' 3–2 home defeat. Why keep that horror image on show?

Houllier is looking dapper, in a blue monogrammed shirt and a striped tie. He looks fitter and healthier than he has done on TV recently, where he has usually been explaining away another painful Liverpool failure. But he doesn't look especially relaxed; in fact he seems a bit agitated, overly conscious that what is required here is a 'performance' of some kind, and that it needs to be carefully monitored and planned because: Anything He Says Might Be Taken Down and Used in Evidence Against Him. The Liverpool press officer tapes the whole thing, which, I guess, is fair enough, given the media snake pit these guys now have to breathe and work in. Sadly, Houllier does seem like a man who has now had too many difficult press conferences and four miserable years of being shafted and misquoted by sections of the British press. It must really piss him off that it all has to be like this. We really don't understand what he has to put up with, and why he sometimes comes over as defensive or evasive. He has certainly lost a little bit of that freewheeling 'Let's talk football' approach from the last time we met. Maybe his illness has tempered his passion, just a little, but I think it is mainly the media trials. It's a shame, but what can you expect? I really don't think it is his fault. I can only assure you that everything you read below is what the great man actually said. Scout's honour.

★

'PLAYERS ARE MACHINES TO WIN'

I begin by asking Houllier about the nature of the modern football manager's job, and also what he had tried to do at Liverpool to transform the club as an organisation. He gives me four things: first, in the immediate term, the search for results; second, work on the lifestyles and ethics of the club and its players; third, the longer-term legacy that a football manager must work for and leave in player development; and, finally, the importance of helping players 'grow' beyond the confines of football. On getting results – something Liverpool had been struggling on in 2002–03, especially at home – he says this:

> I think, first of all, as a manager you need to have a vision, you
> need to know, exactly, where you want to go; that this is the
> target. Then you have to work out the ways to get there. You
> need to be a strategist really, to know the aims and targets. You
> need to know that this will be our purpose; that this is what we
> want to achieve. Nothing is achieved overnight; you have to
> gradually get into it. So, coming back to the role of the
> manager, it is, firstly to generate results. The first mission is to
> get results. Once you get results you get the credibility and
> confidence of your players, the confidence of your staff and the
> board. The board are very good here; this is a special club in
> that respect. You get the fans happy. The results are something

you have to deal with on a weekly basis and you need to get the best results.

This is clearly important, striking the balance between the obvious importance of the next match, but also having a wider vision. Gary McAllister thought that this sort of vision was lacking at Leeds in 1992, when that club had just won the League title but then failed to capitalise. Has Houllier a strategy in case *we* win the League? I hope he has to draw on it soon. On the specifics of the future and of planning for the longer term, we get some familiar Houllier themes:

> Secondly [you must] influence the life of the club. You need to improve the facilities, the philosophy, change the lifestyle of some of the players. That is very important: to influence the professional life of your club. This is why you also need some ethics. I'm pleased to say we have these new facilities, which are very good. We've also influenced the life of the players. That's not perfect yet, because you have to convince people, you don't dictate things to them. Still in that area, you have to make sure that the future of the club is there. The average age of the [Liverpool] team that played last week is 24.8 years. The [opposing] team is 28.9, four years older. When I leave this club I want to make sure that there is still a legacy. I don't want to be known as a manager who spent lots of money and then there is no team. Some players are still early in their development, I would say. When we sign players from Le Havre, who are just 18 or 19, it is because we know they were gems, and when you don't have a lot of money, all you have to do is be clever, to be more creative. Three years ago, when I wanted to buy [Rio] Ferdinand, the price I was quoted was what I was given to rebuild the whole Liverpool team! That is why we bought Hyypiä, Henchoz, and so on. So, you need to prepare for the future. I didn't buy Rivaldo because I thought he was not right for the club. He would have broken the wage scale and also he would have been just a short-notice fix. You need someone who doesn't just come here for the money. He must come here for the challenge. I preferred to find somebody, to develop somebody.

There are a few hard things to pick up on here. No one can doubt the money that has been poured into Melwood recently, which is also an important future investment. These players now have the best, and good facilities attract better players. No debate. There are also a few 'Spice Boy' allusions made by Houllier here to the lifestyles of some Liverpool players in the 1990s, but nothing really to frighten the horses. We all know that players need to be more professional these days. At least Houllier recognises here that persuasion rather than coercion is the key, that players need to learn about a professional's life, again as Gary McAllister did at Leeds, and to such incredible effect. The idea that the club itself has a life, a character, can be traced right back to the eras of Yeats and Brian Hall. Important continuity.

More interesting and a little disturbing is Houllier's very precise focus on the *age* of his own side – and that of the opposition. We have seen this before, but notice here the real precision involved: someone – probably himself – has actually done the calculations, and on the opposition, too, as if this is somehow real, indicative 'science'. Now I would guess that the current average age of the best sides in Europe – Real Madrid, Milan or Juventus, or even Arsenal and Manchester United – is probably around 28 or 29 years. A top football side, a *championship* team, probably has to have exactly that kind of maturity to succeed. (Although Ajax actually seemed to have a younger – and a better – team than even Liverpool in 2003.) But for Houllier this maturity seems to become almost a criticism, the sign of an ageing squad. This is really why he rejects Rivaldo: he's too old and too expensive to join the 'project', and maybe he was only interested in the cash. We want our manager to be planning for the future, of course we do. But with his 'I prefer to develop somebody' approach, will our manager *ever* be happy to boss a mature side like these, especially when most of his real success in the game has come from working with younger players?

He also sends out another important message in his comments above: that this Liverpool now has to shop very cleverly in the global transfer market, and buy for the future at much lower prices. The boys at Le Havre are a good example, though the French club is heading for relegation this season. This shows that, like shopping in the Newmarket yearling sales, buying young football players cheaply is also a risky business. Will they develop? Can they adjust to England? How long will you have to wait? Leeds buying Ferdinand for £15 million was actually not bad business – they sold him for £30 million. Buying young footballers is a similar sort of speculation. Also, can Houllier and his staff really spot young players, like a Bob Paisley could, or even a Dario Gradi? We seem to have rejected plenty recently who eventually went on to make it elsewhere, and the young players brought here have yet to really excite. Time will tell.

THE LIVERPOOL WAY

The third part of the manager's role is developing players. Houllier is not exactly backwards in coming forwards on this point:

> The third thing is you need to help your players and your team to prepare and develop, and to influence that. Not only on the football side, but that is, obviously, 80 per cent of your job. And I can say that Michael Owen, when I came here, was not even 18. At the age of 21 he got the Ballon d'Or [the Golden Ball]; and Murphy is a much better player; Hyypiä, Henchoz, you name them, practically everybody has improved. In fact, when Jamie Redknapp left the club he said: 'I'm very sorry I was so much injured because I feel that, like all the other players, I would have improved my game [at Liverpool] so much as well.' So you need to have your players and the team develop for the better. And be more competitive and improve their game. When we went through a difficult period I was making a point to them that we can celebrate together but we can also suffer together. It was good for the players to know that as well. I'm not the sort of manager who says: 'OK, you're good, you're the best' and then later 'You're bad, you're the worst.' You have to find the balance in man management and, in fact, the players need you when they are going through a difficult period. When Michael was not doing well and not scoring, that's when he needed me. Michael doesn't need me when he's on fire.

Maybe I'm wrong, but I suspect that not too many top football managers would talk publicly in these terms. I don't doubt, for a second, that Gérard has improved all of these players, and that he deserves much credit for it. Michael's work on heading is a case in point, though he seems to have lost faith again in his left foot. But there is also a case for maintaining the public face, the essential deceit, that the game is actually about good players, rather than about the contribution from the back room. The most secure managers usually deflect this kind of talk. It is unusual for a Lippi, or a Wenger, or even a Martin O'Neill to expand like this, for example. Normally, self-deprecation is, properly, the order of the day in these sorts of elite managerial circles. We all know how important Houllier has been on the coaching and technical side here. He has transformed preparation and coaching at Anfield, and we owe him hugely for it. But it is up to the Liverpool players, publicly, to compliment the coaching staff on this sort of input – and the best ones usually do.

Houllier then says something very significant about the importance of the development of players at Liverpool as *men*, as well as footballers. Check this out:

> You also need to have your players improve as men. And I'm pleased to say that some of the players have opened up. You have to be careful: we are not just idols or role models, but we are also men. I like my players to be accessible, reachable: to be nice. Michael Owen is a good example. He is a star on the field and off the field. I want the players to be nice, to be good people, to have respect for each other, but also respect for the girls in the canteen, or the kit manager. I think if you are a nice man, you are a nice player. When you are not nice – well, it's a team thing. When you are nice, people know that, and you have to get the players to work with each other. When they are not nice, they won't work together in the same way. It's as simple as that. It's a team thing. Leadership is about convincing people to work together with *you*, not *for* you. A club is about love, care and forgiveness sometimes. If you don't have those values as well, you lose some kind of enjoyment. The best of people, you get it when they enjoy themselves, when they think they are cared for, and people like them, and so on.

The importance of players 'opening up' is an interesting idea, a sign of growing maturity, perhaps, and something rather alien to the English players. When Houllier says 'accessible' here, I think he really means polite and professional. Owen is hardly accessible. Clearly, the manager would like all of his players to adopt Michael's rather blandly professional 'boy next door' off-field demeanour. I'm not sure I agree. But the idea of young players showing respect to the junior staff and to other people is a good one. It rather begs the 'Lee Bowyer question', of course. ('I was signing a player who had been cleared by the justice, by the way,' says Houllier later. Bowyer just showed a lack of respect to the club, and so the manager killed the deal.) So, too, does his emphasis here on 'nice' men making 'nice' players. This may not have gone down too well in earlier Liverpool teams, but what I think he really means here is that more rounded and secure men make better players and better contributors to the team. I think this is right, though the team also sometimes looks as if it is playing in a coaching straightjacket – individualism is strangled. He also says, intriguingly:

> Players are machines to win: they are built to win. They are fighters, competitors. You need to make sure that you take that

> type of player – say Steven Gerrard's frustration – I want more of
> that, that's good he has this guts about him. But this winning thing
> must not destroy a quality which is very good about men, which
> is that we need to share. We need to contribute to do something.
> A fighter is not a fighter on his own in football. He's not a tennis
> player; he's a fighter in a team. And you will get more out of your
> teammates and out of the team if you are nice to the teammates.
> And you'll get more out of life if you're nice to people.

Broadly, speaking, I think I buy this approach, and I believe in this part of the Houllier project. I also approve of his focus on emotions – that a football club is also about caring, love and forgiveness, sometimes. Does he also mean Steven Gerrard here? Or maybe Dioufy, for his Celtic spitting episode? This is heavy, almost revolutionary, stuff for English football. I wonder if he ever uses it directly with the players. And will it help win us trophies? But, also, is the critical balance between the team and the individual exactly right in this analysis? Can too much emphasis on the collective – always on the team – also suffocate innovation? And has that not been part of our recent problem? Interesting.

'IF YOU'RE STRONG, THEY ARE STRONG'

Isn't it difficult, I ask next, always planning for the future but also having to satisfy the clamour for success now? He's ready for this one, meets it head on with a top-spin forehand:

> We are a victim of our own success here. When you first came to
> see me we had won nothing. In three years we played twice in the
> Champions League, won the UEFA Cup, and we won, altogether,
> six trophies. So in a short period we had massive achievement.
> Some players have improved, some unfortunately had to leave
> because they were too old or were not good enough. But that's
> part of the job. Don't forget we have moved from 54 to 80 points
> in our League performance. For the last four years we have been
> competing for a Champions League place. That's what I call
> consistency. I would like now for the next four years to be
> competing for the top two. That would be a step up.

So this is the new Liverpool agenda: we have been aiming at the top four, now we are going for the top two. Why not just the top? We, the fans, were spoiled in 2001 and probably expected too much, too soon, afterwards. Houllier says, with a smile, that even the stock market doesn't always rise. We are experiencing a blip. OK, but we won't reach 80 points this season. I ask him about the loss of McAllister in all this, and generally about the problem of finding good, experienced leaders. Does Houllier agree that the current Liverpool side misses a player of his quality and type? He does – but only up to a point. Other players now have to step up:

> McAllister is McAllister; he's a gem. It is hard to find a player like that. And you also want somebody who wants a challenge. Macca wanted to come here. So you're right, we miss not only his experience, but also his reassuring calm and his model – his attitude in training, everything. We haven't lost that in training, but on the field and off the field he was very good. We won five trophies with him; he was man of the match in the European final. He was a brain. But now I think we must be careful because if you say you can't play if you don't have this sort of player then you compromise yourself. You basically say we can't play. I personally think that everybody's got to become a leader in the team. Everybody has to bring some response to that. Now we have players who have played over 50 European games, so that becomes useful experience. Zola has produced a very beneficial experience for Chelsea. It helped them go through difficult patches. So what Zola did for them, Gary McAllister did two years ago for us. That's why Alex [Ferguson] is very, very reluctant to let Roy Keane go, and Arsène [Wenger] was the same with [Tony] Adams. Experience is important.

Ah, Zola! What would *he* do for this Liverpool? We talk a little now about players who have left the club. Houllier had warned Sander Westerveld 'in front of a witness' in the summer of 2001 that he wanted to sign a 'new' goalkeeper, who was a better player: 'The name of the goalkeeper I want to sign is – Sander Westerveld.' In other words, Sander had to front up, improve his game, or move out. The improvement never happened. Robbie Fowler's case was different. Robbie didn't want to stay, he was frustrated to be on the bench, and his lifestyle was still not doing him any favours. 'Robbie was the most gifted striker I've ever worked with, maybe alongside Trezeguet,' says Houllier. But it wasn't enough to save him.

What about Houllier's illness? I had read that he had ignored some symptoms because he wanted to appear 'strong' for the players. What did he mean by this? And what decided him to come back, ahead of time, for the Roma game? He has strong views here, and sees himself very much as the figurehead in the club. Maybe he needs to spread the load, give others a bigger role – but that seems unlikely, and not what he would want. He's also rather proud – and why not – at how quickly he was able to return to his job:

> Leadership is transferable. If you're strong, they are strong. If you're weak, they're weak. If you're nervous, they're nervous. If you're tired, they will be tired. You've got to be sharp. It takes a month for every hour of an operation before you can return. My operation took 11-and-a-half hours. I came back after only five months. Maybe I came back too early, for the Roma match. Only Phil [Thompson] knew about it. I said if I could make 1 per cent difference I could come back. It was a very emotional team talk, because it was my first game back. It was difficult not to be *too* emotional. In fairness, I don't think the players listened to the team talk! I just said to them that I wanted to be there because 'I know you are going to be special tonight. I don't want to miss that.' Maybe for the first part of this season I was not quite right. Now I'm all right. I think in this game you can't delegate too much. You've got to be sharp all the time, live with pressure, live with hard work, a lot of things to do. You need to be sharp in your mind and body, everything. But maybe, because of my illness, I'm able to give more time with people now.

Was Houllier surprised by anything he had come across in England since we last spoke and since his illness? It turns out that he has recently experienced both the lows and highs of being under the intense media spotlight. In England, the 'outside world' frequently intrudes into coverage of sport, usually through the special prism of the tabloids. This must be tough to deal with. So there is plenty of pressure, of course, especially from the press, but also strong support at the dark moments, crucially from the highest levels inside the club. Houllier's comments about the Liverpool board are interesting here. The directors have resolutely refused to criticise him, scoffing at the anxiety among the fans and at the panic allegedly generated by the press about Liverpool's form. Instead, they are in it with Houllier for the long term – well, at least for now. He seems to see this sort of situation, essentially, as a kind of loyalty test: a moment for finding out who your friends really are. I suspect Gérard is very big on loyalty. So had he found the pressure alarming, perhaps, especially this season?

No, you always have a lot of pressure. You have more pressure here because when you are at a big club, losing is always a crisis, and when you're Liverpool and you raise the expectation of the fans that increases the pressure. You get pressure from the fans, pressure from the press, and that affects the team when we were going through a difficult period. Then you can count on your friends. The pressure comes from results, and from the financial side. And it's not always about football: it's stories, always stories. Like: 'Owen's former girlfriend and blah, blah, blah . . . that sort of thing, all the time. You know it's going to affect some of your players, so you have to be mentally strong. This season has been interesting in terms of the fact you learn more about people from difficult periods. When we had ten games without a win, never, *never* at any kind of board meeting was something mentioned against the players. When we were not doing well, a member of the board said: 'Don't worry Gérard, do what you have to do. We trust you. It will take time.' When I went out of the Board meeting, I knew we would be successful.

He sees only loyalty from the Liverpool fans, too. He probably cannot begin to imagine the debates that have been going on in pubs and clubs this season, including among those committed diehards. Discussion is incessant about how the team is playing, about the run of poor results, and about Houllier's basic football philosophy. He remembers the Villa League Cup match – the ticket debacle, when Reds fans had to queue for hours – and he still marvels at the fortitude and the devotion of the Liverpool supporters that night:

This is a special club. When we played at Aston Villa in the League Cup, a cold night, very cold night, the fans had to wait practically two hours outside. Can you imagine the fans, one week before Christmas, travelling from Liverpool to be there [in Birmingham] waiting in the cold and supporting and chanting, backing the team? It was a difficult period for us. They pushed us through. I said to the boys: 'We need to win, just for them.'

I gently remind Gérard at this point that I don't have to *imagine* the Liverpool fans at this game: I was there, queuing, emoting and screaming with the best of them. But I also tell him that one of the reasons for the passion and travelling commitment was precisely because of the way the team *played* that night: its attacking verve and determination. Its 'never give up' attitude. And how little we have seen of that stuff from his Liverpool this season. Now we are moving on to the difficult part: I tell him I want to try to understand why he and so many fans seem so at odds on this. I tell him I want to be able to write about this clearly, deal with the issue directly. Liverpool do not always play as they did that night at Villa. This was an exceptional performance. He knows this is coming. He has his materials ready and a twinkle in his eye. He thinks he has knowledge, information, to surprise me:

> Do you know that apart from Manchester United, we are the team with the most shots at goal this season? And people think we are not attacking! We attack, probably too much at times.

This is his opening shot. It's impressive, but familiar. I tell him that we know a little about his use of statistics to 'prove' that Liverpool are actually an attacking machine. But statistics are not always great guides, I say, to the processes, to the chemistry of a match or a season. He twinkles again. These, he points out, are not actually statistics at all:

> These are not statistics. These are *figures*. I can tell you how many goals we have scored this season and how many we have conceded. I can tell you how many goals we have conceded inside the box and outside the box: that's figures, that's facts. Its not stats. Statistics is about trends. I'm talking about facts about the team. When I said that we had so many shots, it's because I *know* we had so many shots. When I know we had so much possession, this is fact. It is not just that we are eager to know that. It's just sometimes you have to check your impressions to make sure you have the facts correct. A couple of times people were saying that so-and-so was not having a good game. I was watching the game and said that was not my impression. So I watched the game again and I could see that I was right. Impressions sometimes can be very subjective, very partial. As the manager, you have to step back and have a different look. But the figures are not guiding my decisions. My decisions are guided by the atmosphere, the roles, the impact, and the influence of players.

Forget the semantics here. Houllier makes it clear that, for him, at least, it is not loyal Liverpool fans who have been complaining about the club's performances. Instead, it is some people working in the press who have developed the idea that Liverpool should just 'attack and attack and

attack'. This sounds like some serious – perhaps even necessary – denial.
And there is more to come. Listen up, you could learn something, *gratis*:

> There are three ways of scoring goals: one is build-up attack,
> which is most of the cases. When you play any team, when they
> lose the ball they all get behind the ball right away. Then you are
> confronted with a situation where you have 10 or 11 men behind
> the ball and you've got to be creative. This is probably where
> McAllister was missed. But, funnily enough 45 per cent of our
> goals were scored from these build-up attacks. Then you have
> breaks, counter-attacks, which are more effective, but it happens
> not so often because teams work hard and get back. We scored 25
> per cent from these. Then you have set plays, where teams score
> 25–30 per cent. What you want to improve is your team to play
> better football in build-up attack, with more safety. And that takes
> time. And I think we have improved in that. It doesn't show in all
> games. The consistency of keeping the ball will come. We had
> some very good spells in 80 per cent of our games. Good
> movement, good passing, and so on. Sometimes you need the
> resilience to dig in and support the difficult moments of the
> game. We were not able to do that this year. We conceded too
> many goals. Sometime it opens up and you can play. But we didn't
> always have the quality of the finish.

So now you can call these goal types from the comfort of the Kop,
count them in yourself. But Houllier is right, of course: having these
sorts of data is fine, as long as they are your servant rather that your
master. But we have really wondered at times this season about how he
uses the percentages. Does he truly shape his approach using all this
stuff? It sometimes feels that way, despite his denials. Now he is really
animated, running through the home games we should have won by
miles – 'Crystal Palace should have been 6–0 at half-time!' – and the
many, many chances we have missed. Missed chances are, for Houllier,
the single main reason why the season started going bad for Liverpool.
That and the fact that key players in the spine of the team have suffered
individual losses of form at critical moments. He is willing to concede,
nevertheless, that we will probably need some 'adjustments' for next
season. I ask him why he thinks people talk so much about Liverpool's
style of play. He begins to soften up a little – but don't talk to Houllier
about width, OK?

Regarding the style of play, yes, we do need a creative player, because our best performances were when we had someone who could provide a link between the midfield and attack. Don't go like those people who talk about width. You have width when you go with wingers. But there are only two or three natural wingers in the world! Sorry, but we don't have wingers. We have players in midfield who can work inside out. Listen, away from home we are third behind Manchester and Arsenal. At home it's not so good. The thing is, we need more creativity around the box. It is no good us having someone swinging in crosses all the time, because Michael is not someone who needs crosses. You have to play different football with Michael. Anyway, you don't see Arsenal scoring a lot of goals with headers. Let the team develop. Let the team go. We have got a young team, and we are getting some experience now in Europe. We need to improve, but we've improved in our ball possession and ball construction; we have improved in creating chances. We still need to improve on how to break down a defence that sits back.

I'm not sure about all these 'improvements' he mentions, but the figures probably tell that to the coaches anyway. This also seems like a genuine concession he is making here: the need for a more creative Liverpool player in midfield. So we will await the next Liverpool signing in huge anticipation. Is he happy with what the Liverpool full-backs offer wide? And what of this season's Liverpool new boys so far? What is the manager's assessment? El Hadji Diouf, for Houllier, has 'great skill' and he will be an 'outstanding player' at the club. He has also suffered from playing in the African championships and the World Cup finals within a six-month period, so there is lots more still to come from him. Salif Diao will add 'strength' to the Liverpool midfield. Bruno Cheyrou 'got injured at the wrong moment' and he had some difficulty when he first came into the English game (I'll say). But he has good skill and a 'great eye for the pass'. Houllier still backs him. On balance, I wouldn't.

The Liverpool manager denies that his team played overdefensively at Boro and claims that we had 'bad luck' in the Champions League (what, against Valencia?). All in all, he says, it has been a season of 'negatives and positives'. I guess that's about right, but there have been too many negatives. Houllier still thinks we have had some 'massive achievements' in his short time at Liverpool, and that's right too. Perhaps with a new McAllister-type midfielder we can pick up again, and have a serious tilt at the title? We need change, and maybe the manager needs to accept, a little more, that he may have been just a little part of the problem this season. But he is unlikely to concede that to me – or to all of you. We also need to stick by the Frenchman, and all of his facts and figures. He is still our future. But our chances of rapid progress depend, in part, on this season's finale.

CHAPTER 10

Eight Cup Finals

23 MARCH 2003: LIVERPOOL 3, LEEDS UNITED 1

Talk of football financial woes! Leeds United are in town, 2003's major, gold-plated football basket case – that is, if you are not counting Leicester City, Sunderland, Derby County or Ipswich Town, of course. The once-lauded – and suddenly loathed – Peter Risdale has now ditched El Tel, who was admittedly doing a risible managerial job in difficult circumstances, and Peter Reid has stepped in as Leeds boss in order to give the reluctant millionaires up front – Cob-on Kewell, and Fat-boy Viduka – just a little more fire in their bellies. He says, does the old Everton powerhouse, that some of the Yorkshire club's internationals have been 'feeling sorry for themselves'.

But not Reidy, of course. Not a bit of it. In fact, his is a typical football tale for the times, a stunning reward for lamentable failure. Reid – a former Kopite – had completely lost it at Sunderland. He had to go, but he left with pockets plied with the green stuff. This *is* football, after all. And since being sacked out of the north-east, Reid has been near unwatchable as a TV pundit recruited, no doubt, by his Merseyside drinking partners Stubbs, Hansen and Lawrenson. And now Reid is lately cast as a short-term saviour for Leeds, set to earn a reported £500,000 bonus, just for keeping these lazy fakers up. This is a job that you or I could probably do, by the way, while simultaneously solving world poverty and whistling 'I'm a Yankee-Doodle-Dandy'. Just two years ago pretty much this same Leeds team were semi-finalists in the Champions

League. They do need a shaking, but at least lucky-boy Reid ends up woeful and penniless here – and thoroughly deserved.

Listen to this: today Liverpool fields the same team in a Premiership match for the first time in 88 starts. *Eighty-eight!* This says either that we just *never* play well, or that our manager likes to tinker endlessly with all the toys in his £100 million playpen. Diouf is spritely here, though his direct Leeds opponent, the Real Madrid man Raul Bravo, is to left-sided defending what Bruno Cheyrou is to *Fight Club*. The Spaniard disappears at half-time. I would be surprised if English football sees him again.

Dioufy and Michael carve out the first goal for the Golden One after 15 Liverpool-dominated minutes in front of the Kop. Michael prods in a pull-back from the right with his *left* foot, if I'm not mistaken. The second Reds goal, after 20 minutes, is a joke effort, but one brilliantly taken by Danny Murphy. The Leeds defenders stop playing on the Liverpool left, expecting Riise to be awarded a foul. But by forgetting the whistler in the black – a juvenile's error this – they simply allow Murphy all the time and space he needs for a curling right-footed strike around defenders from the left corner of the box. Robinson sees it all the way, but is helpless: so, it seems, is this awful Leeds team.

Now this really should be a rout, but Liverpool last scored more than two goals at home way back in September – and Emile has his Row-Z boots on again today, thrashing reasonable chances high into the stands. Also, Houllier's approach to winning football matches is a little like the French sports magazine *L'Equipe's* assessment of Lance Armstrong addressing the Tour de France: 'Everything is calculated. Not an ounce of energy is wasted. Every stage is plotted, carefully planned. No risks. You do enough to secure victory, no more.' But, unlike the bike master, we are seldom in control, and we have precious little of Armstrong's famed iron will. So when the portly Viduka picks up a rebound off Jerzy from a Wilcox cross right on half-time and finishes sweetly at the Anfield Road end, no one here is that surprised. Or that upset, actually. This game was drifting away to a big nothing.

Emile blasts clear openings high and wide after the restart, a man for ever searching for forward partners in the crowd, before Michael brilliantly manoeuvres a dipping cross from the right for Steven Gerrard to side-foot volley home at the far post to put this no-contest finally to bed. Heskey should watch this technique: he could never match it. Nevertheless, it is only Stevie's sixth goal in 48 games, a poor return in a difficult season, and one of the main reasons for our generally inconsistent form. We will need more, much more, of his special kind of energy and decisiveness for the bigger trials to come. On this squalid form, meanwhile, the Merseyside monkey-man Reid will actually have to earn some of his half-a-million give-away smackers. If he fails, Leeds could disappear.

EMILE HESKEY: MYSTERY MAN-CHILD

Of all the many anguished Liverpool conundrums this year, of all the hair-tearing, teeth-grinding, night-howling mysteries and inadequacies of this already punishing season, Emile Ivanhoe Heskey is but the most frustrating, the most disturbing manifestation. Five Premiership goals in 24 games might be acceptable at a top club from a defensive midfielder or even a dangerous centre-half in the Sami Hyypiä mould, but not from a central striker. Not an international, £11 million striker. When Emile joined Liverpool in 2000 he already had plenty of Kop doubters. His touch was poor and the ball was often pumped forward early to the big man – far too early. When Gary McAllister finally lost his legs we also saw a lot more of this aimless, dull stuff than we had ever wanted, or expected, to witness. But Emile still won over most of the objectors with his work ethic, his pace and also his willingness to shoot. And, of course, with his goals.

In his second season, Emile seemed to miss the fatherly Houllier more than most, and his goals and confidence dried up well before the manager's return sparked a few monster performances. More recently, Houllier has parked him, too often, deep on the left side, where this essentially gentle man can too easily hide. Deep down, Heskey knows this. He says, under shy eyes: 'The manager wants me to play in other positions and playing on the left is hard work. I don't know the position and sometimes I get out of position.' He's right. Playing here, Emile's major contribution to Liverpool is actually *defending* in the air from opposing free kicks and corners. This alone seemed to earn him his place in GH's increasingly zany football world, as the manager airily waved away suggestions that he might now turn, instead, to Barca's Rivaldo ('too old') or Real's Savio ('too expensive').

Now he is finally back up front, Heskey's goal potential still seems largely a promise rather than a threat, and his movement in and around the box is actually worse than ever. He *never* anticipates. Houllier must be losing faith in the big man, but he hides it well. In fact, he now tries to bluff a decent closing run out of Emile by placing him in the side for each of the last seven games, a dangerous – possibly reckless – tactic. 'He's a sleeping giant. I'm backing Emile 100 per cent and he knows that,' says the manager rather too forcefully. 'We still have seven games to play and he will play in all seven. His teammates know the work he does; he does a fantastic job for the team. I would admit he had a difficult period after the World Cup, but since the New Year he has done very well.' He needs to spark because nothing is sure at Liverpool for Emile Heskey anymore. Except, it seems, these next seven games.

5 APRIL 2003: MANCHESTER UNITED 4, LIVERPOOL 0

> 'We are the most loved club – and the most hated.'
>
> Gary Neville

The new global game. At Anfield, these days, we have an international fan following: our incomprehensible Scandinavian fanatics, drawn mainly from small, blank towns in Denmark and Norway; the Reds' considerable Irish contingent, of course, right off the ferries and into taxis to Anfield; increasing numbers of Japanese faces, now staring out from the Centenary and from the gloom of the old Main Stand; and the Kop-based green, red-and-black Mönchengladbach contingent, with their 'Ooompa' German songs, beer bellies, pony-tails and daft sleeveless denim jackets. But it is at Old Trafford that you get the real smell (stench?), these days, of a truly global English football club and, it has to be said, the vision of a modern stadium to match. In a few weeks' time the Champions League final will be hosted here, and it will not feel out of place. God help us if United are actually involved. But this stage, with its huge arching white-crane structures, visible for miles, and clean sight lines, now points the way. It is inevitable, I'm afraid, that we must follow or else crumple in United's financial wake.

Increasingly, this ground feels like it could be almost anywhere in Europe, the surrounding steel and glass landscapes and early morning 'home' supporter accents, cameras and dress sense offering few clues on whether we are in the post-industrial north-west of England or in some other nameless and placeless suburban location across the great continental divide. Until, that is, you catch the early morning local chip munchers and flat-vowelled, bellied beer guzzlers outside the nearby Lou Macari fish, pie and lard factory. Welcome to English football – with a continental twist. And it is partly this thinning-out of the local diehards on both sides, the dissolving of some of the heavier local tribalisms of the recent past, that at least allows us to stand, unmolested, on the upper apron behind the scoreboard end this morning, exchanging accented tales of grizzly past visits, and our complaints (mainly from Steve Kelly of *Through the Wind and Rain*) about how Houllier now 'infantalises' his Liverpool players. *What?*

OK, United's fanzine *Big Issue* carries a big piece today about the local hooligan firm and its 'grown-up' relationship with local police football intelligence men, confirming that the United boys are still seen here as cultural heroes and have not yet left these parts. But from where we are you are also more likely to see idiotic United fans in fancy dress, and smartly dressed parents leading muffled-up kids and making their way to the merchandise outlets and, perhaps, even to seats in the home stands. So, the future is also already here. Just get used to it.

Not that *all* the exchanges here are as docile and polite as this. Who could stomach that? After all, this game is vital to both sides. It's important to United because they have clawed back Arsenal's lead at the top, and have lost twice to Liverpool at home in our past two leagues visits, and also recently choked at Cardiff. It matters to Liverpool because of the Dudek humiliation against United at Anfield earlier this season and the fact that big-time European football next season is now on the line. And just to stoke things up, just a touch more, the arch United fan pranksters even stage a ghoulish and unscheduled pre-match performance today. Posing as a joke United charity team, these boys manage to get on the Old Trafford pitch before kick-off and charge up to the scoreboard goal to re-enact 'that' Dudek goal, before parading triumphantly in front of enraged Liverpool fans. For the visitors, this atrocity reads like part of their welcome – part of the United official pre-match entertainment. So, fair-do's to these skilled United urchins: this is a gold-plated winner, a top giggle.

And while the rest of the United fans positively wet themselves with glee at this humiliation of their guests – 'Screw the usual pre-match crap from now on,' you can hear them thinking, 'bring on more of the goon show.' Liverpool Reds around me go ape-shit now, fairly frothing with inter-city hatred and bile. They just don't get the joke, and soon the Munich abuse is on full throttle. It's out of control. Fellahs behind me have totally lost it, are glazed over with rage at this gratuitous insult, while United's (mainly black) stewards look on, smiling. So when it eventually kicks off, this affair has already reached boiling point inside the Liverpool end. Now we really want to *cane* United, stick it right up 'em. We want to hurt them, damage them: we want them to pay. But it isn't going to happen, not today: not with the injured Owen out of the Liverpool team and not with Sami Hyypiä's current poor vein of form. It isn't even going to begin to happen.

Big Sami has had a couple of top seasons at Liverpool, an inspired buy, possibly Houllier's best. But the whisper inside the club now is that he has been coasting this season, believing his own press. Maybe he has also been missing the defensive glue and the covering pace offered by Henchoz. Traore has been an inconsistent replacement in comparison, a young man born to go to ground in all circumstances. But where is the leadership, the passion, the defensive consistency that Sami *had* been providing? Flat-track bully Van Nistelrooy has already been through this Liverpool back-line, but, on just four minutes, he's through again, this time on to a Scholes pass poked through Traore's legs. Sami is grasping and sliding at the diving Dutchman, defeated and on the wrong side. Van Nistelrooy crumples – OK, you're not shocked, but it probably *is* a penalty. It is referee Mike Riley's fifth award for United this season, out of a grand total of six he's given. Are we at all suspicious? Rubber-kneed Ruud and the fearsome Fergie clearly talk Riley's language.

Chances are that we'll be an early goal down, which will be a blow. We can just about live with this, a bad start, but not an irretrievable one. But Riley, urged on by Gary Neville and by howling from the cheap seats, now sends off Hyypiä, which is a misjudgement, the action of a man placed on a big stage and offered ridiculous guidance and powers. Four minutes into a vital collision that 67,000 have travelled distance and stumped up more than £1 million to watch, and with TV millions around the world missing bed and family for this battle, and this official has effectively ended the contest, has killed the entire event cold. After barely 240 seconds. We, the customers, should be able to claim back the entire cost, be allowed to leave now, because this is not what any of us agreed to buy. Mind you, Houllier also helps administer the fatal dosage because, after Van Nistelrooy calmly scores from the spot, Liverpool make their inevitable defensive change.

Milan Baros has been bursting for another first-team try, and is in today for Michael, a big chance in a big game. But now he's avoiding the bench, because he can see Biscan preparing to come on to replace Sami. He knows that those fêted Liverpool goal machines, Heskey and Diouf, will not be sacrificed, so it is he who must take the long walk. It is not a popular decision in the Liverpool end: 'Fucking strangle yerself with that scarf, Houllier, will yer!' This move seems cowardly, and also makes no rational sense. We have to score, after all, and now we have no one on the field to offer even a distant hope. Gérard's default position is always defence, we all know that, but through this substitution we have opted for a dishonourable and certain suicide, rather than the small possibility of escape – albeit from a potentially violent, brutal death.

All this suits United, suits them perfectly. One up against a feared and potent rival, who are now reduced to a threatless ten men, and with Real Madrid to face next week, they don't especially want to go to work right now. They'll happily settle for this scoreline, see off the next hour and 20 minutes playing keep-the-ball if necessary. Steven Gerrard is our only real hope, his energy and his professional and personal Manc-hatred still clear for all to see. But with a punchless and undermanned attack, and a hapless central Liverpool defensive pairing of Traore and Biscan, more home goals simply have to come. And after 65 minutes of boring inequality, Igor clatters into Scholes just inside the Liverpool box, right in front of us. It looks clumsy, ill-timed, rather than intentional or reckless. Mostly, it is unnecessary. Van Nistelrooy scores again. Minutes later, Giggs gets across a sleeping Carragher at the far post and also scores his first league goal in two years, from a Beckham cross, the England man's single contribution to the day's events. So now it's a mauling, an embarrassment. Now all you can do is pray for the final whistle, or else apply the end for yourself.

United get a fourth goal, completing their biggest win over Liverpool for 50 years (that '50 years' label is becoming a bit of a feature of this Liverpool season). I honestly can't tell you how it went in, or even who scored. All right, I'm lying now – it was that horrible clinician, Solskjaer. But I still haven't seen it on TV, and I was nowhere near the ground, or its ugly sounds, when it went in. I was already driving, wondering whether there was still time to make that afternoon's Grand National, a chance to wash this morning's events away. Well, what do you want, blood? Do you think it adds to the story, or makes any clearer the issues we still have to address, to watch United beat us up, to the very last bell? Do you really want me to stand there, listening to our frustrated, angry fans disgrace themselves by singing the terrible 'Munich' song? And do you think it is somehow noble to let the home cheers – and jeers – crash around your shoulders, and to walk outside among the manic home grins, just so you can applaud off the 10 Red men who at least stood firm for an hour – and then folded? Do you think it is easy to stand among such visiting disappointment, such rank hopelessness, for fully 86 dreadful minutes, while you are really just waiting every second for the whole thing to be over? There is no honour in hoping for a 1–0 defeat, so we have to take a 4–0 beating if it comes along. I accept that. But I don't have to watch it all, not every last, bitter minute. You can't make me.

NO GROUND, GO DOWN?

After the disgrace at United, Liverpool now need a willing victim at home, someone to lay down and offer up three easy points. Step up Fulham FC, a team without hope or direction, and **Liverpool 2, Fulham 0** could have been many more but for a heroic display from goalkeeper Taylor and a stream of misses from a returning Michael. Emile Heskey even scores in the first half – but does little else, this time playing wide on the right to allow Baros the forward's run he was denied at Old Trafford. On the hour Owen is put through by Smicer (remember him?) and finally beats the Fulham keeper low to his left to seal this result. The game then drifts away. Liverpool are glad for the points; Fulham seem happy to escape a drubbing. Relegation looks a real prospect for a club with (on this feeble showing) no guts, huge debts, no ground – and no manager.

19 APRIL 2003: EVERTON 1, LIVERPOOL 2

At the FA Cup final (1966) presentation of the teams (as told to Bill Shankly):
Princess Margaret: 'Mr Labone, where is Everton?'
Brian Labone: 'In Liverpool, ma'am.'
Princess Margaret: 'Of course, we had your first team here last year.'

'I was only a kid the last time Liverpool won the League. In fact, I think I was still an Everton fan.'

Michael Owen

Everton have been eyeing this April date, waiting for this local bragging-rights contest, for some time. The Merseyside papers have been full this week of barely contained Bluenose confidence, built around the success of the cold-eyed Moyes, the emergence of the urchin genius Rooney, Liverpool's alarming new vulnerability, and the fact that Everton are suddenly striving for Champions League glory more strongly than their famous neighbours. An Everton win today will, almost certainly, kill off any Anfield Champions League hopes and offer Everton the prospect of the European big time for the first time in more than 30 years. Their fans might even forget the 'lost' European years of the 1980s, but somehow I doubt it. In fact, I don't believe it for one second. So, you could say that this match is important, is *anticipated*, in these parts. And you would be right.

This anticipation explains – if not excuses – the daubing this week, by Liverpudlians, of Dixie Dean's statue and the retaliatory defacing, by Evertonians, of the Hillsborough memorial. Our view, for what it's worth, is that a bit of ritual criminal damage to the icons or properties of a hated local rival before a big fixture like this one is pretty sad, but probably to be expected these days. I suspect most Blues probably feel the same. But the Hillsborough memorial is a little more than just a football property. So, here is a message to the Hillsborough damage crew: next time, if you really have to, go for a Liverpool football target. But don't defile the memory of the dead: just show a little respect, for God's sake.

Those Evertonians involved know just how much this particular blasphemy really offends us: it offers maximum emotional damage – and shock – and, cynically, that's why the Memorial is targeted. The collective Park End chanting of 'Murderers' at Liverpool fans today also ratchets the increasingly poisonous Merseyside derby rivalry up another couple of notches. The *Football Echo* argues we now need a UN-style summit meeting between the two clubs to lance the growing boil of enmity and hatred in the city and that, 'It is no longer safe to attend if you're a visiting fan', which is just rubbish. In fact, this affair still stops way short of the real ugliness of, say, Wednesday v. United in Sheffield, or the violent envy of United v. City in Manchester, or even the territorial rights of the big city Metropolitan rivalry of Arsenal v. Spurs in north London. Reds and Blues in Liverpool will still walk to the match together this afternoon, even if tonight, in town, blood will definitely be spilt over this result. And it *is* getting worse.

David Moyes deserves praise for his stubborn protection of the mute Rooney and his overall dedication to the Everton cause this season. Telling the little Croxteth porker to cut out eating anything after 7 p.m. and colour-coding a bemusing performance chart in his office to map the playing profile of his staff may seem like little more than anal obsession. But the efforts of any football boss willing openly to criticise referee Jeff Winter suggest an honesty and a steely one-eyed glint most fans can easily identify with. No wonder they like him at Goodison. In an era of continental cool, Moyes has more than a touch of the fiery Ferguson temper, allied to the Manchester mad one's utter determination to win. So this new challenge from Everton will not go away – as long, of course, as Moyes stays, and the Blue end of town continues to remains solvent.

Lacking both Hyypiä and Henchoz today, and faced with the physical challenge Everton always provide – 'the fittest in the Premiership' according to Bobby Robson – Liverpool also have to counter Rooney's ability and inventiveness, which means that standing up in the physical contest, and then delivering quality, will distinguish between the clubs today. And we have just enough, even with Heskey replacing the inconsistent Diouf in midfield, and Igor Biscan coming in for the suspended Hyypiä. Strangely, Biscan's early injury and substitution seems to help the Red cause, because the experienced and committed Carragher then moves to centre-back with Traore and Diao comes on to play at right-back – and does so with a calm assurance and a certainty we have seen far too little of in his midfield play. The truth is that, despite Moyes' claims that Everton's 'flair' players simply did not perform today, this Everton have plenty of grunt but still too little big-match experience and guile to really hurt us. More than this, Murphy, Gerrard and Owen, especially, still care enough about this result to raise their game and to take the spoils.

Rooney – now raised, on his 17th birthday, from his initial £90 a week to a cool £13,000 – cares enough all right, and he also has plenty of that streetwise Croxteth 'Fuck you' about him to be both cocky and fearless. He positively scowls at ape-like defenders. So when he ships first-half abuse from front-row Liverpudlians, he offers them a youthful scouser's gob back in return, thus stirring predictable Red whining and loathing in the Bullens Road lower. Modern football fans expect to be able to shout any kind of abuse to young players these days and to receive only stoic good humour in return. It is a grossly unequal contest, of course, a hypocrite's escape. Ex-Bluenose Michael Owen receives plenty of stick here, naturally, but he replies with a goal on the half-hour, one which is mainly down to the little man's pace and determination to cut inside Yobo with a shot from the left. But is also about Richard Wright's lack of concentration and occasional vulnerability – he is much too easily beaten at the near post. It is our only direct strike at goal, but it means that half-time arrives with the unwelcome Red intruders ahead.

Now for some local pantomime. During the interval, a Bluenose in the Park End – no kid, a fellah in his 30s wearing a T-shirt and cut-offs – wanders along the front of the stand, eyeing up Reds in the Bullens Road and signalling a cut-throat job, while pointing outside. He is like a hyperactive child, pumped up with E-numbers, and he is not alone. The Everton stewards, the guardians of our welfare today, simply stand and watch this ridiculous, provocative floorshow, as we do, amused. It is a laugh a minute here, honestly. Treatment must be available.

Back on the park, it also gets a little ghoulish. A rash Jamie Carragher challenge lets Everton back into this game after half-time, the Bootle boy mistiming his lunge on Naysmith, to allow Unsworth the opportunity to score *another* Gladys Street penalty in a Goodison derby. But his fat-arsed joy lasts just five minutes, as does this uneasy Merseyside parity. Hamann soon leads a breakaway charge at the Everton defence, which is interrupted by Weir, but the ball breaks to Danny Murphy near the edge of the Everton box – and no Blue defender presses him. This is just asking for trouble, because this is Murphy's range, his *métier*. He lines up and bends his shot high, in off Wright's left-hand post, before joining the bubbling sunshine celebrations in the Red corner of this ragged, bitter Blue outpost.

Now the Park End faithful, the School of Science irregulars, are furiously urging Liverpool supporters outside for further discussions. Even at this stage they doubt their heroes really have the balls – or the ability – to get back into this. For once, they are good judges. Duncan Ferguson's late introduction produces aimless Everton punts into the Liverpool box, an ugly admission of defeat. Before the end, a Gladys Street pitch runner comically manages to wrap a flapping blue flag around Salif Diao's head, making the Senegalese look a little like an exotic desert nomad. Later still, Weir and Naysmith contrive to get themselves sent off by Paul Durkin, the only sensible referee in the entire Premier League. Reduced to nine men and utterly defeated, the great Blue exodus now begins. The home areas of Goodison are close to empty at the whistle, signalling yet another false, Everton dawn. The ex-Bluenose Carragher, especially, celebrates their humiliation with gusto. Away win.

So it is clear, we are still a class above, and millions of pounds ahead of our near neighbours, who have made up some ground and have a canny new boss and a dangerous new weapon, but still trail. 'I've kept telling you that you have to let him grow,' Moyes complains to the Rooney press corps later, 'but you wouldn't listen.' He'll hurt us in the future, the Croxteth Casual, no doubt at all about that, and he has ten years or more to make his mark. But not today. Back in the Flattie, the gloomy landlord, a Bluenose we spotted earlier in the Park End, serves the ale up and also graciously offers some food. 'Humble pie?' someone asks, archly. As we sit to sup the sweet liquor of victory, a plastic blue trophy also appears on the table, a severed seat from the Upper Bullens which mysteriously 'gave way' during the wild celebrations for Danny Murphy's goal. The demolition of Goodison Park has already prematurely begun: Anfield's Owen and Murphy are the familiar site foremen.

A CATEGORY C LIFE

A well-known Goodison 'face', Andy Nicholls, a Category C hooligan, has just published his colourful memoirs, a heroic story, full of tales of terrace comradeship, unsolicited glassings, collective home slashings, patriotic violence for England and 'Keep Everton White' racism. It is an ugly, vainglorious account and he makes it clear that plenty of lone visitors to Goodison got torn apart by jackals – especially if they were black. School of Science? More like a variation on the Final Solution.

Nicholls laments the decline of Liverpool hooliganism, naturally, while the Blues crews have managed, rather more successfully, to keep the local faith, and also organise the downtown nightclub door security in the city. Happy days. Chapter 12 ('The Blues in Europe') would have been longer, he says apologetically, except the actions of Liverpool fans at Heysel caused Everton and other English clubs to be banned from Europe in the late 1980s. A common Blue refrain this one, a tale of a triumphant Merseyside army denied. We must accept our Heysel dues, and let's be honest, some of our troops are no angels, but judging from these and his other gobshite stories, the European ban on Everton fans in the 1980s probably saved a few foreign fans from the Stanley Knife. The coppers abroad will need to mark some Evertonians down for special attention next season. Judging by this, they will need some watching.

21 APRIL 2003: LIVERPOOL 2, CHARLTON ATHLETIC 1

This is a really poor performance, an insult to the home crowd, especially after the gutsy Liverpool show at Goodison only two days before. Maybe it is simple tiredness, or the problem of raising the game for another 'ordinary' home match. Whatever the reason, this could actually have been a home defeat, and one to a Charlton team boasting just one point from their last six games. Worse, this is now typical 2002–03 Liverpool home form. Forget the first half – I already have. After his Everton heroics, Jimmy Traore shows his catastrophic weaknesses once more today, gifting the visitors an early second-half goal by actually falling over the ball, like a pub amateur, and allowing the grateful Bartlett a clear run on goal. Now it almost gets funny, because Jimmy lies distraught in the Anfield grass long after Jerzy has parried the Bartlett shot into the home net. Perhaps he's hoping the game might continue around him while he quietly digs his escape tunnel? No such luck.

But the real Liverpool failings, once more, are further forward. We create next to nothing. Diouf is again anonymous; Heskey, and his half-time replacement Baros, brainless; and Murphy is also poor – but he is, surely, allowed the occasional stinker now? Not according to Kopites near us, who only see Murphy's lack of pace, and judge his unwillingness to hide to be an obvious failing. Thommo's not impressed either, giving Murphy such a mouthful when the midfielder is reluctantly substituted that the Crewe man tosses a water bottle right back at the gobby coach. 'You need characters like that,' Houllier says, approvingly, later, so maybe Danny should have gone the whole way and gubbed Thompson. The Kirkby mouth probably deserved it.

My guess is that Murphy has actually tried to reason with the coaching staff at this moment: 'OK, fair enough, I'm playing like a complete tosser – but look at who you are bringing on!' His replacement, Bruno

Cheyrou, changes little, as usual, and when Hyypiä bundles in a late – and totally undeserved – equaliser from a corner and Gerrard flick-on in front of the Kop, it comes as a complete surprise to us all, and a real body blow to the visitors. Nevertheless, Euell still has time to force two last-gasp saves in the Liverpool area, before Steven Gerrard gallops down the left, and cuts between Young and Robinson before threading a shot under Dean Kiely and into the far corner. Robbery! I'm too embarrassed to celebrate, too sorry for the visitors – suckers. Houllier says, limply: 'We kept going to the end.' He's right, because we could have collectively left the pitch at any moment saying: 'Give Charlton the game, we are truly fucking hopeless.' But we kept going to the end – and stole the points. No one ever said the beautiful game was fair, certainly not our manager. Here's the proof.

I CAN MANAGE

Letter to the *Football Echo*, 19 April 2003:

If I was Gérard Houllier, I would sign the following players for next season:
Trabelsi (right-back) the same style as Lillian Thuram
Mexes (centre-back) the future Sami Hyypiä
Joaquin (right winger) the new wonder boy of Spanish football
Cole (central midfield) tear any defence apart
Ronaldinho (up front) Houllier should have the necessary contacts
Van der Vaart (striker) comparable to Zinedine Zidane.

What, no new *left*-back?

Ninety per cent of football managers are under pressure 95 per cent of the time, and *Le Boss* has had his fair share of advice and criticism at L4 this season, much of it from us. I hold my hand up here: we forget, sometimes, that he missed most of the last campaign because of illness. We demand instant success, and expect him to buy all the major available stars and see it as a lack of managerial imagination or drive if we fail to bid, or if favoured players choose to go elsewhere. But top football players are much more in charge these days: if they don't want to come, or if they ask for ludicrous deals, you just have to let it go, look elsewhere. Liverpool have no magical allure anymore, and no bottomless pockets in the global era.

THE LIVERPOOL WAY

At the bottom, things are even more difficult, of course. Glenn Roeder, at West Ham, has struggled all season, barely able to win a match at home, where the pressure is at its greatest. And now it has taken its full toll. Ironically, it is after a rare Hammers home win, against Boro, that Roeder's system finally gives in. He has a diagnosed blockage in the brain and is tonight in intensive care. Houllier, naturally, has already sent him a message of support. Roeder has seemed a lonely, intense man all season, not great qualities for this stressful line of work. He is well liked in the game and is regarded as honest and decent by journalists. He probably should be coaching rather than taking all the front-line crap, which requires a thicker skin and a ruthless streak. Now he has almost given the sport his life. He'll try to come back. But enough, as they say, is probably enough.

26 APRIL 2003: WEST BROMWICH ALBION 0, LIVERPOOL 6
Owen: 15, 49, 61, 67; Baros: 47, 84.
Attendance: 27,128 (West Bromwich Albion are relegated.)

GÉRARD HOULLIER'S BOARD OF CHALK.
France's master tactician solves another footballing conundrum

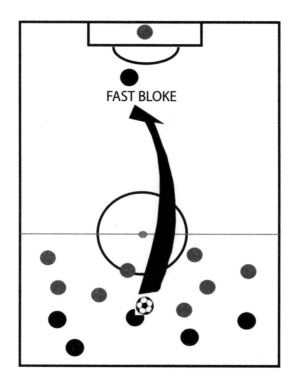

FAST BLOKE

What do you call a side that can't deal with my tactics? Relegated! Ha! See, it's not all about tactical wizardry chez Houllier, I've got a sense of humour too. It was very pleasing to see my football philosophies so savagely proved at Les Aubepines, with my little fast bloke positively running riot. Stick that up your Baggies, as Roy Keane might say. It's just a shame there aren't more First Division sides in the Champions League, although if we keep on expanding that competition at the current rate it'll happen eventually. What havoc we will wreak then!

The Guardian, 28 April 2003

3 MAY 2003: LIVERPOOL 1, MANCHESTER CITY 2

After the Liverpool slaughter of the relegated innocents at the Hawthorns – where a clinical finisher might have scored six or seven of the chances missed by Milan Baros alone – this last home fixture might look, simply, like the visit of a usually accommodating Man. City, a stitched-on three points, before the Champions League final showdown away next week at Chelsea. But most Liverpool fans read this match slightly differently: it is, after all, Robbie Fowler's return to Anfield.

OK, Robbie struggled at Leeds United, had a stop–go transfer to City, and now looks like he still lacks fitness and form in Moss Side, though Keegan is making all the right noises about how Fowler might link up well in the longer term with another recent reluctant Anfield departee, the dangerous Nicolas Anelka. The mind games kick in early on: 'We never wanted Robbie to leave,' says Houllier ingenuously before this match-up, perhaps already fearing the worst. 'He probably thought that because of his reputation and stature here he had to be in the first team. But I believe he made a mistake in leaving us. He should have been a bit more patient.'

Which is all hooey. Asking a man of Fowler's reputation and stature – and incredible Liverpool goal-scoring record – to be 'a bit more patient' is a little like asking Paul Merson to wait until the final race before getting on. Look, Robbie needed to play first-team games at Liverpool, for all sorts of reasons, and Gérard wanted him away from Melwood, once again, for all sorts of reasons. So why not just be straight, for once? City, a relaxed footballing side, and with an avowed Fowler fan at the helm, might be just what Robbie needs right now. But, of course, we don't really need to see any of this 'new dawn' stuff happening for him today. Today, we want to see the usual City show at Anfield: expansive but fruitless up front, and wide-eyed and thoroughly legless at the back. Robbie can have his one goal, late on at the Kop end, but only if we can have a few ourselves beforehand. Not that any of this goes exactly to plan. These are the reasons why:

• First, City have the crabby Peter Schmeichel in goal in his last away match in England, and the boring, brilliant get makes at least four top saves, including a shot from Diouf that no bulging 39-year-old has the right even to attempt to save.

• Second, instead of their usual flaccid midfield, City today field a young terrier in the target zone, Barton, who scraps for everything, works his socks off. Steven Gerrard can't shake him.

• Third, Liverpool are denied a sure-fire first-half penalty, on Baros, and City are later awarded a scratchy one.

• Fourth, a nervous Liverpool fail to settle for a point when they know that Chelsea are losing away to West Ham and that a home draw would mean the same next week in London would now be enough for us.

• Fifth – and here's the killer that you knew would come – City have two quality ex-Liverpool players in their ranks, Robbie Fowler and Nicolas Anelka. After today, Anelka will have claimed 14 Premiership goals for City this season, compared to just three for his Anfield replacement Diouf. Anelka claims Houllier let him down on his agreement to sign at Liverpool last summer when he desperately wanted to stay. Go figure it out for yourselves.

Naturally, Robbie gets his old chant from the Kop at the start, swiftly followed by a louder, rather guilty, song for Michael, our new local hero. We don't threaten that much, but following the first-half Schmeichel heroics, Milan Baros finally puts Liverpool ahead on the hour, fed by Diouf. Fowler claims, not unreasonably, that Hamann has fouled the ex-Liverpool man earlier in the build-up, but referee Neal Barry is unimpressed, and this one goal really should really be enough. You think? At home? Traore soon shows more defensive vulnerability by trying to make up for his lack of strength in tangling crudely with Anelka in the home box. Lots of referees would let this mess pass, especially under the collective scrutiny of a tetchy Kop, but this joker takes pity on our reject Frenchman and offers him the spot. He takes it: – Robbie ostentatiously ignores the resultant City celebrations, jogging back alone to the centre-circle. Respect.

Nerves really start to play a part now, because while City suddenly look carefree and fluent, Liverpool look edgy and without a convincing shape, but still striving for a winning goal. The early leavers are already starting to drift away, and rumbling uncertainty is spreading around the ground like low thunder, when City claim a late winner. Fowler is involved, naturally, linking cleverly this time with Wright Phillips, who allows Bernabia to put Anelka free, wide on the Liverpool right. Carragher is lost. We can already tell what is coming next, sure as night follows day: a true striker's finish, gliding low across Dudek.

Now this is a real dagger, and payback time for Houllier's chicanery with Anelka last summer, while also chasing Cisse and eventually ending up with the, thus far, impotent Diouf. Later Houllier is visibly furious with TV interviewers who want to press him on this issue. 'What? Me, make a mistake?' He's fuming, lost it. Perhaps because this Anelka goal – which may yet cost us £20 million, a Champions League slot, and any real chance of making key summer signings – displays all the lateral movement and the certainty of execution that Liverpool have lacked from forward players throughout the season. We have now dropped an astonishing 22 points at home, mainly through this lack of intelligent mobility, sterile attacking and abject finishing.

As Anelka is giving it the big one, right in front of the emptying Kemlyn – and why not – Robbie Fowler shows no real interest in this shock City win. To be fair, he has not played well and actually looks a little embarrassed at the final outcome: he wants this to end quickly, as we all do. This is still *his* crowd and club, after all, if no longer his team, and a home defeat here still hurts. (Am I imagining all this, engaging in some kind of infantile projection?) This all means that Liverpool will now need to win at Chelsea after all, our nemesis, in a fourth-place winner-takes-all play-off next weekend, an unequal contest that will absolutely shape our future. 'We like cup finals,' says Houllier, ruefully. Deep down, he probably knows we've already blown it.

THE FA: CHAMPIONS OF THE GRASS ROOTS

Southampton will meet Arsenal in the 2003 FA Cup final at the Millennium Stadium, and the Saints fluff their lines by losing 6–1 in the Highbury League rehearsal. So don't bet on Strachan going 'too open' now when the two teams meet again in a fortnight's time. But even as the Cardiff FA climax looms, Diarmuid Crowley, sales director, gestures towards a building site where the famous twin towers used to stand, and outlines plans for the new Wembley Stadium, now due for opening in sunny Brent in 2006. More than £750 million of football's money will have been ploughed into this cash-guzzling overblown monster by then. Meanwhile, local parks' changing-rooms are rotting and local Sunday football clubs search for level playing fields. A question of national FA priorities? You decide.

Today, the Wembley 'premium seats' scheme is being launched by the FA, so reach for your wallets. This little baby involves a one-off payment up front for a licence (a licence?) and then annual payments for 10 years for specified seats for 12, gold star events each season: the FA and Worthington Cup finals; play-offs; England internationals; and ... er ... the rugby league Challenge Cup final? There are 17,000 of these seats, costing, at the top end, £16,100 for a 10-year licence, and a further £5,450 per season for each seat. I make this about an £80,000 spend in all: for *one* Wembley seat. You could argue, I think it is reasonable to say, that this scheme is probably aimed at a fairly exclusive clientele.

So soon it will be the Royal Opera one week and next, perhaps, Reading v. Sheffield United in the Football League play-offs. Perhaps the high spenders will keep ordinary ticket prices down, as the FA claims, but we have all heard that empty promise before. And will this new Wembley focus on the corporate elites also alter the stadium atmosphere? 'No,' says Jonathon Hill, marketing and communications director, not entirely reassuringly. 'We believe that everyone coming to the stadium will be real fans of football.' Jim Royle, TV sit-com star and Liverpool football fan, comments, sagely: 'My arse!'

11 MAY 2003: CHELSEA 2, LIVERPOOL 1

'You are dead, awaiting burial, but you must somehow dredge up the strength to carry on to the finish.'

José Miguel Echavarri on the Tour de France.

'I wouldn't say it's a disappointing season.'

Gérard Houllier

At £40 a shot you might expect Stamford Bridge, on this sunny Sunday afternoon, to be on the exclusive side, too, but all the usual Merseyside ragamuffins and grifters are here, Liverpool accents dominating the away end at a London venue for once. Somehow we end up, pre-match, in a cavernous gay bar in Earl's Court, where a tattooed biker with handle-bar whiskers lights up a nine-inch Corona, just in case we hadn't got the point already. But we have other issues to consider: namely, how to wrestle three points from a Chelsea side who need only to draw and who are fired up and desperate to claim *our* Champions League spot. 'I am very tired of seeing the Champions League only on my television,' says the appealing Ranieri. 'I know Liverpool very well,' he goes on, clearly not impressed. 'They don't like to attack – but they will have to attack us.' Hmmmm.

These matches are increasingly serious matters, especially in an era in which all your top players, and their many advisers, expect you to be competing, year in, year out, with the game's Euro elite. How else can you pay their stratospheric salaries? How else, too, are these fragile men able to hold up their heads during international training weekends, especially with United stealing yet another title from under Arsenal's noses? Alan Hansen calls it correctly: 'The difference between playing in the Champions League and not for an international player can be as significant as the gulf between playing in the Premiership and the First Division is for others.' He means that international places will also be at stake for Euro 2004, and no continental or top-notch British-based player will prefer to sign for puny UEFA Cup hopefuls in 2003, over a cashed-up, media wise, Champions League entrant. So there is big pressure here.

'The culture of this club is about the Champions League,' says Houllier before the off. 'The players here talk about the Champions League. We want to win the big one. It's possible, provided we can keep the nucleus of this team and reinforce it with one or two players of quality.' (One or two – is he dreaming?) And, of course, this must be our aim, distant as this target seems right now. But lose today and we are out of the major summer transfer bidding. Worse, lose this sort of game too often, and Steven Gerrard, Michael Owen and others will also have to consider their options. Houllier now says Liverpool are still three years behind United, but Michael, for one, has only two years left on his contract. How does this work? Owen said this week: 'I only have two years to win the title with Liverpool . . . I'm 23 now, so it's going to have to be in the next couple of years.' Business, after all, is business.

No one really fancies us to win today, not really. Our record here is terrible. It is a mystery how entirely different groups of Liverpool players and coaches, down the years, can still find it so difficult to get a result at a place we were dreading visiting more than 30 years ago. And even the Chelsea stadium is changed now, no longer the open dust bowl, the west London wind tunnel of years gone by. Now it is a tight venue, decent pitch, with fans close up to the action. Maybe new players just pick it up, at Melwood and Anfield, these deep trails of impacted anxiety, the fear and uncertainty about visits to Chelsea, that are left behind by ghosts of previous Liverpool squads. We often thrash Chelsea at home, and yet have no price away. Not that too much has changed in the fans' away sections here, apart from the price and a welcome relative decline in the hometown nihilism and violence more characteristic of the 'good old days'. What are our extra facilities for paying the away fans' levy? It seems to be an old wallpaper table at the back of the stand, presumably for the purpose of resting hot drinks. How they think of everything here.

For all Houllier's talk about the strength of the current Liverpool squad, a few injuries and suspensions too soon reduce us to poor options. Injuries to Hamann and Smicer mean Diao is preferred to Heskey in midfield, an obvious error, and the departing Patrik Berger even makes it to the bench, a man with little to play for at Liverpool, apart from avoiding injury. Cheyrou and Biscan also fill the away dugout, so cute managerial switches are not going to win this game for the visitors. But we do, at least, get a start. Chelsea – with Cole and Zola on the bench, by the way – look nervous, and Murphy's swinging free kick is poorly defended, allowing a startled Hyypiä to glance home a header.

Perhaps we can hang on now, frustrate Chelsea for a while and get the home supporters on their backs. We do just that: for three minutes. Baros should really hold on to a clearance from a Chelsea corner but, instead, he allows Gronkjaer to return a cross into the Liverpool box, as defenders are still trying to clear their lines. Salif Diao, for too many times already in his brief Reds career, is poorly positioned and muscled out in the air, this time by Dessailly, who steers a clever header low and beyond Jerzy Dudek.

Steven Gerrard is trying to stir us now, determined and committed as usual, but Liverpool can never hold the ball high enough up the pitch to be dangerous, with the slight and haphazard Baros stifled and bullied by the sheer aggression and strength of Gallas and Dessailly. Petit is also starting to dominate midfield for Chelsea and Gronkjaer continues to look dangerous down the home right. In front of us the Dutchman now plays a simple exchange with Melchiot from a Chelsea throw-in and then eases past a dreaming Riise. Traore is next in line, but he seems to fall backwards and down in front of the attacker – can no one coach this kid to stand up? – this allows Gronkjaer to lazily bend his shot through the air above the defender's body and around Dudek into the far corner of the net.

Excuse me? Have Chelsea actually *won* the League, because this stadium now starts to rock around us with unrestrained joy. Only 27 minutes gone, and the rational heads in the away end, by contrast, already know this is over. We have as much chance of claiming two unanswered goals here as Graeme Le Saux has of joining Robbie

Fowler's book group. Heskey replaces the outclassed Diao at half-time and the cast-off Berger soon gets his chance in place of the pathetic, wafer-thin El Hadj Diouf, which means he is the preferred option to Cheyrou. Bruno's own late (and anonymous) entry into proceedings sums up the manager's main challenge for next season: it is make something impressive out of the £20 million spent on these three, substandard imports. Or get rid of them.

Owen misses a difficult second-half chance, Melchiot strikes a Liverpool post, and Zola makes Lovejoy monkeys out of both Carragher and Murphy. (Where is *our* Zola?) At the bitter end, and before the obnoxious Chelsea parades and flag-waving, a fired-up, frustrated Steven Gerrard goes hunting and is rightly sent off for clattering high into Le Saux. Red 17 doesn't even look at the referee: he wants to be off this field, away from all these Red faint-hearts and losers. He is applauded off by us, the sad remaining Liverpool loyalists, the mugs who hoped for guts and passion from everyone in Red today. Even Houllier refuses to criticise Gerrard later: 'I sometimes wish we had a couple more like him.' Too true – but he also needs to keep his head.

But what really hurts us, the fans, as we travel home on a tube full of Reds supporters, who are by now deep in themselves with anger and despair, is that in a match that we just had to win to reach our target – a match in which no other outcome would do – we have managed only three on-target attempts on goal, including Hyypiä's scoring header. Cudicini has made no saves. Once again, we have played with no real urgency, bite or belief. Irrespective of all Houllier's vapid arguments about statistics or figures, this feels too much now like normal Liverpool service. The truth is that we were simply not equipped, either mentally or technically, to be really positive against decent opponents and to take the acceptable risks we needed to in search of the goals we just had to get. We were not brave enough or good enough to succeed. Period.

CLOSING LINES

So there it is, in black and white. Sixty-four points. The final Premier League table does not lie: ask Ronnie Moran or Bob Paisley, or any of the coaching staff in the Liverpool Boot Room, or even those in Houllier's Melwood Bunker today (though the manager still mumbles about the points we 'should' have had). Having started the season with real championship hopes, the 2003 Liverpool are currently only the fifth best team in England, having assembled, along the way, the worst Anfield home record for 49 years. While Gérard Houllier has performed wonders in transforming this club, especially in addressing, head on, the new culture of decline in L4 and the faults in attitude and coaching, he has also spent a net £64 million in transfers over four years in getting us here: to fifth place in the Premiership League. Perhaps the harsh truth is that he has a good serve, but no convincing game. We have won cups on the way, of course, and enjoyed glorious nights at home and abroad; no one could deny that. But the League is our workplace, our bread and butter. This is what we pay for, and how we want to be known. At the moment, we are shamed by our output.

Let me put it more plainly: we really do want to win this title again, much more than we might dream about ever winning the Champions League. So time is running out for Gérard to show us that he has both the knowledge and the nerve to deliver on this difficult agenda. No one doubts, for a second, that he has rectified the moral health of Liverpool football club, and has improved its organisation and administration, and that its players are more professional and better prepared now than they have been in the past, in order better to meet the demands of a new era. No one doubts, either, Houllier's ruthlessness and his determination to win. We have seen enough of that to know he is serious. What is less clear is whether he has the courage and the judgement to build a truly great team, a championship team. One that can think on its own feet and which is allowed to play beyond the umbilical cord of its maker. One that is confident and skilled enough to take risks – and to come through.

A social psychologist at Southampton University, Dr Mark van Vugt, has found that if you look at the turnover of players in club squads in the Premiership over the past four seasons, the clubs with the lowest turnover tend to do best. He concludes that: 'Rather than investing in new players and changing their squad around, clubs should develop the team skills of their current players to ensure that everyone is familiar with each other's game. There is an optimum stability because you do need some innovation in the team, but it shouldn't be the silly numbers we've seen in recent years.' Now, you can raise all sorts of objections about research of this kind, not least the fact that it is actually the struggling teams who tend to change players as they search desperately for a formula to try to keep them out of the relegation zone.

So, does this sort of work simply measure the thrashing around of the stragglers in *response* to crises, rather than offering a way of avoiding them? Also, buying good players is a favoured strategy in football after a satisfying and successful season. You have to buy when you look attractive: it is a signal of club ambition, and also a warning to established players

236

who might have thought that they had already done enough. So, the buying of new players is not necessarily the problem. It is more the judgement involved in your purchases, but also the performance of your reliable assets, the players who had taken you forward in the first place. Liverpool have struggled here on both fronts in 2002–03.

Houllier likes to joke about how, when you sign African players, you have to hope they don't have too many 'African days' when playing. He is right to be concerned. The new Senegalese at Liverpool still have much to prove, not least whether they have the heart, pace and skill to play consistently well in this League, a league in which matches often kick off in third gear and get quicker and more physical as they approach the climax. As a teacher and amateur footballer in Liverpool – a striker, no less – Houllier was noted for his own physical approach to the sport, surprising locals who thought that continentals could never match up to a traditional English idea of a bustling centre-forward. He once turned up to school, after a heavy Saturday battle, with stitches to the forehead, so Houllier knows well, and enjoys, the physicality of the English game. And yet, his own recruited 'touch' players – Diomède, Smicer, Cheyrou, Litmanen and even Camara – have pretty much all failed this critical test. His judgement here still seems unproven, and could potentially be a major problem.

Also, in 2002–03 what the Americans would call the club's 'go to' guys, their experienced and reliable match winners or defenders, simply did not match up to the challenge. Houllier's response was that this was a World Cup hangover, though in some cases – Hyypiä, Owen and Gerrard, for example – other issues also seemed in play. Keeping players up to a consistent level is probably much harder now than it was in the Shankly era. How do you motivate these millionaires today? Failure at one club only seems to open up an opportunity somewhere else. And leaving Liverpool is no longer quite the dagger to a professional's heart it may once have been in the 1960s, 1970s or 1980s. Times change.

More than all of these questions: can the manager release the current Liverpool team to play the sort of decisive, progressive football the club's followers want to see and the sort which is actually required now to win the Premiership in England? It is a great quality, to hate to lose – Liverpool championship teams of the past have been built around it – but these days you also need to love to win almost as much. Indeed, despite Houllier's boasts about the certainty of Liverpool winning the title under his stewardship, the final table of 2002–03 suggests the existence of a number of mini-leagues within the top level in England at the moment.

THE LIVERPOOL WAY

Clearly, at the top at the moment, in their own personal battle, stand Ferguson and Wenger, Manchester United and Arsenal, both struggling in Europe, sure, but both with the sort of defensive hardness and the attacking vim necessary to crush most of their English rivals. United's new challenge is to replace talisman Roy Keane and, more immediately, the Madrid-bound David Beckham. In the summer of 2003 they were in search of Brazilians and a new direction. Arsenal's challenge was to find a convincing defensive partner for Campbell, a solid replacement for Seaman in goal – the German Lehmann has arrived – and someone to take over Bergkamp's slipping mantle as 'inventor' of the game at Highbury. All this while eyeing Chelsea's threatening rise and managing a necessary move to a stadium they cannot really afford. Both these clubs are vulnerable to challenges from below. But from where?

At the second level come Newcastle United, Chelsea and Liverpool, but there is much less solidity here. After all, Leeds United were in this rank just two seasons ago. But these clubs have a core of quality players and a greater financial resolve than Leeds. In the north-east, Bobby Robson is threatening to put together a strong young team, but how long can the 70-year-old manager realistically go on? Alan Shearer, Newcastle's totem, is also coming into his dotage, and Robson might also be storing up problems with his growing group of 'Spice Boys' (mark II) of Bellamy, Dyer, Woodgate and now the dangerous Bowyer. Without Shearer and Speed, Newcastle look undercooked – exciting, but brittle, especially with the uncertain Given in goal.

And then there is Chelsea. They have Dessailly, Le Saux and Hasselbaink all beginning to look rather worn – and Zola is gone. Convincing and creative forwards will have to be found to supplement the pace and tricks of Damien Duff. But they do have the impressive Cudicini in goal, Terry and Gallas at the back, and also Lampard and Petit are beginning to cut it in midfield. And now they also have many Russian millions to call upon, though spending extensively on players does not always guarantee a decent team. Champions also have to have the desire and the collective know-how.

But both these clubs, crucially, have Champions League places in 2003–04 – which means top players might be tempted if the money is right. On the other hand, neither club has won the English title in decades. And history is not always bunkum in football.

This leaves Liverpool – assuming you discount Blackburn Rovers, the Everton revival and the Leeds relegation escape as possible preludes to a serious challenge next time. I do. Houllier's new Liverpool require, above

238

all, a change in managerial philosophy, as well as the recruitment of a top midfield/attacking brain to complement Hamann's defensive experience, Gerrard's huge promise and Murphy's reliability and quality. Another McAllister, in fact: the signal for a strong return to the Liverpool Way. The signing of attacking full-back Steve Finnan from Fulham and the enigmatic but talented Harry Kewell from Leeds certainly adds a new, more creative face to the Liverpool squad. Kewell can actually go past defenders, at least. And the move, controversially, made young Harry, and also his agent, very rich men.

A centre-back (for cover) and an imposing, intelligent striker who can score goals would also improve Liverpool's prospects (as if you didn't know already). Some players will leave – Berger, Heggem and Diomède certainly, and perhaps Vignal, Biscan and Babbel. Possibly even Smicer and Cheyrou, too – but the savings here will be largely in wages. And Houllier will claim he still needs his big squad to fight on all fronts. Can the Liverpool manager successfully mould the right sort of quality needed for a serious title challenge in 2003–04 and for the new European football order that will surely follow, who knows when? With Newcastle United young and ambitious and Chelsea high spending and dangerous, even getting into the Champions League places in 2004 might be much tougher than before. The pressure never slackens.

More importantly, can Gérard Houllier also graduate from a knowledgeable and respected international coach, if one with the reputation of a rather defensive football technician and match analyst, to become a truly mature and secure European-class football manager, a man capable of shaping a really competitive and experienced elite side in the new era? In short, can he finally join the really hard men, the big league of Ferguson and Wenger and all those chain-smoking continental football eggheads? Can he deliver at a club at the very highest level? I want to believe in him, I really do. We can only hope that he has all the answers. We, the fans, always have hope, of course. *Allez les Rouges!*

FA PREMIER FINAL LEAGUE TABLE AT 12 MAY 2003

	P	W	D	L	F	A	GD	Pts
MAN. UNITED	38	25	8	5	74	34	40	83
ARSENAL	38	23	9	6	85	42	43	78
NEWCASTLE U.	38	21	6	11	63	48	15	69
CHELSEA	38	19	10	9	68	38	30	67
LIVERPOOL	**38**	**18**	**10**	**10**	**61**	**41**	**20**	**64**
BLACKBURN R.	38	16	12	10	52	43	9	60
EVERTON	38	17	8	13	48	49	-1	59
SOUTHAMPTON	38	13	12	12	43	46	-3	52
MAN. CITY	38	15	6	17	47	54	-7	51
TOTTENHAM	38	14	8	16	51	62	-11	50
MIDDLESBRO.	38	13	10	15	48	44	4	49
CHARLTON	38	14	7	17	45	56	-11	49
BIRMINGHAM C.	38	13	9	16	41	49	-8	48
FULHAM	38	13	9	16	41	50	-9	48
LEEDS U.	38	14	5	19	58	57	1	47
ASTON VILLA	38	12	9	17	42	47	-5	45
BOLTON W.	38	10	14	14	41	51	-10	44
WEST HAM	38	10	12	16	42	59	-17	42
WEST BROM.	38	6	8	24	29	65	-36	26
SUNDERLAND	30	4	7	27	21	65	-44	19